CW00925371

HAKLUYT SOCIETY

COUNCIL AND OFFICERS, 1978–79

PRESIDENT
Professor GLYNDWR WILLIAMS

VICE-PRESIDENTS
Professor C. F. BECKINGHAM   Professor C. R. BOXER, F.B.A.
Sir ALAN BURNS, G.C.M.G.   G. R. CRONE   Dr E. S. DE BEER, C.B.E., F.B.A.
Sir GILBERT LAITHWAITE, G.C.M.G., K.C.B., K.C.I.E., C.S.I.
Professor D. B. QUINN

COUNCIL (with date of election)

Dr K. R. ANDREWS (1978)	†Sir EDWARD MUIR, K.C.B. (1974)
Dr J. R. BOCKSTOCE (1978)	Dr H. C. PORTER (1978)
Dr R. C. BRIDGES (1976)	PAUL PUTZ (1977)
P. R. COTTRELL (1978)	Royal Geographical Society
Professor J. S. CUMMINS (1973)	(Mrs DOROTHY MIDDLETON)
STEPHEN EASTON (1975)	Dr GEOFFREY SCAMMELL (1974)
BASIL GREENHILL, C.M.G. (1977)	Dr SUSAN SKILLITER (1975)
P. H. HULTON (1974)	Dr J. W. STOYE (1975)
M. J. MOYNIHAN (1976)	Dr HELEN WALLIS (1977)

TRUSTEES
Sir ALAN BURNS, G.C.M.G.
Dr E. S. DE BEER, C.B.E., F.B.A.
Sir PHILIP HAY, K.C.V.O., T.D.
Sir GILBERT LAITHWAITE, G.C.M.G., K.C.B., K.C.I.E., C.S.I.

HONORARY TREASURER
J. F. MAGGS

HONORARY SECRETARIES
Dr T. E. ARMSTRONG, Scott Polar Research Institute, Cambridge CB2 1ER
Professor EILA M. J. CAMPBELL, Birkbeck College, London WC1E 7HX

HON. SECRETARIES FOR OVERSEAS
Australia: D. McD. HUNT, The State Library of N.S.W., Macquarie Street, Sydney, N.S.W. 2000
Canada: Professor J. B. BIRD, McGill University, Montreal
India: Dr S. GOPAL, Historical Division, Ministry of External Affairs, 3 Man Singh Road, New Delhi
South Africa: Dr F. B. BRADLOW, P.O. Box 341, Cape Town 8000
New Zealand: J. E. TRAUE, The Alexander Turnbull Library, P.O. Box 12-349, Wellington C.1
U.S.A.: R. ARMSTRONG, Boston Athenaeum, 10½ Beacon Street, Boston, Massachusetts 02108

ADMINISTRATIVE ASSISTANT
Mrs ALEXA BARROW, Hakluyt Society, c/o The Map Library, The British Library, Reference Division, Great Russell Street, London WC1B 3DG

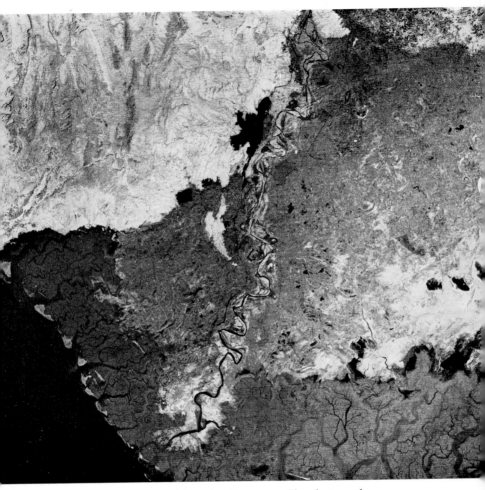

The Delta of the Indus. From a satellite photograph.

THE PERIPLUS OF
THE ERYTHRAEAN SEA

by an unknown author

WITH SOME EXTRACTS FROM AGATHARKHIDĒS
'ON THE ERYTHRAEAN SEA'

Translated and edited by
†G. W. B. HUNTINGFORD

THE HAKLUYT SOCIETY
LONDON
1980

© The Hakluyt Society 1980

ISBN 0 904180 05 0

Printed in Great Britain
by Robert MacLehose and Company Limited
Printers to the University of Glasgow

Published by the Hakluyt Society
c/o The British Library
London WC1B 3DG

HOC OPVSCVLVM
MEMORIAE PATRIS MEI
DILECTISSIMI ET ERVDITISSIMI
DISCIPLINAE EIVS GRATVS
DEDICAVI

Th' extreme of cultivated lands survey,
The painted Scythians, and the realms of day;
All trees allotted keep their several coasts,
India alone the sable ebon boasts;
Sabaea bears the branch of frankincense.
And shall I sing, how teeming trees dispense,
Rich fragrant balms in many a trickling tear,
With soft Acanthus' berries, never sear?
From Aethiop woods, where woolly leaves encrease,
How Syrians comb the vegetable fleece?
Or shall I tell how India hangs her woods,
Bound of this earth, o'er Ocean's unknown floods?

VERGIL, *Georgics*, II. 114–123,
translated by the Rev. Joseph Warton, 1753

Ceu septem surgens sedatis amnibus altus
Per tacitum Ganges, aut pingui flumine Nilus,
Cum refluit campis, et iam se condidit alveo.

VERGIL, *Aeneid*, IX. 30–33

In medio glaebis redolentibus area dives
Praebet odoratas messes; hic mitis amomi,
Hic casiae matura seges.

CLAUDIAN, *Epithalamium de nuptiis Honorii Augusti*, 92–94

Contents

ILLUSTRATIONS AND MAPS *page* ix

PREFATORY NOTE xi

PREFACE AND ACKNOWLEDGEMENTS xiii

INTRODUCTION 1

NOTE ON SOME FEATURES OF THE
TRANSLATION 16

TOPOGRAPHICAL SUMMARY 17

THE PERIPLUS OF THE ERYTHRAEAN
SEA 19
Notes on the text of the *Periplus* 58

APPENDICES
1 The topography of the *Periplus* 77
    1. The start of the journey and the ancient canals 77
    2. Summary of routes: 81
        (1) Africa 83
        (2) Arabia and India 84
    3. Local topography: 86
        I. The African coast to Rhapta 86
        II. The Arabian coast to Omana 100
        III. The coasts of Persia and India 106

2 The products of the Erythraean area   122
   Glossary of Imports and Exports: 129
        I. Clothing material   129
       II. Vegetable products   132
      III. Ivory, horn, and shell   137
       IV. Hardware   138
        V. Precious stones   139
       VI. Miscellaneous   140
3 The ethnology and history of the area covered by the
   Periplus   143
4 Shipping   158
5 Elephant-hunting   166
6 The mountain of the moon   173

EXTRACTS FROM AGATHARKHIDĒS
'ON THE ERYTHRAEAN SEA'   177
Notes on Agatharkhidēs   194

BIBLIOGRAPHY   198

INDEX OF PLACES, TRIBES, AND
PERSONS NAMED IN THE TEXT   205

INDEX OF GREEK WORDS   209

INDEX OF TRADE-GOODS   210

GENERAL INDEX   215

Illustrations and Maps

The Delta of the Indus   *frontispiece*
From a satellite photograph

Fig. 1   Aduli and the throne of Ptolemy   *facing page*   20
From: McCrindle (ed.), *Christian Topography of Cosmas*
(Hakluyt Society, 1897)

Fig. 2   The harbour of Berbera (Malaō) in 1944   *page*   25
From a sketch by G.W.B.H.

Fig. 3   Cape Gardafui (Arōmatōn akron), 1938   25
From a sketch by G.W.B.H.

Fig. 4   Ras Filuk (Cape Elephas), 1938   27
From a sketch by G.W.B.H.

Fig. 5   Ras Shenagef (Tabai akrōtērion), 1938   27
From a sketch by G.W.B.H.

Fig. 6   Egyptian ship used for the voyage
to Punt   *facing page*   158
B. Landström, *Ships of the Pharaohs*, 1970

Fig. 7   *Galawa* at Dar es-salaam, 1926 (1, 2);
attachment to boom and float, outrigger
canoe, Zanzibar, 1926 (3)   *facing page*   159
From photographs by James Hornell

Fig. 8   East African sewn boat, *mtepe*   *page*   160
After a drawing in Grottanelli, *Pescatori dell'Oceano Indico*
(1955)

Fig. 9   East African dug-out canoes: (a) *mtumbwi* type;
(b) outriggers with *galawa* type   161
From sketches by G.W.B.H.

ILLUSTRATIONS AND MAPS

Map 1 General map of the Erythraean Sea   *facing page* 19
Map 2 Sketch map of the Arsinoē Canal   *page* 78
Map 3 The Red Sea   82
Map 4 Adouli and Alalaiou   88
Map 5 The Straits of Bab al-mandab   91
Map 6 The Courses of Azania   96
Map 7 The Puralaōn Islands   98
Map 8 States and kingdoms in Africa and Arabia
        known to the Author of the *Periplus*   101
Map 9 India as known to the Author of the *Periplus*   107
Map 10 The Gulf of Cambay   111
Map 11 Mouziris and Nelkunda   117

Prefatory Note

DR HUNTINGFORD died on 19 February 1978. He was already mortally ill when he completed this book and, although he was able to make some corrections to the galley-proofs, he asked me to be responsible for the final stages of publication. I have taken the opportunity to include some valuable corrections to the translation and to the notes on the text which were very kindly sent to me by Professor Giuseppe Giangrande, whom Dr Huntingford had been consulting on the interpretation of difficult passages. Professor Giangrande has explained the most important of these in articles in *Mnemosyne*, XXVIII (1975), 293–5, in *The Journal of Hellenic Studies*, XCVI (1976), 154–7, and in one to be published in *Museum Philologum Londiniense*, V (1979). I have also corrected a few *lapsus calami* and rectified some inconsistencies in transliteration and presentation. The bibliographical references were checked by Mr Michael Pollock and Mrs Irene Pollock.

Dr Huntingford had been interested in the *Periplus* since he first went to Africa in 1920. His illness and the restricted library facilities of Málaga, where he was living, prevented him from elaborating some of his arguments as he would have wished. It should be remembered, however, that the identifications he proposed are the considered judgments of a scholar with an intimate knowledge of the topography and ethnography of East Africa, who had reflected for nearly sixty years on the problems presented by this text.

C. F. BECKINGHAM

Preface and Acknowledgements

THERE are several texts of the *Periplus of the Erythraean Sea* of varying merit, as well as several translations; a list will be found in the Bibliography. The latest, and definitive, text, is that by Hjalmar Frisk (1927), which contains a detailed study of the text and its grammatical and lexical problems. I have used this text for my translation, and wish to acknowledge my debt to it.

In preparing the book my greatest obligations are perhaps to Professor Charles Beckingham, who not only provided me with xerox copies of Frisk's book and of J. W. McCrindle's *Commerce and Navigation of the Erythraean Sea* (both long out of print, though the latter has been recently reprinted), but also spent much time and trouble in giving me help of other kinds, and was indefatigable in answering questions and making enquiries. To Professor Eila Campbell I am also indebted for much help, and the great amount of trouble she has taken which made my task much easier, as well as for providing me with a set of maps of the Erythraean area. I have also to thank Mrs Waddell, formerly of Málaga, for a set of recent Indian Government Tourist Maps; and I have the further pleasure of acknowledging the help which I have received from Colonel H. W. Wagstaff, R.E., C.S.I., M.C., and his wife (who is a daughter of the late Sir John Marshall, C.I.E.).

In more technical matters, my thanks are due to Professor Giuseppe Giangrande of the University of London, who was kind enough to read my translation and make a number of helpful suggestions; to Professor A. F. L. Beeston of the

University of Oxford for a note on the date of the *Periplus*; and to Dr A. D. H. Bivar of the University of London for much detailed information on the Western Indian section of the *Periplus*, as well as for lending me offprints. I have also to thank Mr Neville Chittick for information about the East African coast, and the owners of Mr James Hornell's photographs of canoes for permission to reproduce them in this book. The frontispiece is reproduced by courtesy of the National Aeronautics and Space Administration (NASA) and the U.S. Geological Survey, EROS Data Center; and figure 6 by that of Rahm and Stenström Interpublishing AB.

Málaga, 1975   G.W.B.H.

Introduction

THE ERYTHRAEAN SEA was the name given by the Greeks to the whole of the vast sea which comprises the Indian Ocean and its branches the Red Sea and the Persian Gulf; and in this sense it was understood by the author of the 'Periplus of the Erythraean Sea'. Some ancient writers, however, did not include the Red Sea or the Persian Gulf, and Hērodotos distinguished between the Red Sea, which he called the Arabian Gulf, and the Erythraean Sea. The Greek word *eruthra* means 'red', but there was much uncertainty among ancient writers as to the origin and significance of the term. Agatharkhidēs of Knidos, whose account of the Red Sea coast of Africa, as quoted by Phōtios, is printed in this book, devoted considerable space to show that the name did not mean *red* sea, but that it was derived from a mythical Persian called Eruthras. A more recent suggestion is that the colour name is derived from the 'red Homēritae' of the Yemen:[1] Pliny says that 'we call it *rubrum* (red), but the Greeks, *erythraeum*, from king Erythras, or, as others say, from thinking that such a colour is due to the reflexion of the sun; others again, from the nature of the water'.[2] Perhaps after all the name was really taken from some fancied colour of the water (a theory mentioned and rejected by Agatharkhidēs), or from the heat of the region, where the unpleasant affliction known as 'prickly heat' is common.

The Indian Ocean was virtually unknown to the ancient Greek geographers except at second hand. Hērodotos describes the first circumnavigation of Africa, made by order of the

[1] *Guida dell' Africa Orientale Italiana* (Milan, 1938), p. 126.
[2] Pliny, *Nat. Hist.*, VI, 28.

I

Egyptian king Nekhō II in the sixth century B.C., though he doubted the statement of the leaders that they had the sun upon their right hand. This voyage, however, was made, not by Greeks or Egyptians, but by Phoenician sailors, and there seems to be no doubt that they did sail right round Africa, as is made clear by Hērodotos, who wrote

As for Libya [i.e. the continent of Africa], we know it to be washed on all sides by the sea, except where it is attached to Asia. This discovery was first made by Necos, the Egyptian king, who on desisting from the canal which he had begun between the Nile and the Arabian Gulf, sent to sea a number of ships manned by Phoenicians, with orders to make for the Pillars of Hercules, and to return to Egypt through them, and by the Mediterranean. The Phoenicians took their departure from Egypt by way of the Erythraean Sea, and so sailed into the southern ocean. When autumn came, they went ashore, wherever they might be, and having sown a tract of land with corn, waited until the grain was fit to cut. Having reaped it, they again set sail; and thus it came to pass that two whole years went by, and it was not until the third year that they doubled the Pillars of Hercules, and made good their voyage home. On their return they declared—I for my part do not believe them—that in sailing round Libya they had the sun upon their right hand. In this way was the extent of Libya first discovered.[1]

For many centuries this story was not believed, perhaps because Hērodotos doubted the statement about the sun being on their right hand. Even Ptolemy thought that somewhere south of Cape Prason (possibly Cape Delgado) the coast of Africa turned eastwards and joined Asia, thus enclosing the Indian Ocean.[2]

Except for the voyage of Nearkhos, who took Alexander's fleet from the Indus to the Euphrates along the coast of Makran into the Persian Gulf (and of course added nothing to confirm that Africa was a continent) we have no certain evidence of

[1] Hērodotos, II, 42; trans. by G. Rawlinson.
[2] It is clear that the author of the *Periplus* did believe that Africa was a separate continent, as can be seen from chapter 18 (*see* p. 31 below).

Greek fleets sailing in the Indian Ocean, and no certain evidence of ships from the Mediterranean entering the Red Sea through the Isthmus of Suez even after the opening of Trajan's canal.

Geographers like Eratosthenēs, Marinos of Tyre, Claudius Ptolemy, and the others who followed them, relied on second-hand information, having themselves no personal knowledge of the area. It is true that sailors and others with Greek names occur occasionally—*apparent rari nantes in gurgite vasto*—like Timosthenēs in the 3rd century B.C., Arkhippos in the 2nd century B.C., Hippalos before the *Periplus* was written, and Diogenēs and Theophilos who gave information to Marinos of Tyre. Timosthenēs came from Rhodes, and as admiral of the fleet to Ptolemy II he may have known part of the Indian Ocean, and perhaps described it in one of the works attributed to him. Hippalos, Diogenēs, and Theophilos certainly knew the area from personal experience. Perhaps we should add to these the names of Sarapiōn and Nikōn, who occur in chapter 15 of the *Periplus* attached to two of the 'courses of Azania'. An inscription of the mid-first century B.C. found at Philae names one Sarapiōn son of Drakōn the Thēbarkhos or military governor of the Thebaïd 'on the Indian and Erythraean Sea',[1] whom we mention here merely to show that Sarapiōn was a Greek personal name, and that the first element in *Sarapiōn*'s Course is not necessarily a distorted form of a native name, as McCrindle thought.[2] Of Nikōn nothing is known, but the name is Greek.

Writers on geography like Pliny and Ptolemy, and their successors, Agathēmeros and Markianos of Hērakleia, had no personal knowledge of the Indian Ocean. Ptolemy, it is true, worked at Alexandria, as did Agatharkhidēs; and Strabō may have accompanied Aelius Gallus on his Arabian expedition in

[1] W. Dittenberger, *Orientis Graeci Inscriptiones Selectae*, 1 (Leipzig, 1903), no. 190.

[2] J. W. McCrindle, *The Commerce and Navigation of the Erythraean Sea* (Bombay, 1879), p. 67.

24 B.C. But the only writer with personal knowledge of the Indian Ocean whose work has survived was the anonymous author of the *Periplus*. Ptolemy based his *Geographia* on the lost work of Marinos of Tyre, and these two works were the first attempts at comprehensive and scientific description. But those who followed them, no matter what language they wrote in, were mere compilers who took their material from Ptolemy and rather unsuccessfully epitomized it. They are hardly worth serious study. (The work attributed to Agathēmeros, indeed, names the river Kottiaris in the land of the Sinai (following Ptolemy: *Geographia* VII. 3, 3); and Markianos refers to the courses of Azania, which he may have got from the *Periplus*.)

Knowledge of the Indian Ocean was thus derived from traders living in or at least starting from Egypt, whose point of departure for the East was on the Red Sea coast, for although ships from the Mediterranean could reach the Red Sea after Trajan's time, it seems unlikely that a great many did so. Nor did the ancient Egyptians venture—at least in Ptolemaic times— into the Indian Ocean beyond the Gulf of Aden.[1]

This vast ocean was in fact the preserve of Arab and Indian navigators, who discovered how to make use of the monsoons, which made it possible to sail across the ocean instead of travelling round the coasts; and this secret seems to have been carefully guarded till it was accidentally discovered by a more than usually enterprising 'foreign' navigator named Hippalos. Trade during most of the period of the Roman Empire was probably in the hands of men from Egypt, either Greeks or Egyptians, and Arabs and Indians.

Dr Gervase Mathew has suggested that Greek ships first went south of Cape Gardafui in the 3rd century B.C., and that Graeco-Roman fleets had at one time sailed annually to India, though they had practically ceased to do so by the 6th century A.D., whence the surname of Indikopleustēs (Sailor to India)

[1] We exclude Kosmas, because, although he certainly knew the Indian Ocean, he was much later; he appears to have been an Egyptian.

4

given to Kosmas owing to the rarity of such journeys by that time.[1] We may note that the traffic (mentioned by Strabō) of 120 ships a year[2] was carried by ships based on Muos Hormos and not coming direct to India from the Mediterranean, since Trajan's canal was not then completed.

It seems clear that in the time of the author of the *Periplus* the canal from the Nile to the Bitter Lakes had not been extended to the Red Sea, whence the choice of Muos Hormos, though ships could sail between Arsinoē and the Nile. Any Greeks or Romans who sailed the Indian Ocean before the time of Trajan must therefore have used ships built in Egypt. After the completion of the canal to Klusma near Suez on the Red Sea doubtless ships did come through from the Mediterranean, and in the course of time Klusma took the place of Muos Hormos and Berenikē for some if not all of the produce brought from the East. But no matter how many ships may have sailed through the canal to India, and irrespective of whether they were owned or manned by Mediterranean people, no account of their voyages has survived.

In the absence, therefore, of any first-hand description, apart from the *Periplus*, we must consider ourselves lucky to have this text, short as it is, preserved apparently complete, a text moreover which shows every sign of being the work of a man who had himself been to most of the places he mentions, even if he did not know very much about the remoter eastern parts of the world.

This little work, the *Periplus of the Erythraean Sea*, belongs to a class of writings in Greek of which several examples are known, all of which bear the title περίπλους, *Periplus* or 'circumnavigation'. Among them are the following:

1. A 'Periplus of the Seas of Europe, Asia, and Africa', attributed to Skulax of Karuanda (5th century B.C., though the existing text was probably written later).

[1] R. Oliver and G. Mathew, *History of East Africa* (Oxford, 1963), I, 98.
[2] Strabō, *Geographia*, bk. II. Strabō died about A.D. 20.

2. More than one Periplus has been attributed to Timosthenēs of Rhodes, admiral of the fleet to Ptolemy II (3rd century B.C.) who also wrote a book 'On Harbours'. All his works are lost, but Pliny names him in his list of sources.

3. An anonymous 'Periplus of the Euxine Sea', of uncertain date.

4. A 'Periplus of Europe, Asia, and Africa' by Mnaseas of Patara, perhaps of the 2nd century B.C., but now lost.

5. A 'Periplus of the Inner Sea' (the Mediterranean) by Menippos of Pergamon (early 1st century A.D.), of which a few fragments have been preserved.

6. A 'Periplus of the Euxine Sea', by Arrian (2nd century A.D.), the historian of Alexander the Great. He was for a long time credited with the 'Periplus of the Erythraean Sea'.

7. There is also a 'Periplus of Africa' attributed to a Carthaginian named Hanno (perhaps of the 5th century B.C.) originally written in Punic, but surviving in a Greek version. This name occurs in Pliny's list of sources.

Nothing is known of the author of the *Periplus of the Erythraean Sea* (which henceforth will be referred to as *PME*, the abbreviation of the Latin title of the work, *Periplus Maris Erythraei*). The work was for a long time attributed to Arrian simply because his 'Periplus of the Euxine Sea' came next to it in the better of the only two manuscripts which contain it, known as Heidelberg 398. This MS contains also the Periplus of Hanno, as well as another genuine work of Arrian, his *Kunēgetikos*, a book on hunting, written as a supplement to Xenophōn's work on the same subject. Arrian of Nikomēdeia in Asia Minor flourished in the 2nd century A.D. He was a pupil and friend of Epiktētos, and was one of the best Greek writers of his time. He chose Xenophōn as his model, and early in his career published his master's lectures at Athens, where he won a great reputation. His literary style and abilities are so different from those of the author of the *PME* that it is difficult to understand how it could ever have been attributed to him. Moreover, the language is totally different. It is true that both authors wrote in 'Greek', but Arrian wrote in Attic Greek, while the *PME* is written in a post-classical form of Greek known as the κοινή (*koinē* or 'common' language), which, if imitated by a schoolboy in a Greek prose, would certainly bring upon him the wrath of his teacher. And of course it goes without saying that such a book was not welcome in the purer field of classical studies, nor admitted into any school syllabus. At the time when the best editors of the *PME* were at work, like Fabricius[1] and Müller,[2] little study had been made of the *koinē*, and they tended to regard many of its forms as incorrect or ungrammatical, and thus felt compelled to emend many passages unnecessarily.

We do not even know whether the author of the *PME* was a Greek or a Greek-speaking Egyptian, though there are some indications which point vaguely to the former. He gives the names of three of the months in the Hellenized forms of their Latin names, as well as the Egyptian equivalents: Ἰανουάριος Januarius, Egyptian *Tubi*; Ἰούλιος Julius, Egyptian *Epiphi*; and Σεπτέμβριος Septembrius, Egyptian *Thoth*. The expression in chapter 29 'among us in Egypt' does not necessarily indicate any more than that he lived in Egypt; and as to his writing in Greek, it must be remembered that the *koinē* was in those parts more of a lingua franca than was Latin or Egyptian. The somewhat irrelevant chapter 47, which, although it mentions Poklaïs as a trading centre, goes out of its way to bring in Alexander the Great and his invasion of India, does rather suggest that the author was a Greek, even though he got his facts wrong about the extent of Alexander's conquest. Our author was in fact a trader, possibly a shipmaster, κυβερνήτης, and what he wrote was simply a trader's guide to the coasts of the Erythraean Sea, giving information about the ports, harbours, roadsteads, and marts, together with their imports and exports (the former a very necessary item of knowledge in

[1] B. Fabricius, *Arriani Periplus Maris Erythraei* (Dresden, 1849).
[2] C. Müller, *Geographi Graeci Minores*, vol. I (Paris, 1855).

7

primitive countries), as well as navigational aids such as how to enter difficult harbours, and how to recognise the signs of coming storms and the approach of land—in fact it is an early example of a combined trade directory and *Admiralty Handbook.*

II

The only clues to the date of the *PME* are contained in four passages, none of which is by itself conclusive. They are:

(1) Chapter 19. . . . Λευκὴ κώμη δἰ ἧς ἐστὶν εἰς Πέτραν πρὸς Μαλίχαν βασιλέα Ναβαταίων, ‹ἀνάβασις› '. . . Leukē Kōmē ('White Village') from which there is ⟨a route inland⟩ to Petra, to Malikhas king of the Nabataioi.' The fact that the MS reading is ἀναβαταιως, corrected by the second hand to ναβαταίων is immaterial, since the mention of Petra and Malikhas make the author's meaning quite clear.

(2) Chapter 26, referring to Eudaimōn Arabia. Νῦν δὲ οὐ πρὸ πολλοῦ τῶν ἡμετέρων χρόνων Καῖσαρ αὐτὴν κατεστρέψατο 'But now, not very long before our time Caesar subdued it.'

(3) Chapter 41. ἡ ἤπειρος τῆς 'Αριακῆς χώρας, τῆς τε Μανβάνου βασιλείας ἀρχή. 'The mainland of the country of Ariakē and the beginning of the kingdom of Manbanos.'

(4) Chapter 52. Καλλίενα πόλις, ἡ ἐπὶ τῶν Σαραγάνου τοῦ πρεσβυτέρου χρόνων ἐμπόριον ἔνθεσμον γενομένη· μετὰ γὰρ τὸ κατασχεῖν αὐτὴν Σανδάνην ἐκωλύθη ἐπὶ πολύ. 'The city of Kalliena, which in the time of the elder Saraganēs became a legal mart, but since it came under Sandanēs ⟨the trade⟩ has been much hindered.'

We may now examine these four passages one by one.

(1) A. von Gutschmid[1] gives a list of kings of Nabataia in which occur three kings bearing different forms of the name we

---

[1] In Euting, *Nabatäische Inschriften aus Arabien* (Berlin, 1885), pp. 81-9.

find in the *PME*: Mâliku I, who occurs A.D. 39–59; Malchos II
(Μάλιχος), d. 77; Malchos III, the last king but one before the
conquest of Petra by A. Cornelius Palma in 106. Professor
Beeston[1] refers to Malikhas I 'who reigned in the first century
B.C.' and is thus clearly excluded, and adds that the Malikhas II
who died in 77 seems to fit the statement in the *PME*. He also
cites the criticism by Jacqueline Pirenne, who argues that the
political and navigational data in the *PME* are wholly different
from those of Pliny, and reflect a much later period.[2] He goes
on to cite J. Starcky, who on the basis of a papyrus document
found in 1954 written in a palaeographic style more recent than
the time of Malikhas II refers to another king Malikhas[3] which
suggests to Beeston that we must deduce the existence of a
Malikhas III as a vassal of Rome subsequent to the Roman
annexation of 106. Since we appear to have already three kings
called Malikhas, this last should, if he existed, be Malikhas IV.
He also notes that Jacqueline Pirenne says that since the *PME*
does not mention the state of Qataban, which she considers
disappeared about A.D. 250, this implies a late 3rd century date
for the *PME*, in which she is supported by J. Ryckmans.[4] But
the fact that the *PME* does not mention Qataban by name
seems to the present writer immaterial. It does not mention by
name the Khatramōtitai either, though it names their king
Eleazos. The mention of Petra and Malikhas suggests that the
book might have been written before the overthrow of
Nabataia; but we must remember that Malikhas or Malkhos is
not really a personal name, but a title.

(2) The date of the subduction, conquest, or overthrow of
Eudaimōn Arabia does not seem to me quite so important as it
once did. If we knew exactly what οὐ πρὸ πολλοῦ implied, it

---

[1] In a private communication to the present editor.
[2] *Le Royaume Sud-Arabe de Qatabân et sa datation*, Bibliothèque du *Muséon*,
47, Louvain, 1961, pp. 167–93.
[3] *Revue Biblique*, 1954, pp. 161–81.
[4] Ryckmans, J., *Oriens Antiquus*, III (Rome, 1964), pp. 1–24.

might help; but 'not very long before our time' is too vague. The only known military activities of the Romans in Arabia are the expedition of Aelius Gallus about 24 B.C., and Trajan's conquest of Nabataia in 106. The last was confined to the northern part of Arabia, and according to Strabō the furthest south reached by Aelius Gallus was a place called Marsuabai, which may have been near but not identical with Mariaba (Marib). The latter is at least 200 miles north of Aden, and if Gallus had subdued Aden, Strabō would surely have said so. I feel that καῖσαρ should be regarded as a miswriting for some name or title that the scribe did not understand. McCrindle indeed suggested ἐλισαρ[1] which could be the name or title of a ruler of one of the inland states; but on the whole it is best to disregard this passage as a clue to the date of the PME.

(3) King Manbanos is certainly Nahapāna, and there are dates, in inscriptions referring to him, of A.D. 119 and 123; but there is no evidence as to how long he had been reigning then,[2] while MacDowall and Wilson claim that c. A.D. 95 is virtually certain for his accession (p. 238). Taking the reference of Malikhas of Petra as giving a *terminus ante quem* of A.D. 106, and the reference to Nahapāna as implying a date after his accession, they date the PME to about A.D. 100.[3]

(4) Saraganēs is the Gautamīputra Śrī Śātakarṇī who fought Nahapāna till c. A.D. 138, while Sandanēs appears to have been the ruler of Kalliena in the time of the author of the PME, but there is nothing to show that Sandanēs was not a contemporary of Saraganēs, and MacDowall dated the PME to A.D. 120–30 on the evidence of this chapter 52.[4]

The evidence supplied by these four passages does not give us

---

[1] McCrindle, *Commerce*, p. 8.

[2] In a private communication from Bivar to the present editor.

[3] D. W. MacDowall and N. G. Wilson, 'The references to the Kuṣānas', *Num. Chron.*, 7 series, x (1970), 239.

[4] D. W. MacDowall, 'The Early Western Satraps', *Num. Chron.*, 7 series, IV (1964), 280.

anything like a clear date, and the most we can say is that the book may have been written—according to this evidence—between A.D. 95 and 130.

From the geographical evidence, one fact does seem to stand out: the *PME* was written after the publication of Pliny's *Naturalis Historia* in A.D. 77, since Pliny's description of the East African coast stops before Cape Gardafui at the *promontorium et portus Mossylicus, quo cinnamomum devehitur,* though he does add *aliqui unum Aethiopiae oppidum ultra ponunt in litore Baragaza*[1] ('some place another town of Ethiopia, Baragaza, on the coast beyond'), which, since he has quite a lot to say about India as far south as the kingdom of Pandion, must be a misplacing of Barugaza on the other side of the Indian Ocean. The *PME* and Ptolemy do not mention any 'Baragaza' on the African coast, and after naming Mosullon continue as far south as Rhapta and Menouthias, Ptolemy having in fact seven more names after Mosullon than the *PME*: Kobē, Panōn Kōmē, Zingis, Notou Keras ('headland of the south wind'), Essina, and Toniki, while the *PME* has Tabai which is not in Ptolemy.

However, it is not really Ptolemy that we have to deal with, but the lost work of his immediate predecessor Marinos of Tyre. It is quite clear that much of Ptolemy's *Geographia* is based on the work of Marinos,[2] especially the part dealing with the east coast of Africa south of Gardafui, for he twice names Marinos as the authority for certain statements made by two men with Greek names, Diogenēs and Theophilos, on which see below, Appendix 6. It is believed that Ptolemy was working at Alexandria in A.D. 139, and he appears to have survived Antoninus Pius who died in A.D. 161.[2] Marinos must therefore, if the earlier date is correct, have been working perhaps as late

[1] This may also be responsible for his *oppidum Gaza*, though this might conceivably represent the Tapatēgē of the *PME*, chap. 11, if Müller's conjecture *Gaza pēgē* (Gaza spring) is right. (*Geog.* I, p. 266.)

[2] W. Smith, *Dict. of Greek and Roman Biography*, art. Ptolemaeus, Claudius; *Paulys Real-Encyclopädie der classischen Altertumswissenschaft*. Neue Bearbeitung, Bd 23 (Stuttgart, 1959), art. Ptolemaios, Klaudios.

as about A.D. 130. So it is a fair assumption that the *PME* was not in existence in Pliny's lifetime, and was probably (from the geographical evidence) written before Marinos wrote his book. If the *PME* had been in existence in Pliny's day, it would almost certainly have been known to that omnivorous and indefatigable collector of information. Schoff assigns the *PME* to A.D. 60, and argues that though it was in existence in Pliny's day, 'a man of Pliny's standing would have been apt to refrain from mentioning by name a writer with no literary reputation in Roman society'.[1] This feeble argument ignores the fact that Pliny was careful to give the names of his authorities for each book of his *Naturalis Historia*, those for the sixth book being fifteen Roman and thirty-seven Greek writers, some of whom had not only no literary reputation in Rome, but were probably quite unknown in ordinary literary circles. Schoff's further argument that Pliny may have used the *PME* without mentioning the author's name is again futile, because if he did so he would certainly have included the places beyond Portus Mossylicus. The fact is that it is possible on the available evidence to give only an approximate date to the book, and the evidence would suggest some time between A.D. 95 and 130.

III

There are only two manuscripts of the *PME* and both are late. The better of the two is at Heidelberg: *Codex Palatinus Graecus* 398 (fol. 40v–54v), of the 10th century; the other is in the British Library: Add. MS 19391, of the 14th or 15th century. The later MS is merely a copy, with a few important corrections, of the Heidelberg MS, and in the words of Hjalmar Frisk, 'du reste assez mauvaise'.[2] The text was published by Frisk in 1927 (at Göteborg), with the title *Le Périple de la Mer Erythrée*.

[1] W. H. Schoff, *The Periplus of the Erythraean Sea* (New York, 1912), p. 15.
[2] Frisk, p. 32.

The book contains a detailed study of the text and language, of a high order of scholarship and written in French. Those who want further information on this aspect of the *PME* are referred to this work. I have made my translation from Frisk's text.

The text in MS Heidelberg 398 was written by two different hands. The first wrote in minuscules, with many marginal notes in small uncials and a number of corrections. The second hand added further corrections. Frisk considered that the divergences of MS 19391 from MS 398 are due mostly to the negligence of the copyist, though occasionally there are correct conjectures in the emendation of errors in MS 398, of which Frisk gives some examples, such as ἐνδικὸς in chapter 6, corrected in MS 19391 to ἰνδικὸς; and παρεσταμέναι in chapter 34, corrected to παρατεταμέναι. Frisk's conclusion from a comparison of the two texts was that the corrections in MS 398 by the second hand were later than the date of MS 19391. It is of interest to note that several words—names of places and products—are written without an accent, because they were either corrupted or else unknown to the copyist. Among them are Ἀργαλου, ἀσυφη, δουακα, γιζειρ, μοκροτου, μαγλα, τοπαρον.

The *PME* has been printed several times,[1] and in fact it is the best known of the surviving works of its kind. The earliest modern edition was published by Sigismund Gelenius in 1553; he attributed it to Arrian for the reason already given. The next four editors also attributed it to Arrian, and it was not till Carl Müller produced a greatly improved text in his *Geographi Graeci Minores* (1855) that Arrian's authorship was seriously questioned. There have also been at least three translations into English. The first, in 1807, was by William Vincent, Dean of Westminster; the second, the best of the three, in 1879, by J. W. McCrindle, Principal of the Government College, Patna, in 1879; and the third, in 1912, by W. H. Schoff, which Dr Gervase Mathew said 'should be used with caution;

[1] See below, p. 198.

it is a free translation of an imaginatively emended text'.[1]

As a supplement to the *PME* I have added a translation of certain chapters from Agatharkhidēs' description of the African coast of the Red Sea, which I believe has never been previously published in English. Agatharkhidēs of Knidos was a grammarian of the second century B.C. who wrote a book called περὶ τῆς ἐρυθρᾶς θαλάσσης ('On the Erythraean Sea') now lost, and surviving only in an epitome made by Phōtios.[2] This work is, in effect, an ethnological sketch giving but few geographical names. It is, however, the first book written about the Red Sea, and contains some interesting material, especially about the 'Trōglodytes'. It has also an intelligent classification of the races which lived to the south of Egypt.

Agatharkhidēs belonged to the Peripatetic School of philosophy, and wrote several books on history and geography. During part of his life he was guardian to one of the sons of Ptolemy VII Phuskōn (143–116 B.C.). His work on the Erythraean Sea was published about 113 B.C.; the rest of his works, which included a book on Asia, a book on Europe, another on the Trōglodytes, a book on history, and others, are all lost. Unlike the author of the *PME* he was a scholar, and wrote in Attic Greek. 'His style, according to Phōtios, was dignified and perspicuous, and abounded in sententious passages. . . . In the composition of his speeches he was an imitator of Thucydides.'[3]

---

[1] Mathew, Gervase, *History of East Africa*, p. 94.

[2] Phōtios, Patriarch of Constantinople in the 9th century A.D. wrote a book called Μυριοβίβλιον ἢ Βιβλιοθήκη (Muriobiblion or Bibliothēkē) which contains extracts from many ancient writers whose works are now lost. The work of Agatharkhidēs is in codex 250. The complete text of Phōtios was published by Bekker (Berlin 1824–5). The extracts from Agatharkhidēs given in this book are taken from Müller's *Geographi Graeci Minores*. The work appears to have been in five books, but Phōtios gives extracts from Books I and V only. There seems to be little doubt that Strabō, who was born in 64 B.C., used the text of Agatharkhidēs, though he has added names and other details which are lacking in the earlier work.

[3] Greenhill, W. A., *Dictionary Greek and Roman Biography*, I (1844), p. 61.

In justification of the brevity of this Introduction, we should perhaps say that much of the material which is often included in an introduction is placed after the translation in the form of Appendices, and thus the order of the book is as follows:

After a summary of the topography comes the translation of the text, and, separately, the notes. Only marginal glosses and scholia are placed as footnotes to the translation. Then comes Appendix 1, divided into: (a) a brief account of the start of the journey from the Red Sea Coast of Egypt, and of the ancient canals from the Nile to the Red Sea; (b) an outline of the routes from Egypt along the African, Arabian, and Indian coasts; and (c) a more detailed study of the local topography, arranged, not as an alphabetical gazetteer, but in the order in which the places occur in the narrative. There follows, in Appendix 2, a glossary of imports and exports, divided into six sections according to the nature of the trade-goods. Appendices 3–6 deal respectively with the ethnology and history of the area concerned as far as it affects the *Periplus*, and with shipping, elephant-hunting and the Mountains of the Moon.

In the translation we have followed McCrindle's plan of listing the trade-goods in the text, together with the Greek words used to describe them, and in Appendix 2 the Greek words are given after their English equivalents. Since the lists of trade-goods are in alphabetical order there is no separate English index of them, but instead there is one of the Greek words. Lastly there is the English version of the selections from Agatharkhidēs, with separate notes.

Note on some Features of the Translation

1   Words added to complete the sense are given in ⟨   ⟩.

2   The Greek words used in the text for trade goods are added in the cases in which they occur in the text, i.e. nominative, accusative, genitive; this applies also to the Glossary of Imports and Exports.

3   Superior numerals refer to the Notes which follow the translation.

4   Some glosses which had crept into the text are given as footnotes; Frisk includes them in his text between square brackets [ ] or daggers † †. Some marginal glosses are also included in footnotes. These are indicated by an asterisk *.

Topographical Summary

AFRICA

1* Muos Hormos (near Qosseir)
   Bernikē (in Foul Bay)
2 †Barbaroi
   †Ikhthuophagoi
   †Agriophagoi
   †Moskhophagoi
   Meroē
3 Ptolemaïs Thērōn (Aqiq)
4 Adouli (Zulla)
   Oreinē (Dissei)
   Didōros' Island (Delemme)
   Koloē (Qohayto)
   Axōmite metropolis (Aksum)
   Kuēneion (Sennar)
   Alalaiou Islands (Dahlak)
5 Great sandbank (in Hawakil Bay)
7 Aualitēs (Zeyla)
8 Malaō (Berbera)
9 Moundou (Heis or Mait)
10 Mosullon (Bandar Kasim)
11 Cape Elephas (Ras Filuk)
   Akannai (Bandar Alula)
12 Arōmatōn Emporion (Olok)
   Tabai (Tohen)
13 Opōnē (Ras Hafūn)
15 Bluffs and Strands of Azania
    (Hafūn to Mogadishu)
   Courses of Azania
    (Mogadishu to Kwaihu)
   Puralaōn Islands
    (Pate, Manda, Lamu)
   The Channel (Siyu channel)
   Menouthias (Zanzibar or Pemba)
16 Rhapta (perhaps in Rufiji delta)

ARABIA

19 Leukē Kōmē (Yanbu' al-bahr)
20 Burnt Island (Zebayir)
21 Mouza (Maushij)
22 Sauē (Udain)
23 Saphar (near Yerim)
25 Diodōros Island (Perim)
   Okēlis (Sheikh Sa'id)
26 Eudaimōn Arabia (Aden)
27 Kanē (Hisn Ghurab)
   Isle of Birds (Sikha)
   Troullas (Halania)
   Saubatha (Shabwa)
29 Sakhalitēs Bay
30 Suagros (Ras Fartak)
   Dioskouridou Island (Socotra)
32 Omana (Oman)
   Moskha (perhaps Salala)
33 Asikhōnos (Ras Hasik)
   Isles of Zēnobios (Kuria Muria)
   Sarapis' Island (Masira)
34 Kalaiou Isles (Fahal, Daimaniyat,
    etc.)
35 Asabōn (Cape Musandam)
   Semiramis Height (Larak Is.?)
   Apologou (al-Ubulla)
   Pasinou Kharax (Jabal Khiyabar)

INDIA

37 Hōraia

★ Figures are chapter numbers.   † Peoples.

INDIA—*contd.*

38 Sinthos river (Indus)
   Barbarikon
   Minnagar (Mandasor)
40 Eirinon (Rann of Kutch)
   Barakē gulf (Gulf of Kutch)
41 Surastrēnē (Kathiawar)
   Astakapra (Hathab near
   Bhavnagar)
   Papikē (near Astakapra)
42 (Bay of Cambay)
   Baiōnēs Island (Peram)
   Maïs river (Mahi)
   Lamnaios river (Narbada or
   Narmada)
43 Hērōnē shoal
   Kammōni
46 Barugaza (Broach)
47 Proklaïs (Chārsadda)
48 Ozēnē (Ujjain)
50 Dakhinabadēs (Deccan)
51 Paithana (Paithan)
   Tagara (Ter (Thair))
52 Akabarou
   Souppara
   Kalliena (Kalyāna near Bombay)
53 Sēmulla (Chaul)
   Mandagora (Bankot)
   Palaipatmai (Dabhol)
   Melizeigara (Jaigarh)
   Buzantion (Vijayadurg)
   Toparon (Jamsanda)

   Erannoboas (Malvan)
   Sēsekreienai (Vengurla Rocks)
   Aigidiōn Island (Anjediva)
   Kaineitōn Island (Oyster Rock)
   White Island (Hog Island or
   Pigeon Island)
   Naoura (Cannanore)
   Tundis (Tanor)
   Limurikē (Damirikē, the Tamil
   coast)
   Nelkunda (Kottayam)
55 Bakarē (Vaikkarai)
58 Red Mountain (Red Cliffs near
   Quilon)
   Balita (Trivandrum or Manpalli)
   Komar, Komarei (Cape
   Comorin)
59 Kolkhoi (Korkai)
   Argalou (Uraiyur)
60 Kamara (Kaviripaddinam)
   Podoukē (Arikamedu)
   Sōpatma (near Madras)
61 Palaisimoundou (Ceylon)
62 Masalia (Masulipatam)
   Dēsarēnē (perhaps Orissa)
63 Gangēs town
   Gangēs river (Ganges, Ganga)

FURTHER ASIA
   Khrusē (Burma and South-east
   Asia)
64 Thina (China)

The Periplus of the Erythraean Sea

CHAPTER 1

AMONG the established harbours of the Erythraean Sea[1]★
and the marts round it, the first is the Egyptian harbour of
Muos Hormos. Those who sail from here come, after
1800 stades,[2] to Bernikē on the right hand. The harbours
of both are on the edge of Egypt, and lie in bays of the
Erythraean Sea.

Muos Hormos
Bernikē

CHAPTER 2

Still on the right hand from Bernikē and adjoining it, is
the land of the Barbaroi.[1] The maritime parts are inhabited
by the Ikhthuophagoi[2] who dwell in enclosures scattered
here and there in the narrow inlets; the country inland is
occupied by the Barbaroi and those who live beyond
them, the Agriophagoi[3] and the Moskhophagoi,[4] under
the rule of chiefs. Behind them in the interior to the west
⟨is the metropolis called Meroē.⟩[5]

Barbaroi
Ikhthuophagoi

Agriophagoi
Moskhophagoi

Meroē

CHAPTER 3

After the Moskhophagoi there is beside the sea a small

★ Notes on the Periplus appear on p. 58.

Ptolemaïs
Thērōn

mart, distant about 4000 stades,★ called Ptolemaïs of the Huntings, which the hunters of the king in the times of the Ptolemies used as their base. At this mart there is true tortoiseshell, χελώνην ἀληθινὴν καὶ χερσαίαν, and a little land tortoise, white and with smaller shells. A little ivory ἐλέφας, is also found here, like that of Adouli. The place has no harbour and can be reached only by small boats.¹

CHAPTER 4

After Ptolemaïs of the Huntings, at a distance of about 3000 stades, there is the customary mart of Adouli, lying in a deep bay that runs southwards; in front of it is an island called Oreinē, which is about 200 stades out in the sea from the inmost part of the bay, lying along the mainland on both sides, where ships entering anchor on account of attacks from the mainland. For at one time they used to anchor right inside the bay at the island called Of Didōros along the mainland where there was a crossing on foot, by means of which the Barbaroi living there attacked the island. And opposite Oreinē on the mainland, twenty stades from the sea, is Adouli, a village of moderate size, from which to Koloē, an inland city and the first ivory market, it is a journey of three days; and from this, another five days to the metropolis called the Axōmite,¹ to which is brought all the ivory from beyond the Nile through the district called Kuēneion, and thence to Adouli. For the whole quantity of elephant and rhinoceros which is killed grazes in the interior, though occasionally they are seen by the sea round about Adouli. Out to sea beyond this mart, on the right, lie several small

Adouli

Oreinē

Didōros'
Island

Adouli
Koloē

Aksum
Kuenēion

★ Interpolated gloss before σταδίους: τὸ πέρας τῆς ἀνακομιδῆς, 'the end of the importation' (?).

FIG. 1. Aduli and the throne of Ptolemy

This is a picture possibly made from sketches by Cosmas, and reproduced from McCrindle's translation of *The Christian Topography of Cosmas* (Hakluyt Soc., 1897). The wording is: 1. 'The city Adoulē'; 2. 'Road leading from Adoule to Axomē'; 3. 'Ethiopians travelling on foot'; 4. 'Ptolemaïc throne'. There is another version of this drawing in MS Cod. Vat. Gr. 699, which shows the throne from a different angle with a tablet lying across it and another tablet standing beside it; there are four figures of 'Ethiopians travelling', and on the left side are the words, reading from the top, *TEΛWNION ΓABAZAC*, 'custom-house of Gabaza'; *AIΔOYΛIS*, 'Aidoulis'; *ΘAΛACCA*, 'sea'; and, at the bottom, *CAMIΔI*, 'Samidi', which I cannot identify. Unfortunately this picture is not clear enough to reproduce, but McCrindle's drawing gives a good enough idea of it.

sandy islands called Alalaiou, where there is tortoiseshell, Alalaiou
Islands χελώνην, which is brought to the mart by the Ikhthuophagoi.

CHAPTER 5

And at a distance of nearly 800 stades there is another very deep bay, at the mouth of which on the right hand is a great sandbank, in the depth of which is found deposited the opsian stone,[1] which occurs in this place only. Zōskalēs rules[2] these parts, from the Moskhophagoi to the other Barbaria, mean[3] ⟨in his way⟩ of life and with an eye on the main chance, but otherwise high-minded, and skilled in Greek letters.

CHAPTER 6

To these places are imported:
  Barbaric unfulled cloth made in Egypt ἱμάτια
    Βαρβαρικὰ ἄγναφα.
  Arsinoïtic[1] robes ἀρσινοϊτικαὶ στολαί.
  Spurious[2] coloured cloaks ἀβόλλαι χρωμάτινοι νόθοι.
  Linen λέντια.
  Fringed mantles δικρόσσια.
  Several sorts of glassware λιθίας ὑαλῆς.
  Imitation murrhine ware made in Diospolis[3] μορρίνης.
  Ōrokhalkos ὠρόχαλκος, which they use for ornaments
    and for cutting ⟨to serve⟩ as money.
  Material called 'copper cooked in honey' μελίεφθα
    χαλκᾶ for cooking-pots and for cutting into armlets
    and anklets for women.
  Iron σίδηρος used for spears both for hunting elephants
    and other animals and for war.

Axes πελύκια.

Adzes σκέπαρνα.

Swords μάχαιραι.

Big round drinking-cups of bronze ποτήρια χαλκᾶ στρογγύλα.

A little money δηνάριον, for foreigners who live there.

Ladikean⁴ and Italian wine οἶνος, but not much.

For the king are imported:
Silver and gold objects ἀργυρώματα καὶ χρυσώματα, made in the design of the country.

Cloaks of cloth ἱματίων ἀβόλλαι.

Unlined garments γαυνάκαι, not of much value.

Likewise from the inner parts of Ariakē:
Indian iron and steel σίδηρος καὶ στόμωμα.

The broader Indian cloth called monakhē μοναχή.

Cloth called sagmatogēnai σαγματογῆναι.

Belts περιζώματα.

Garments called gaunakai γαυνάκαι.

Mallow-cloth μολόχινα.

A little muslin σινδόναι.

Coloured lac λάκκος χρωμάτινος.

The exports from these places are:
Ivory ἐλέφας.

Tortoiseshell χελώνη.

Rhinoceros horn⁵ ῥινόκερως.

The greater part is brought from Egypt to the mar between the month of January and the month o September, that is, from Tubi to Thōth. The best time fo the trade from Egypt is about the month of September.

CHAPTER 7

From here the Arabian Gulf stretches eastward, and nea Aualitēs becomes narrowest. After about 4000 stades thos

22

who sail eastwards along the same coast find the other Barbaric marts called 'Those beyond ⟨the straits⟩', lying one after another; these have harbours with anchorages and roadsteads ⟨which can be used⟩ at suitable times. The first is that called Aualitēs, near which is the shortest Aualitēs crossing from Arabia to the other side.¹ At this place is the small mart of Aualitēs, reached by rafts² and small boats. There are imported here:

Various kinds of glassware ὑαλῆ λιθία.

Unripe olives from Diopolis χυλὸς ὄμφακος.

Miscellaneous dressed Barbaric clothing ἱμάτια βαρβαρικὰ.

Corn σῖτος.

Wine οἶνος.

A little tin κασσίτερος.

From here are exported, sometimes by the Barbaroi ⟨themselves⟩ on rafts to Okēlis and Mouza:

Spices ἀρώματα.

A little ivory ἐλέφας.

Tortoiseshell χελώνη.

A very little myrrh, σμύρνα, but better than the other. The Barbaroi who live in the place are more stubborn.³

CHAPTER 8

After Aualitēs there is another mart, different from it, called Malaō, distant about 800 stades by sailing. The Malaō harbour is exposed to the sea, ⟨but⟩ sheltered by a projection running out from the east. The inhabitants are more peaceful. There are imported to this place the afore-mentioned things, and also:

Many tunics χιτῶνες.

Dressed and dyed Arsinoïtic cloaks σάγοι.

Drinking-cups ποτήρια.
A little meliephtha μελίεφθα.
Iron σίδηρος.
Coinage, δηνάριον, but not much.
Gold and silver χρυσοῦν δὲ καὶ ἀργυροῦν.
There are exported from these places:
Myrrh σμύρνα.
A little incense ⟨called⟩ 'from beyond the straits',
λίβανος ὁ περατικὸς.
The harder kasia κασία σκληροτέρα.
Douaka δουακα.
Kankamon κάγκαμον.
Makeir μάκειρ, sent over to Arabia.
Occasionally slaves σώματα.

CHAPTER 9

Moundou

From Malaō it is two courses to the mart of Moundou, where ships anchor more safely by an island lying very close to the land. The imports to this are as aforesaid, and from it are likewise exported the same goods, ⟨and⟩ fragrant gum called mokrotou μοκροτου. The inhabitants who trade here are more stubborn.

CHAPTER 10

Mosullon

From Moundou sailing eastwards likewise after two or nearly three courses lies Mosullon on a harbourless shore. There are imported to it the afore-mentioned goods, and objects of silver, σκεύη ἀργυρᾶ, a little iron, and precious stones. From these places a large amount of kasia, κασίας

24

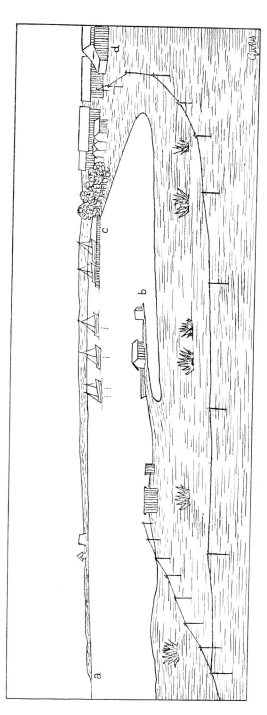

FIG. 2. The harbour of Berbera (Malaō) in 1944   a = Ras   b = Shaab pier   c = Pier and Customs   d = Native town

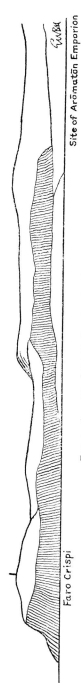

FIG. 3. Cape Gardafui (Arōmatōn akron), 1938

Faro Crispi

Site of Arōmatōn Emporion

χύμα, is exported, on account of which larger ships are needed at the mart; and other ⟨exports⟩ are fragrant gums, ἐνωδία, and spices, ἀρώματα, a few small tortoises, χελωνάρια, and the fragrant gum mokrotou, inferior to that from Moundou, and 'incense from beyond the straits', λίβανος ὁ περατικός, and occasionally ivory and myrrh.

CHAPTER 11

Cape
Elephas

Akannai

From Mosullon, after sailing two courses, are what they call Neiloptolemaiou, and Tapatēgē, and the Little Laurel Grove, and the headland Elephas, and a large laurel grove* called Akannai, in which alone is produced the greatest quantity of the best 'incense from beyond the straits'.

CHAPTER 12

Mart of
Spices

And after this, the land now turning away to the south, is the Mart of the Spices[1] and the precipitous headland which is the eastern end of the Barbarian mainland.[2] The harbour, exposed to the sea, is dangerous at certain times since the place lies open to the north wind. A local sign of approaching storm is the greater disturbance in the depth of the sea and a change of colour.[3] When this happens, all take shelter by the great promontory, a place of shelter

---

* Interpolated gloss between ἐλέφας and καὶ δαφνῶνα μέγαν: ἀπὸ ὀπώνης εἰς νότον προχωρεῖ εἶτα εἰς λίβα ἡ χώρα ποταμὸν ἔχει τὸν λεγόμενον ἐλέφαντα, 'from Opōnē the country turns away to the south and then to the south-west, ⟨and⟩ has a river called Elephas'.

26

FIG. 4. Ras Filuk (Cape Elephas), 1938

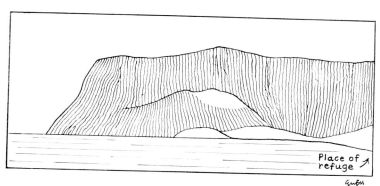

FIG. 5. Ras Shenagef (Tabai akrōtērion), 1938

Tabai

called Tabai. There are imported to the mart the goods aforesaid; and there are produced in it:

Kasia κασία.

Gizeir γιζειρ.

Asuphē ἀσυφη.

Arōma ἄρωμα.[4]

Magla μαγλα.

Motō μοτὼ.

Frankincense λίβανος.

CHAPTER 13

Opōnē

From Tabai, after sailing along the peninsula for 400 stades, drawn by the current, they come to another mart, Opōnē,[1] to which are brought the aforesaid imports. A great deal of kasia is produced in it, and spice, ἄρωμα, and motō, μοτὼ, and better slaves, δουλικὰ, which are sent mostly to Egypt, and a great deal of tortoiseshell, better than the other.

CHAPTER 14

The voyage from Egypt to all these marts beyond the straits is made in the month of July, that is Epiphi. It is customary to bring local products from the inner parts of Ariakē and Barugaza to these marts beyond the straits:

Corn σῖτος.

Rice ὄρυζα.

Ghi βούτυρον.

Sesame oil ἔλαιον σησάμινον.

The cloth called monakhē and sagmatogēnē μοναχὴ, σαγματογήνη.

Belts περιζώματα.

Honey-cane called sakkhari μέλι τὸ καλάμινον τὸ λεγόμενον σάκχαρι.

And some traders sail direct to these marts; others exchange their goods while sailing along the coast. The country is not ruled ⟨by one chief⟩, but each mart is under its own chief.

CHAPTER 15

From Opōnē the coast stretches away more to the south, and first are what are called the Lesser and Greater Bluffs of Azania,[1] where there are anchorages, extending for six courses towards the south-west. Then the Lesser and Greater Strands, of another six courses, and after them in succession the courses of Azania, the first called Sarapiōn's, then that of Nikōn, after which there are several rivers and a series of other roadsteads separated by several stations and courses of a day, seven in all, as far as the Puralaōn islands and what is called The Channel, from which a little to the south-west, after two courses of a night and day along the Ausineitic coast, the island of Menouthias is encountered, about 3000 stades from the mainland, low and covered with trees, in which are rivers and many kinds of bird, and mountain tortoise. Of wild animals there are none except crocodiles; but they hurt no man. There are in it small boats sewn and made from one piece of wood,[2] which are used for fishing and catching marine tortoises. In this island they catch them [i.e. fish] with a local form of basket trap[3] instead of nets

Bluffs of Azania

Strands

Courses of Azania

Puralaōn Islands

Menouthias

29

stretched across the mouths of the openings along the foreshore.

CHAPTER 16

Rhapta

From here after two courses off the mainland lies the last mart of Azania, called Rhapta, which has its name from the aforementioned sewn boats, where there is a great deal of ivory and tortoiseshell. The natives of this country have very large bodies and piratical habits[1]; and each place likewise has its own chief. The Mopharitic chief rules it according to an ancient agreement by which it falls under the kingdom which has become first in Arabia. Under the king the people of Mouza hold it by payment of tribute, and send ships with captains and agents who are mostly Arabs, and are familiar through residence and intermarriage with the nature of the places and their language.

CHAPTER 17

There are brought to these marts things made specially in Mouza:

Spears λόγχη.
Axes πελύκια.
Small swords μαχαίρια.
Awls ὀπήτια.
Several kinds of glassware λιθίας ὑαλῆς.

And to some places wine, οἶνος and corn, σῖτος not much, nor for trade, but for expenses in making friends with the Barbaroi. There are exported from these places a great deal of ivory, though it is inferior to that of Adouli,

30

and rhinoceros horn, and tortoiseshell, next in demand to that from India, and a little coconut, ναύπλιος.[1]

CHAPTER 18

And these are almost the last marts of Azania on the right hand ⟨coming⟩ from the land of Bernikē. For after these places the unexplored ocean curves round to the west, and extending southwards in the opposite direction from Aithiopia and Libya and Africa, mingles with the western sea.

CHAPTER 19

On the left from Bernikē, two or three days run from Muos Hormos eastwards, crossing the gulf which lies alongside, there is another harbour with a fort, called Leukē Kōmē, from which there is ⟨a route inland⟩ to Petra, to Malikhas king of the Nabataioi. It has some reputation for the ships, though ⟨they are⟩ not large ones, ⟨which come⟩ loaded from Arabia. For this reason a Collector[1] of a tax of a quarter on imported merchandise is posted there, and for security a centurion[2] with a garrison.

Leukē Kōmē

CHAPTER 20

Immediately after this place and contiguous with it is the land of Arabia, for most of its length stretching along the Erythraean Sea. Different tribes inhabit it, differing in speech ⟨from each other⟩, some partly, others completely. Likewise[1] along the sea occur the enclosures of the Ikhthuophagoi; and higher up ⟨inland⟩ are villages and

Arabia

31

nomadic encampments inhabited by scoundrelly people who speak two languages; and those who stray from the middle course[2] and fall into their hands are either plundered, or, if they survive from shipwrecks, are carried into slavery. For this reason they are continually being made prisoners by the chiefs and kings of Arabia. They are called Kanraïtai. Thus, on the whole, this voyage along the coast of the Arabian mainland is dangerous, the country being without harbours, with bad anchorages and a foul shore, unapproachable by reason of rocks, and in every way formidable. For this reason, on coming near it we hold to the middle course,[*] and press on all the more as far as the Burnt Island, after which are continuous regions of civilized people with nomadic herds of cattle and camels.

Kanraïtai

Burnt Island

CHAPTER 21

After these ⟨regions⟩, in the furthest bay on the left hand of this sea is Mouza, an established mart beside the sea, distant from Bernikē, for those sailing south, at least 12,000 stades.[1] The whole place is full of Arabs, shipmasters and sailors, and hums with business; for they use their own ships[2] for commerce with the opposite coast and with Barugaza.

Mouza

CHAPTER 22

Three days from this is situated the city Sauē in the country called that of Mapharitis; the ruler[1] who lives there is called Kholaibos.

Sauē in Mapharitis

★ Interpolated gloss after μέσον πλοῦν κατέχομεν: εἰς τὴν Ἀραβικὴν χώραν, 'towards the Arabian country'.

32

CHAPTER 23

And after another nine days is the metropolis Saphar, in which ⟨lives⟩ Kharibaēl the lawful king of two tribes, the Homērite and that lying beside it called Sabaïte; he is ⟨called⟩ 'Friend of the Emperors' on account of ⟨his⟩ continual embassies and gifts.

Saphar

Homēritai

Sabaïtai

CHAPTER 24

The mart of Mouza is harbourless, but has good moorings out in the sea because of the sandbanks which provide anchorages. The imports here include:

Mouza

Good quality and common purple cloth πορφύρα.

Arabian sleeved clothing both unlined and common with check patterns and interwoven with gold ἱματισμὸς 'Αραβικὸς χειριδωτός, ὅ τε ἁπλοῦς καὶ ὁ κοινὸς καὶ σκοτουλᾶτος καὶ διάχρυσος.

Saffron κρόκος.

Kuperos κύπερος.

Cotton cloth ὀθόνιον.

Cloaks ἀβόλλαι.

Blankets λώδικες, not many, single and local.

Striped sashes ζῶναι σκιωταί.

A moderate amount of perfume μύρον.

Sufficient coinage χρῆμα.

Wine οἶνος.

Corn, σῖτος, not much, for the country produces a moderate amount of corn and plenty of wine.

To the king and the chief ⟨of Mouza⟩ are given horses, and pack-mules, ἡμίονοι νωτηγοὶ and gold plate, χρυσώματα, and chased silver ware τορευτὰ ἀργυρώματα, and

33

expensive clothing ἱματισμὸς, and objects of copper, χαλκουργήματα. The exports from here are local products: selected myrrh, staktē στακτή, both Abeiraian and Minaian ἀβειραία καὶ μιναία, marble λύγδος, and also all the things before-mentioned from Adouli on the other side. The voyage to here[1] is best made about the month of September, which is Thōth; but there is nothing to prevent it from being made sooner.

CHAPTER 25

After this, sailing along the coast for about 300 stades, the Arabian mainland and the opposite coast of Barbaria near Aualitēs now come near each other. There is a channel, not very long, which brings ⟨the waters of⟩ the sea together and shuts them in a narrow strait.[1] Here, in the middle of the strait, which is 60 stades long,[2] the island of Diodōros interrupts the channel. For this reason the passage through it is rough, the water being blown upon ⟨by the winds⟩ from the neighbouring hills. On this strait is Okēlis, a village of Arabs beside the sea, under the same chief ⟨as Mouza⟩, not so much a mart as an anchorage and watering-place, and the first landfall for those sailing into the gulf.

Diodōros'
Island

CHAPTER 26

After Okēlis the sea widens again to the east and soon the open sea becomes visible, and at about 1200 stades is the village of Eudaimōn Arabia beside the sea, belonging to the same king Kharibaēl, with convenient harbourage and a better water supply than Okēlis. At this time it lies at the

Eudaimōn
Arabia

34

entrance to a bay, where the land begins to recede.
Eudaimōn Arabia was called Eudaimōn when in former
days it was a city, when men had not voyaged from India
to Egypt, and those from Egypt had not ventured to sail
to the places further inside the sea-corridor, but came here
where the cargoes from both ⟨India and Egypt⟩ were
received, just as Alexandreia receives them, both from
overseas and from Egypt itself. But now, not very long
before our time, Caesar destroyed it.[1]

CHAPTER 27

After Eudaimōn Arabia there is a long line of continuous
beaches, and a bay, stretching for 2000 stades or more,
with Nomads and Ikhthuophagoi living in villages along
the coast; and after a projecting headland, there is another
mart beside the sea called Kanē, of the kingdom of   Kanē
Eleazos—the frankincense country. Opposite to it are two
desert islands, one called Of the Birds, the other Troullas,   Troullas
120 stades from Kanē. Lying above it inland is the
metropolis of Saubatha, in which the king lives. All the   Saubatha
frankincense produced in the country is brought here, as
to a warehouse, by camels and locally-made rafts of skin
floated on inflated hides, and boats. It[1] has reciprocal
dealings with the marts on the opposite side, of Barugaza
and Skuthia and Omana, and the neighbouring regions of
Persis.

CHAPTER 28

There are brought to this place from Egypt in like   Kanē
manner:

A little wheat, πυρὸς, and wine as to Mouza.

Arabian clothing, both unlined and common, and much of it spurious, ἱματισμὸς ἀραβικὸς ὁμοίως καὶ κοινὸς καὶ ἁπλοῦς κὰι ὁ νόθος περισσότερος.

Copper χαλκὸς.

Tin κασσίτερος.

Coral κοράλλιον.

Storax στύραξ.

and the rest as to Mouza, but more chased silverware ἀργυρώματα τετορευμένα, and money χρήματα, for the king, as well as horses, statues, ἀνδριάντες, and excellent unlined clothing ἱματισμὸς ἁπλοῦς. From here is exported local produce: frankincense λίβανος, and aloes ἀλόη, and the rest of the things which are shared with the other marts. The voyage is best made at the same season as that to Mouza, or earlier.

CHAPTER 29

Sakhalitēs

After Kanē the land draws back considerably, and another very deep bay called Sakhalitēs follows, and the country is called Libanōtophoros; ⟨it is⟩ mountainous and inaccessible, with a dense and cloudy atmosphere on account of the trees which bear frankincense. The incense-bearing trees are not very large, nor tall, and they bear the solidified incense on the bark, just as some of the trees among us in Egypt weep gum. The incense is handled by the royal slaves and men who have been sent there as punishment. The place is fearfully unhealthy, and pestilential even to those who sail past it; to those who work there it is always fatal; and in addition they are killed off by sheer lack of food.

36

CHAPTER 30

And here is the greatest headland of the bay, looking towards the east, called Suagros, on which is the fort of Suagros the country, and a harbour and a warehouse for the incense which has been collected. And opposite to it, in the sea, is the island called Dioskouridou, half way Dioskouridou between it and the Cape of Spices on the other side,[1] but near Suagros. ⟨This island⟩ is very large and ⟨mainly⟩ desert and damp ground, having rivers in it, and crocodiles, and a great many snakes, and giant lizards the flesh of which is eaten and the fat melted and used instead of oil. The island produces neither vine nor grain. They are a mixed people, consisting of Arabs and Indians, and a few Greeks who have sailed out ⟨there⟩ for trade. The island produces the true tortoise χελώνην ἀληθινὴν, the land tortoise, χελώνην χερσαίαν, and the white, καὶ τὴν λευκήν, which is plentiful and of good quality and profitable on account of its large shell. There is, too, mountain tortoise, χελώνην τὴν ὀρεινὴν, with a very large and thick shell; the parts towards the belly do not allow of cutting on account of their toughness; the ⟨backs[2]⟩ are cut up for boxes, plates, cake dishes, and other similar things. Cinnabar, κιννάβαρι, known as 'Indian' is also produced in the island, collected from the trees ⟨drop by⟩ drop.

CHAPTER 31

It happens that just as Azania is under Kharibaēl and the Mapharitic chief, so the island ⟨of Dioskouridou⟩ is under Dioskouridou the king of Libanōtophoros. There used to be business connexions with some ⟨traders⟩ from Mouza and ⟨some⟩ of those sailing from Limurikē and Barugaza, who put in there by chance, and bartered rice and wheat, σῖτον, and Indian cloth, ὀθόνιον ἰνδικὸν, and female slaves σώματα θηλυκὰ—which are rarely brought there—for large quantities of tortoiseshell as a return cargo; but now under the kings the coast of the island is farmed out and guarded.

CHAPTER 32

Moskha

After Suagros the bay continues, cutting deep into the mainland of Omana, with a passage across it of 600 stades; and after it, for another 500 stades, are high, rocky, and precipitous mountains where men live in caves. After them is a harbour appointed for the loading of Sakhalitic frankincense, σαχαλίτου λιβάνου, called Moskha, to which some ships come regularly from Kanē, and others sailing along the coast from Limurikē or Barugaza winter there in late seasons and in exchange for cloth, ὀθόνιον, wheat, σῖτον, and oil, ἔλαιον, they take in from the king's officers, as a return cargo, frankincense—generally that produced in the Sakhalitic region—at a mole which is ruinous and which is unguarded, being under the protection of the gods which guard this place. For neither secretly nor openly can it be loaded on a ship without royal permission; and if anyone takes up ⟨even⟩ a grain, the ship cannot sail, inasmuch as such sailing is against the will of the gods.

CHAPTER 33

Asikhōnos

From Moskha harbour, after about another 1500 stades, as far as Asikhōnos, a mountain range stretches along the land, and at the furthest part of it, lie seven islands in a row, called Of Zēnobios, after which an uncivilized territory lies along the coast, no longer belonging to the same kingdom, but already under that of Persis. ⟨A ship⟩ sailing beyond along the coast for about 2000 stades from ⟨the islands⟩ of Zēnobios encounters an island called Of Sarapis, which is about 120 stades from the land. The inhabitants live in three villages, and the people, the Ikhthuophagoi, are sacred, and use the Arabic language, and ⟨wear⟩ loin-cloths ⟨made of⟩ palm-leaves. The island has sufficient tortoiseshell and of good quality. Light boats and towed vessels are regularly fitted out in Kanē to come here.

Zēnobios' Isles

Sarapis' Island

Sacred Ikhthuophagoi

CHAPTER 34

Sailing round the bay along the neighbouring mainland, now going northwards towards the entrance of the Persian Sea, lie many islands called the Kalaiou islands, stretched along the land for about 2000 stades. The people who inhabit them suffer from a disease of the eye.[1]

Kalaiou Isles

CHAPTER 35

Near the furthest headland of the Kalaiou Islands and the mountain called Kalon there comes, not far beyond, the mouth of the Persian ⟨Gulf⟩, where there are many pearl fisheries.[1] On the left hand side of this mouth are the very great mountains Asabōn, and on the right, straight on and in full view, is another round mountain called Of

Kalon Mt.

Asabōn Mts.

39

Semiramis
Mt.

Semiramis; and the centre of the passage through the mouth is about 60 stades, beyond which the very great and very wide Persian Gulf extends into the innermost parts. At its extreme end is an established mart called

Apologou
Pasinou
Kharax

Apologou, lying near Pasinou Kharax and the river Euphratēs.

CHAPTER 36

Sailing along the coast through the mouth of the gulf, after six courses there is another mart of Persis called

Ommana,
Omana

Ommana. Ships customarily come to it from Barugaza— to both these Persian marts [i.e. Omana and Apologou]—, big ships ⟨loaded⟩ with copper, χαλκοῦ,

Sandal wood ξύλων σανταλίνων.

Timber baulks δοκῶν.

Sailyards κεράτων.

Beams[1] of shisham ⎫
and sticks of ebony ⎭ φαλάγγων σησαμίνων καὶ ἐβενίνων.

To Omana ⟨also⟩ comes frankincense from Kanē; and from Omana local sewn boats called madarate[2] are exported to Arabia. From both marts are sent to Barugaza and Arabia much pearl, πινικὸν, though inferior to the Indian, and purple dye, πορφύρα, local clothing, ἱματισμὸς ἐντόπιος and wine, quantities of dates, φοῖνιξ, and gold, and slaves, σώματα.

CHAPTER 37

From here the
route crosses
to Asia

Parsidai
Gedrōsians

After the region of Omana, in like manner, the ⟨country⟩ of the Parsidai, of another kingdom, lies parallel, with a large bay called Of the Gedrōsians, in the middle of which a headland stretches into the bay. And nearby is a river

which has an entry for ships; and a little way from the
mouth is the mart called Hōraia, and behind it an inland   Hōraia
city, seven days' journey from the sea, where is the
kingdom called ⟨Rhambakia⟩. The country produces   Rhambakia
much corn, and wine and rice and dates, but the mainland
nothing but bdella, βδέλλα.

CHAPTER 38

After this region the mainland disappears into the distance
eastwards owing to the depth of the bays, and there
succeed the coast parts of Skuthia, which stretch towards   Skuthia
the north and are very low-lying. From them comes the
river Sinthos,[1] the greatest of the rivers which flow into   Sinthos River
the Erythraean Sea, bringing down to the sea such a vast
amount of water that far out, and before land appears in
sight, the water of the sea is white with it. And now a sign
of approaching land for those coming in from the sea is
the ⟨sight of⟩ snakes which come from the deep water to
meet them. There is a similar sign further up off the coast
of Persia; they are called graai.[2] This river has seven
mouths, narrow and full of shoals, and there is no passage
through except by the middle one, where there is a mart
by the sea called Barbarikon. Off it lies a small island, and   Barbarikon
behind, inland, Minnagar, the metropolis of Skuthia. The   Minnagar
country is ruled by the Parthians, who are continually
expelling each other.

CHAPTER 39

Ships therefore come to a safe anchorage at Barbarikē, and   Barbarikē
all cargoes are carried up the river for the king.[1] There is

brought to the mart a fair amount of unlined clothing and a little spurious ἱματισμὸς ἁπλοῦς . . . καὶ νόθος.

Brocades, πολύμιτα.
Chrysoliths χρυσόλιθον.
Coral κοράλλιον.
Storax στύραξ.
Frankincense λίβανος.
Glass vessels ὑαλᾶ σκεύη.
Silver plate ἀργυρώματα.
Money χρῆμα.
Wine, but not much οἶνος.
Cargoes for exchange consist of
Kostos κόστος.
Bdella βδέλλα.
Lukion λύκιον.
Spikenard νάρδος.
Turquoise Καλλεανὸς λίθος.
Lapislazuli σάπφειρος.
Chinese skins σιρικὰ δέρματα.
Cloth ὀθόνιον.
Chinese yarn νῆμα σιρικὸν.
Indian ink² ἰνδικὸν μέλαν.

Those who sail with the Indian ⟨winds⟩³ put to sea about the month of July, which is Epiphi. The voyage is risky, but with these ⟨winds⟩ it is the most direct and shortest.

CHAPTER 40

Eirinon

After the river Sinthos there is another gulf ⟨running⟩ northwards, not yet explored. It is called Eirinon. One might say that in reality ⟨there are two bays⟩ one small and the other large. The sea in both is shoaly with continuous shifting whirlpools far from the land, so that

42

often, when the shore is not even in sight, ships run aground; and if they are pushed further in by the current they are wrecked. Beyond this bay is a headland curving round from Eirinon towards the east and then to the south and then to the west, enclosing the gulf called Barakē, Barakē containing seven islands; those who get caught near its beginning escape by turning back and ⟨going⟩ a little out to sea. Those who are shut within the belly of Barakē[1] are utterly lost, for the waves are large and very heavy, the sea is troubled and turbid, with racing[2] whirlpools and violent currents. The bottom in some places ⟨drops⟩ steeply, in others it is rocky and sharp, so that the cables of the anchors lying alongside the ships, which anchors are dropped in order to hold out against the current, are cut, or some of them are chafed on the sea-bed. The indication that the sailors are approaching these two types of ground ⟨which make the sea-bottom⟩ is the ⟨appearance of⟩ very large black snakes coming out to meet them. In the parts beyond here and round Barugaza they are smaller, greenish in colour, turning to gold.[3]

CHAPTER 41

After Barakē, ⟨going⟩ straight on, is the bay of Barugaza, Barugaza and the mainland of the country of Ariakē,[1] and the Ariakē beginning of the kingdom of Manbanos, and of the whole of India. The inland part of this, continuous with Skuthia, is called Abēria, and the part by the sea, Surastrēnē. The Abēria region ⟨of Surastrēnē⟩ produces much corn, σίτου, and Surastrēnē rice and sesamum oil and ghi and flax-cloth,[2] καρπάσου, and the common Indian cloth made from it, ὀθονίων τῶν χυδαίων. There are in it great herds of cattle, and men with very large bodies and black skins. The metropolis of

43

Minnagara

the country is Minnagara, from which a great deal of cloth is brought down to Barugaza. Round about are preserved to this day memorials of the expedition of Alexander[3]—old temples, the sites of camps, and very large wells. The navigation along this coast from Barbarikē towards Astakapra opposite Barugaza and the headland called Papikē is 3000 stades.

Astakapra

Papikē

CHAPTER 42

Baiōnēs
Island

Maïs R.

After this there is another bay on this side of the waves ⟨of the sea⟩, going towards the north, at the mouth of which is an island called Baiōnēs, and right at its end a very large river called Maïs. Those who sail to Barugaza pass through this bay, the breadth of which is about 300 stades, leaving behind on the left hand the island with its summit just visible, then east to the mouth of the river of Barugaza. This river is called Lamnaios.

Lamnaios R.

CHAPTER 43

Entry to
Barugaza

Hērōnē
Shoal
Kammōni

Papikē

The bay which ⟨leads⟩ to Barugaza being narrow, it is difficult for those coming in from the sea to enter, whether they happen to come by the right or left ⟨passage⟩, though the latter approach is better. For on the right hand near the mouth of the bay there lies a rough and rocky strip called Hērōnē, opposite the village of Kammōni; and on the left, opposite this, the headland before Astakapra called Papikē, where there is a bad anchorage owing to the current which surges round it and because the anchor-cables are cut by the roughness and rockiness of the sea-bottom. And even if one gets through into the bay, the mouth of the river by Barugaza is difficult to find because the country is low, and nothing can be observed with certainty till one is nearer; and even when it is found, the entrance is dangerous because of the shoals in the river round about it.

CHAPTER 44

Because of this, the royal fishermen of the district round the entrance go up with fully-manned long ships called trappaga and kotumba[1] as far as Surastrēnē to meet ⟨incoming ships⟩ which they pilot to Barugaza. For they lead them straight from the mouth of the bay with ⟨their own⟩ crews through the shoals and tow[2] them to berths already appointed, taking them up when the tide begins to rise, and at high tide mooring them at their berths and basins. The basins are the deepest parts of the river up to Barugaza, this being on the river upstream, about 300 stades from the mouth.

CHAPTER 45

The whole land of India has a great many rivers, and there is a great ebb and flow of tides, the high tides increasing at new moon and at full moon for three days, lessening during the intervening periods of the moon. At Barugaza the ⟨alternation⟩ is much greater, so that of a sudden the sea-bottom can be seen and parts of the land are dry where a little before ⟨ships⟩ were sailing; and when the tide comes in from the sea the water of the rivers is forced back more strongly than in the normal flow, for many stades.

Barugaza

45

CHAPTER 46

Barugaza

For this reason, the approach and departure of ships is dangerous for the inexperienced who are coming into the mart for the first time. Because the violent movement ⟨of the water⟩ when the tide is already rising cannot be withstood, and anchors do not hold, ships are caught by its force and are turned sideways by the violence of the current, driven on to the shoals, and wrecked. The smaller ⟨boats⟩ indeed are capsized. Those that have turned into the creeks during the ebb of the tide, unless they are propped upright, are filled with water from the first head of the current when the rising tide suddenly returns. For the sea water comes in with such violence at the new moon, especially if the flood is at night, that, even if ⟨a ship⟩ begins its entry when the sea is still calm, all at once there is borne in from the mouth ⟨of the bay a sound like⟩ the shouting of an army heard from afar, and immediately the sea rushes in over the shoals with a hissing roar.

CHAPTER 47

Aratrioi
Arakhousioi
Gandaraoi
Proklaïs
Boukephalos
Baktrianoi

Behind Barugaza inland lie several tribes, such as those of the Aratrioi, the Arakhousioi, and the Gandaraoi, and ⟨of the district⟩ of Proklaïs, in which is the ⟨town of⟩ Boukephalos Alexandreia.[1] Above these is the very warlike nation of the Baktrianoi, who are under their own king.[2] From these parts Alexander set out and reached as far as the Gangēs,[3] leaving on one side Limurikē and the southern parts of India; and till now are current in Barugaza ancient coins stamped with Greek letters—the

46

inscriptions of Apollodotos and Menander who reigned after ⟨the time⟩ of Alexander.

CHAPTER 48

In this ⟨region⟩ and to the east ⟨of Barugaza⟩ is a city called Ozēnē,¹ which was previously a seat of govern- Ozēnē ment, from which everything that makes for the well-being of the country and of our trade is brought down to Barugaza:

Onyx stones ὀνυχίνη λιθία.
Murrhine ware μουρρίνη.
Indian muslins σινδόνες ἰνδικαὶ.
Mallow-cloth μολόχιναι.
Ordinary cloth in plenty χυδαῖον ὀθόνιον.

Through it is also brought down from the higher parts through Proklaïs spikenard ⟨of the varieties called⟩ Kattubourinē, Patropapigē, and Kabalitē, νάρδος ἡ καττυβουρίνη καὶ ἡ πατροπαπίγη καὶ ἡ καβαλίτη,² and ⟨spikenard⟩ from the adjoining ⟨country of⟩ Skuthia, as well as kostos and bdella.

CHAPTER 49

Wine is imported into the mart ⟨of Barugaza⟩, chiefly Barugaza Italian, and also some Laodikean and Arabian; and

Copper χαλκὸς.
Tin κασσίτερος.
Lead μόλυβος.
Coral κοράλλιον.
Chrysoliths χρυσόλιθον.

Unlined cloth and spurious ⟨cloth⟩ of all kinds
ἱματισμὸς ἁπλοῦς καὶ νόθος.

Damask girdles of a cubit's length πολύμιται ζῶναι.

Storax στύραξ.

Sweet clover μελίλωτον.

Crude glass ὕελος ἀργὴ.

Red orpiment σανδαράκη.

Antimony στίμι.

Gold and silver money δηνάριον which can be exchanged with much profit for the local currency.

Perfume μύρον, neither costly nor too much.

To the king are brought on those occasions

Expensive silver plate ἀργυρώματα.

Musicians μουσικὰ.

Pretty girls for the harem παρθένοι εὐειδεῖς πρὸς
παλλακείαν.

First quality wine οἶνος.

Unlined clothing of price ἱματισμὸς ἁπλοῦς

Choice perfumes μύρον.

From the place are exported:

Spikenard νάρδος.

Kostos κόστος.

Bdella βδέλλα.

Ivory ἐλέφας.

Onyx stones ὀνυχίνη λιθία.

Myrrh σμύρνα.

Lukion λύκιον.

All sorts of cloth ὀθόνιον παντοῖον.

Silks σηρικὸν.

Mallow-cloth μολόχινον.

⟨Silk⟩ yarn νῆμα.

Long pepper πέπερι μακρὸν.

and goods brought in from other marts. In the season men
sail from Egypt to the mart ⟨of Barugaza⟩ about the
month of July, that is Epiphi.

CHAPTER 50

From Barugaza the adjoining mainland stretches from the north to the south, for which reason the country is called Dakhinabadēs, since dakhanos is what the south is called in their language. The inland part of this region encompasses many lands as well as deserts and great mountains, and wild animals of many kinds: leopards, and tigers, and elephants, very large snakes, hyaenas,[1] and many species of baboon; and there are many populous tribes as far as the Gangēs.

Dakhinabadēs

CHAPTER 51

In Dakhinabadēs itself there are two very celebrated marts, Paithana,[1] twenty days south of Barugaza, and ten days eastward from it the second very large city Tagara.[1] From them is brought down to Barugaza in waggons which travel through vast areas without roads—from Paithana a great deal of onyx stone, and from Tagara much common cloth, ὀθόνιον χυδαῖον, all sorts of muslins, σινδόνων παντοῖα, mallow-cloth, μολόχινα, and some other goods which are brought there from places along the coast. The whole coasting voyage as far as Limurikē is 7000 stades, but more to the Strand.[2]

Paithana

Tagara

CHAPTER 52

The local marts here are, one after the other, Akabarou, Souppara, and the city of Kalliena, which in the time of

Akabarou

Souppara

Kalliena

49

the elder Saraganēs became a legal mart; but since it came under Sandanēs ⟨the trade⟩ has been much hindered, and Greek ships which by chance enter these places are sent under guard to Barugaza.

CHAPTER 53

Sēmulla
Mandagora
Palaipatmai
Melizeigara
Buzantion
Toparon
Erannoboas
Islands
Naoura
Tundis
Mouziris
Nelkunda

After Kalliena there are other local marts: Sēmulla, and Mandagora, and Palaipatmai, and Melizeigara, and Buzantion, Toparon, and Erannoboas. Then are the islands called Sēsekreienai and Of the Aigidioi[1] and Of the Kaineitai,[2] opposite what is called the Peninsula—places where there are pirates; and after the last, the White Island. Then Naoura and Tundis, the first marts of Limurikē; and after them Mouziris and Nelkunda, which are now busy places.

CHAPTER 54

Tundis

Mouziris

Nelkunda

Tundis is in the kingdom of Kēprobotos, and is a well-known village beside the sea. Mouziris, belonging to the same kingdom, is a flourishing ⟨place⟩ with ships from Ariakē coming to it, and also Greeks. It stands on a river,[1] and is 500 stades distant from Tundis by river and by sea, and 20 stades from the mouth of the river. Nelkunda is nearly 500 stades from Mouziris, and likewise the same distance by river or by sea. It belongs to another kingdom, that of Pandion, and it too stands on a river,[2] about 120 stades from the sea.

CHAPTER 55

At the mouth of this river there lies another village ⟨called⟩ Bakarē, to which they send down the ships from Nelkunda before putting out to sea; and they lie in the roadstead for loading cargoes, since the river is full of mud-flats and the channels between them are shallow. The kings of both marts[1] live inland. And to those coming in from the open sea a sign of the approach of land is ⟨the sight of⟩ snakes coming out to meet them, black in colour but shorter ⟨than those near Barakē⟩, and with dragon-like heads and blood-red eyes.[2]

Bakarē

CHAPTER 56

Large ships sail to these ports on account of the large quantity of pepper and malabathron. Imports to this[1] are principally:

Imports to Limurikē

Large quantities of coinage χρήματα.

Chrysolith χρυσόλιθα.

Unlined clothing, but not much ἱματισμὸς ἁπλοῦς.

Damasks πολύμιτα.

Antimony στῖμι.

Coral κοράλλιον.

Crude glass ὕελος ἀργή.

Copper χαλκός.

Tin κασσίτερος.

Lead μόλιβος.

Wine, but not much—the same amount arrives as is available in Barugaza, οἶνος.

Red orpiment σανδαράκη.

Yellow orpiment ἀρσενικόν.

Wheat enough for a ship's crew, since the merchants d<
not stock it, σῖτος.
The exports are pepper, grown in quantity only in on
place near these marts and called kottanaric,[2] πέπερι . .
λεγομένη κοτταναρικῇ. Also exported are pearls, μαργαρίτη
in some quantity and of excellent quality. Also:
Ivory ἐλέφας.
Chinese cloth ὀθόνια σηρικὰ.
Gangitic spikenard νάρδος ἡ γαγγιτικὴ
Malabathron μαλάβαθρον from the interior, brought t
the same port.
Precious stones of all kinds λιθία διαφανὴς παντοῖα.
Diamonds ἀδάμας.
Sapphires[3] ὑάκινθος.
Tortoiseshell χελώνη both from Khrusē and from th
islands lying off Limurikē itself.
The season for sailing to here, for those coming fror
Egypt, is about the month of July, that is Epiphi.

CHAPTER 57

Navigator
Hippalos

The whole of the circumnavigation described from Kan
and Eudaimōn Arabia was formerly made in small shij
by sailing round the bays; but Hippalos[1]* was the fir<
navigator who, by observing the position of the marts an
the character of the sea, discovered a route across th
ocean. Since then, when the winds blow locally from th
ocean according to season, as with us, when the monsoo
in the Indian ocean appears to be south-west, it is calle
Hippalos wind
Hippalos from the name of the man who discovered th
passage across. From then till now, some sail direct fror

* Marginal gloss: περὶ ἱππάλου κυβερνήτου ἀρίστου, 'about Hippalos,
very good navigator'.

52

Kanē, others from Arōmata, those sailing to Limurikē turning the bows of the ship against the wind, and those going to Barugaza or to Skuthia hold out to the contrary for not more than three days, and for the rest of the voyage keep their own courses clear of land, sailing past the bays which have been mentioned.[2]

CHAPTER 58

Beyond Bakarē is what is called the Red Mountain, and another country extends . . .[1] called Paralia, towards the south. The first place, called Balita, has a good harbour and a village by the sea. Beyond this is another place called Komar, where are a fort[2] and a harbour, to which come those who, intending to lead dedicated lives, are cleansed and remain celibate; and similarly women. For it is related that the Goddess[3] abode there at one time, and was ritually cleansed.

Red Mountain
Paralia
Balita

Komar

CHAPTER 59

From Komarei the country extends towards Kolkhoi, where diving for pearls is carried on ($\kappa o \lambda \acute{u} \mu \beta \eta \sigma \iota s \ \tau o \hat{v} \ \pi \iota \nu \iota \kappa o \hat{v}$), the work being done by convicts. It is in the kingdom of Pandion. After Kolkhoi comes a Coast-land ($\dot{a} \iota \gamma \iota a \lambda \dot{o} s$) lying round a bay, with an inland region called Argalou. In one place here are brought pearls, $\pi \iota \nu \iota \kappa \acute{o} \nu$, collected in this richly endowed land.[1] The muslins called Argaritid, $\sigma \iota \nu \delta \acute{o} \nu \epsilon s \ a \acute{\iota} \ \dot{a} \rho \gamma a \rho \acute{\iota} \tau \iota \delta \epsilon s$, are exported from here.

Kolkhoi

CHAPTER 60

Kamara
Podoukē
Sōpatma

Among the marts and harbours in this region to which come those who sail from Limurikē and the north, the more important, in the order in which they occur, are the marts of Kamara and Podoukē and Sōpatma, where are local ships which sail along the coast as far as Limurikē, and others which are very large vessels made of single logs bound together and called Sangara;[1] those that cross over to Khrusē and the Gangēs are called Kolandiophōnta[2] and are the largest. Everything made in Limurikē is brought to these places,[3] and nearly all the money which flows annually from Egypt, together with the many kinds of produce of Limurikē which are supplied through the Coast-land.

CHAPTER 61

Palaisi-
moundou *or*
Taprobanē

Concerning the land after this, the course now turning towards the east, the island called Palaisimoundou lies out at sea towards the west, known to the natives of old as Taprobanē. Its northern part is civilized, and the passage to it is long,[1] and it is so large that it reaches nearly to the coast of Azania opposite.[2] It produces pearls, πινικὸν, and precious stones, λιθία διαφανὴς, and muslins, σινδόνες, and tortoiseshell, χελῶναι.

CHAPTER 62

Masalia

Round about these places, stretching far inland and some way along the coast, is the land of Masalia, where much

54

muslin is produced. Beyond it, to the east and going through the adjacent bay, is the country of Dēsarēnē, _{Dēsarēnē} which produces the ivory called bōsarē, βωσαρή. Beyond it, the course bending to the north, are many barbarous tribes, among which are the Kirradai with squeezed _{Kirradai} noses,[1] and savage; and another tribe, that of the Bargusoi, _{Bargusoi} and that of the Hippioprosōpoi* who are said to be _{Hippio-} cannibals. _{prosōpoi}

CHAPTER 63

After these one turns towards the east, sailing with the ocean on the right hand, and the remaining parts on the *Town of* left hand, and Gangēs appears in sight; and beyond it Gangēs the last of the mainland towards the east, Khrusē. The Khrusē river near it, also called Gangēs,† has a rise and fall like Gangēs River that of the Nile; it is the greatest of the ⟨rivers⟩ of India, and on it is a mart with the same name as the river, Gangēs, through which are exported malabathron, μαλάβαθρον, and Gangitic spikenard, ἡ γαγγιτικὴ νάρδος, and pearls and very fine quality muslins called Gangitic, σινδόνες αἱ γαγγιτικαὶ λεγόμεναι. It is said that there are gold-mines in the area, and a gold coin called kaltis.[1] Down the river is an island‡ in the ocean, the last part of the inhabited world towards the east; it is called Khrusē, Khrusē and has the best tortoiseshell of all places on the Erythraean Sea.

* Interpolated gloss after ἱππιοπροσώπων: μακροπροσώπων, 'long-faced'.
† Marginal gloss: γάγγης ποταμὸς πλημυρῶν ὡς ὁ νεῖλος, 'river Gangēs with flooding like the Nile'.
‡ Marginal gloss: νῆσος ἀνατολικωτάτη παρὰ τόν ὠκεανόν, 'the most easterly island alongside the ocean'.

CHAPTER 64

Thina

Beyond this country, now under the very north, the sea outside coming to an end somewhere, there lies a very great inland city called Thina,[1] from which raw silk and silk yarn, τό τε ἔριον καὶ τὸ νῆμα, and Chinese cloth, ὀθόνιον τὸ σηρικὸν, are brought overland to Barugaza through the Baktrians, and again to Limurikē by way of the river Gangēs. This Thina[2] is not easy to reach. People seldom come from it, and not many go there. The country lies under the Little Bear, and it is said to border on the parts of Pontos and the Caspian Sea where the coast-line has changed direction, and the nearby Lake Maiōtis, which disembogues into the ocean.[3]

CHAPTER 65

Sēsatai

Every year there comes to the boundary of Thina a certain tribe, stunted of body and with very broad faces and completely flat noses, and with white skins, and of a wild nature, called Sēsatai.[1] They come with their women and children carrying great packs, plaited baskets full of ⟨what look like⟩ fresh vine-leaves. They stay in some place on the border between their people and those of Thina, and hold a festival there for several days, spreading out ⟨the contents of⟩ the baskets before them and then withdrawing to their own side. The others,[2] looking on, come together to the place and collect what has been spread out. They pull out strips of cane-fibre, called petroi, πέτρους, gently fold the leaves and making them into round bundles string them together with cane-fibres. There are three kinds: that from the larger leaves, called the large-bundle malabathron, τὸ ἁδρόσφαιρον μαλάβαθρον, that from the medium-sized leaves, called the medium-bundle, τὸ μεσόσφαιρον [μαλάβαθρον], and that from the smaller called the small-bundle, τὸ μικρόσφαιρον. In this way are the three kinds of malabathron produced; and they are then brought to India by those who prepare them.

CHAPTER 66

The lands beyond these places, on account of excessive winters, hard frosts, and inaccessible country, are un-explored—perhaps also on account of some divine power of the gods.★

★ The scribe has added as a tail-piece: διώρθωται οὐ πρὸς σπουδαῖον ἀντίγραφον, 'the correctors did not copy well'. The same statement occurs at the end of the text of the Periplus of the Euxine Sea, 'd'où résulte que ces deux opuscules proviennent du même modèle' (Frisk, 33, n. 1).

Notes on the text of the *Periplus*

Chapter 1

1 Three words are used in the *PME* for 'harbour': λιμήν
(*limēn*), ὅρμος (*hormos*), and ἀγκυροβόλιον (*ankurobolion*). The
first is defined by Liddell and Scott as 'harbour, haven, creek';
the second as 'roadstead, anchorage, . . . esp. the inner part of a
harbour'; and the third as 'anchorage' (i.e. a place where the
anchor is cast). With this mixture of meanings it is not
surprising that the author of the *PME* was not always as clear
as he might have been to the modern commentator. Most of
the places are referred to simply as *emporia* or marts; but in
fifteen cases a word for 'harbour' is used:

   Hormos: Malaō, Arōmatōn Emporion, Leukē Kōmē, Okēlis,
      Eudaimōn Arabia, Komar, Podoukē, Sōpatma.
   Limēn: Muos Hormos, Bernikē, Suagros, Moskha, Komar.
   Ankurobolion: Mouza, Aualitēs.
In some cases the last term may justifiably be translated
'roadstead'; Malaō, on the other hand, is called a *hormos*, though
it is not a roadstead, having a sheltered inner harbour, as have
Muos Hormos and Bernikē. Mouza and Aualitēs are rightly
called anchorages, though the former is also said to be *alimenos*,
that is 'harbourless', but at the same time *euormos*, 'with good
mooring'; the verbs *diormizein* and *hormein*, each used three
times in the text, both mean 'to moor'.

2 There were three types of stade (στάδιον) current in the
1st century A.D.: The Philetairian, with 8 stades to the English
mile; the Olympic, with 9 stades to the mile; and that of

Eratosthenēs with 10 to the mile. For this translation the last reckoning has been adopted.

Chapter 2

1 Barbarikē, Βαρβαρικὴ χώρα, is the land of the Barbaroi, Βάρβαροι, a term that may be interpreted as 'Berbers', whose name is possibly the origin of the Greek word Βάρβαρος. The word Βαρβαρικὴ gave rise to a curious error in the MS; having through miswriting become Βαρική, someone wrote in the margin τίς ἡ Βαρικὴ χώρα; 'what is the Barikē country?', whence it crept into the text as τισηβαρικὴ (Frisk, p. 35). The word occurs in several names which exist today, like Berbera, the modern name for Malaō; Berber on the Nile north of Khartum; and the ethnic name Berber. The Berbers are a people of Hamitic stock and thus akin to the ancient and modern inhabitants of North-east Africa.

2 Ikhthuophagoi, ἰχθυοφάγοι, 'fish-eaters'.

3 Agriophagoi, ἀγριοφάγοι, 'eaters of wild animals'.

4 Moskhophagoi, μοσχοφάγοι, 'eaters of wild plants' (μόσχος = young shoot).

5 The text is corrupt here, and Μερόη is an emendation by Schwanbeck.

Chapter 3

1 The wording of the text makes it clear that since the time of the Ptolemies, and the consequent loss of the elephant trade, this mart had decayed considerably.

Chapter 4

1 In the 6th century one Nonnosos was sent by Justinian as ambassador to Kaïsos, the Homērite rebel who took refuge in

Aksum about A.D. 560, and he wrote a book about his travels. He says that Adoulis was fifteen days by road from Aksum, and that near a place called Auē between the coast and Aksum he saw a herd of nearly 5000 elephants grazing in the plain (*see:* Phōtios, *Bibliothēkē*, cod. 3).

Chapter 5

1 The opsian stone (ὀψιανὸς λίθος) is obsidian, which Pliny says was found in Ethiopia (*Nat. Hist.* XXXVI, 67). It was found by Salt in Hawakil Bay north of Mersa Fatma, where it occurred in lumps of 2 to 4 inches in diameter, though the local people said that a few miles inland much bigger pieces were found. (Salt, *A Voyage to Abyssinia and Travels into the Interior of that Country*, 1814, p. 192.)

2 The word used here for 'rules' is βασιλεύει, which does not necessarily mean 'is king' or 'reigns'; and the same verb is used in two other places with the same meaning: (1) chap. 14: οὐ βασιλεύεται δὲ ὁ τόπος, 'the country is not ruled ⟨by one chief⟩'; (2) chap. 38: βασιλεύεται δὲ ὑπὸ πάρθων, 'is ruled by the Parthians'.

3 The words of the text are ἀκριβὴς μὲν τοῦ βίου... γενναῖος δὲ περὶ τά λοιπά. The word ἀκριβὴς means also 'high-minded', but the μὲν ... δὲ ... suggest that the author meant 'mean'.

Chapter 6

1 Robes from Arsinoē near Suez.

2 ἀβόλλαι νόθοι χρωμάτινοι. I have translated νόθοι by 'spurious' here and in chapters 28, 39, and 49—ἱματισμὸς νόθος. McCrindle (p. 50) regarded the whole word as meaning something made in imitation of a better quality, and I use 'spurious' in this sense in all four places.

60

3 Diospolis (Diopolis) was between Abydos and Tentira in the Thebaïd (Wesseling, *Vetera Romanorum Itineraria* (Amsterdam, 1735), p. 159).

4 Ladikean refers to wine from Laodikeia, a place by the sea in Syria, the modern Ladhikiya, the centre of a wine-producing area which supplied wine to Alexandria.

5 Pliny adds, as exports, hippopotamus hides, monkeys, and slaves (*Nat. Hist.* VI, 34).

Chapter 7

1 The distance from Aualitēs to the nearest point on the Arabian coast is about 100 miles, though the shortest distance between Africa and Arabia is actually about 18 miles, between Okēlis and the opposite coast. See note 2 to chapter 25.

2 σχεδία. Pliny mentions Arabs called Ascitae who lived in islands at the south end of the Red Sea and committed acts of piracy, sailing on rafts made of inflated skins (ἀσκός, askos) (*Nat. Hist.* VI, 34).

3 Somewhere on this part of the coast the brig *Mary Ann* was wrecked in 1825 and its crew murdered by the local inhabitants.

Chapter 12

1 Ἀρωμάτων ἐμπόριον.

2 The spice trade had begun some centuries before Christ, and Greeks, or men with Greek names, were taking part in it, like the Arkhippos who about 150 B.C. lent money to five men for a voyage to this area to buy spices (U. Wilcken, 'Punt-Fahrten in der Ptolemäerzeit', *Zeitschrift für ägyptische Sprache und Altertumskunde*, LX (1925), 86–102, summarized in *Ancient Egypt*, 1926, I, p. 31).

3 Somewhere in these parts Kosmas Indikopleustēs saw flocks of birds called *souspha* which indicated that land was near.

4 The MS has ἄρωμα, which Müller altered to an unknown ἀρηβώ.

Chapter 13

1 It was to Punt that Queen Hatshepsut of the XVIIIth Egyptian dynasty sent the expedition which is recorded on the walls of the temple of Dair al Bahari at Thebes.

Chapter 15

1 It has been claimed that the name Azania is of Arabic origin, from '*ajam*, foreigner, not an Arab. But there is no valid reason why it should not for once be a Greek word, derived from the verb ἀζαίνειν, 'to dry, parch up', of which a form ἀζάνειν occurs in one of the Homeric hymns (*Venus* 270). Pliny has *azanium mare* (*Nat. Hist.* VI, 34), 'Azanian Sea', and also *azaniae nuces*, 'dried-up pine-cones' (*Nat. Hist.* XVI, 44). Since much of the Azania of the *PME*, which began in the neighbourhood of Opōnē (as also according to Ptolemy I. 17, 9) is a very dry country, this meaning is appropriate.

2 On sewn boats, see below, pp. 158–60.

3 γυργάθοις. Probably one or both of the kinds of trap still used on the East African coast and called *dema* in Swahili (Bajuni *yema*). This is in the shape of a hexagonal parallelepiped, one side of which has a re-entrant through which fish can enter but not get out. The trap is baited with a dead fish and tied to a buoy (V. L. Grottanelli, *Pescatori dell' Oceano Indico*, Roma, 1955, p. 114).

Chapter 16

1 The word in the MSS is ὁρατοὶ for which Müller conjectured πειραταί, the form accepted by Frisk (which I have adopted). Professor Giangrande has suggested ἀρόται instead (in a paper published in *Mnemosyne*, XXVIII, 1975, from which he has kindly permitted me to quote) which, as he says, is less palaeographically violent. But there is no evidence that the people were not pirates or were even law-abiding, though there must have been some law and order in Rhapta itself, as is clear from the last part of the chapter. But this does not necessarily exclude the existence of piracy. The problem is, what is the precise meaning of ἀρόται if we accept it in place of πειραταί? One naturally connects ἀρόω and its derivatives with ploughing rather than with mere hand tilling of the soil, and there is no evidence that the plough reached further south than the Kāfā and Gurāgē countries in southern Ethiopia till it was introduced into East Africa by Europeans in the 20th century; and the word used by the Swahili for 'plough' was *jembe*, 'hoe' (or its local equivalent). Yet since this chapter is the first place in which agriculture is mentioned, *assuming that ἀρόται is the correct reading*, we should have to take it in its less common meaning of 'people who till by hand', although in the New Testament γεωργός is used several times to mean 'farm labourer', 'husbandman', 'farmer'. The Latin version of Stuck as printed in Hudson's *Geographiae veteris Scriptores Graeci Minores* (1698) simply omits it, and writes *illius regionis incolae vastissimis sunt corporibus*. Müller's version of the words which follow πειραταί (κατὰ τὸν τόπον ἕκαστος ὁμοίως τιθέμενοι τυράννοις) is '*suo singuli loco tyrannorum res suas agentes*', which seems to read more into the text than is justified. (We render them 'each place likewise has its own chief'.) Giangrande takes them to mean that each man is the absolute ruler of his own piece of territory, which is an unlikely situation in East Africa

as far as we know from ethnographical studies. It must be admitted, however, that we know nothing about the people who lived in the Rhapta coast area at the time the *PME* was written, and it is possible that they may have had both ploughs and individual land tenure, though in my view unlikely. The *Aethiopes aroteres* of Pliny who, he says, lived above the *oppidum Aduliton* (Adouli), do not come into the picture, because they lived in the 'plough zone' (*Nat. Hist.* VI, 34). After due consideration of the words 'pirates' and 'ploughmen/tillers' I prefer the first, in spite of its being 'palaeographically violent'.

Chapter 17

1   Though ναύπλιος is unknown with the meaning of 'coconut', a word *nauplius* is recorded by Pliny (*Nat. Hist.* IX, 49) as the name of an *animal sepiae simile*—'a creature like a cuttle-fish'; but this is hardly the meaning here. See p. 132.

Chapter 19

1   παραλήπτης. Whether he was the Annius Plocamus mentioned by Pliny (*Nat. Hist.* VI, 24) who farmed the taxes in the Red Sea area is unknown, but it was the unnamed freedman of Annius Plocamus who made navigational history by being carried from the Persian Gulf by the winds past Carmania to Hippuros a port of Ceylon on the fifteenth day. A graffito recently found on the Koptos–Bernikē road mentions one Lysas (freedman) of P. Annius Plocamus (Λυσᾶς Ποπλίου Ἀννίου πλοκάμου) (D. Meredith in *J. Roman Stud.* XLIII, 1953, p. 38, quoted by Innes Miller, *Spice Trade* (1969), p. 16).

2   ἑκατοντάρχης = commander of a hundred men.

Chapter 20

1   i.e. as on the African coast.
2   i.e. go off course.

Chapter 21

1   This is certainly an overestimate, whatever may have been the exact value of the stade, since the distance from Bernikē to Mouza is approximately 900 miles.
2   ἐξαρτισμοῖς, lit. 'equipment', a word apparently peculiar to the *PME*.

Chapter 22

1   τύραννος.

Chapter 24

1   i.e. from Egypt.

Chapter 25

1   The straits of Bab al-mandab, 'gate of lamentation'.
2   The shortest *distance* between Africa and Arabia at the Straits is 18 miles, from Mulhule in Africa to a point close to Sheikh Sa'id in Arabia. The *length* i.e. the narrowest part (A–B in Map 5), may be put at about 6 miles, or sixty stades.

Chapter 26

1   See above, pp. 8–10.

Chapter 27

1   The region round Kanē.

Chapter 30

1   'Aρωμάτων ἐμπόριον, Olok near Cape Gardafui.
2   The word νῶτα, 'backs', was supplied by an earlier commentator, Bernhardy.

Chapter 34

1   ἡμέρας οὐ πολύ τι βλέποντες. McCrindle (*Commerce*, p. 101) translates: 'See imperfectly in the daylight'. Frisk (*Le Périple*, p. 113) suggests that this may indicate nyctalopia, night-blindness, or the inability to see clearly except at night, or else possibly some disease like trachoma. The word πονηροὶ, which in medical language denotes those suffering from an eye disease, could also mean 'rogues'.

Chapter 35

1   Lit. 'diving-places for seeking pearl shells'.

Chapter 36

1   The word used in the text, φαλάγγων, means round sticks or logs.
2   See below, p. 162.

Chapter 38

1 Sinthos is from Sanskrit *sindhu*, 'the sea', which became *hindu* in Old Persian, whence the Greek form *Indos* meaning the river, and *Indoi*, 'Indians'.

2 On this subject, Pliny writes of snakes being washed out to sea in the Persian Gulf (*Nat. Hist.* VI, 31). The word in the text, γράαι, may perhaps be compared with the Greek γραῖαι, defined by Liddell and Scott as 'sea-crab', which may not be its original or only meaning. McCrindle, however, derives the word from Sanskrit *graha*, 'alligator' (*Commerce*, p. 108).

Chapter 39

1 The king of Skuthia.

2 Indian ink or Chinese ink. Both McCrindle (*Commerce*, p. 109) and *Hobson-Jobson* (p. 437) prefer to understand indigo (*indigofera tinctoria* Linn.), though μέλαν was the Greek word for ink.

3 The expression ἰνδικοί ἄνεμοι, 'Indian winds', would naturally be shortened by sailors, as in other examples in the *PME* where adjectives are used elliptically as substantives. Cf. Βασιλικός, 'royal (servant)' (chap. 32); πινικόν, 'pearl' (chap. 36). *See also:* Frisk, *Le Périple*, pp. 93, 99.

Chapter 40

1 Τὴν τοῦ Βαράκου κοιλίαν.

2 The adjective is ἐλαφράς, *elaphras*, meaning 'agile', for which in this context 'racing' is perhaps a fair translation,

67

though in chapter 55 it appears to mean 'shallow', in which sense McCrindle takes it (*Commerce*, p. 136).

3 On snakes at sea, see note 2 to chapter 38.

Chapter 41

1 Ariakē is another elliptic expression using the adjective as a substantive (see note 3 to chapter 39).

2 Κάρπασος, *karpasos*, means flax, which has been grown in India for many centuries. Linen was made from two varieties, called *atasī* and *kṣumā*; the adjectival form of the latter, *kṣauma*, means linen made from *atasī* fibre (V. A. Smith, *The Early History of India*, Oxford, 1924, p. 102).

3 Alexander's Indian expedition was made in the years 327 to 325 B.C.

Chapter 44

1 See below, p. 162.

2 Almeida gives confirmation that towing was not unknown in the Indian Ocean: 'a pinnace . . . had in tow a boat (*batel*) as big as a ship (*navio*) and so loaded with goods that the ship could hardly haul it' (C. F. Beckingham and G. W. B. Huntingford, *Some Records of Ethiopia*, Hakluyt Society, London, 1954, p. 175). This was going from Bassein to Socotra.

Chapter 47

1 The tribes named in this chapter, and the towns of Proklaïs (properly Poklaïs) and Boukephalos were far inland, and not visited by traders to the coast.

2   The words of Frisk's text are ἔθνος Βακτριανῶν, ὑπὸ βασιλέα
ὄντων ἴδιον [τόπον]. These I have rendered 'nation of the
Baktrianoi, who are under their own king'; McCrindle
(*Commerce*, p. 121) has 'governed by their own independent
sovereign'. Frisk (*Le Périple*, p. 16) in his apparatus criticus has:
'ὄντων Müller: οὖσαν [τόπον] Stuck.' The text is obviously
corrupt, and more recently various attempts have been made
to correct it. The latest work on this passage is in MacDowall
and Wilson, 'The references to the Kuṣāṇas in the *Periplus*',
Num. Chron., 7 ser. x (1970), pp. 222–3. Here they propose as
the MS reading: οὖσαν ἴδιον τόπον and quote the following
emendations: (1) κούσαν, Kennedy in *J.R.A.S.* 1913, p. 127;
(2) ἦσαν διόδοτον, J. A. B. Palmer in *Classical Q.* (1949), p. 61 ff.;
(3) κούσαν . . . ὄν or ὄντα, their own, *loc. cit.*, p. 224. From the
evidence of coins they consider that ⟨κ⟩ούσαν refers to the
Kushans, and 'in the misunderstanding and morphology of the
unfamiliar Kuṣāṇa name, we have the key to the original name
in *Periplus* 47, ΗΓΑΙΟΣ that became corrupted to the puzzling
ΙΔΙΟΣ' (*loc. cit.*, p. 225), ΗΓΑΙΟΣ (ηγαιος) representing the
name of a known Kushān king Hēraios. Accordingly they
translate the passage thus: 'all these races being under a Kuṣāṇa
king Heraios', and on the evidence they produce they deduce
a date of c. A.D. 100 for the *PME*. (In an earlier paper, however,
MacDowall suggested c. 120–30, on the evidence of the
reference to Nahapāna, *Num. Chron.*, 7 ser. IV, 1964, p. 280).
I myself am not convinced by the introduction of Hēraios
on somewhat imaginative evidence; and chapter 47 is largely
irrelevant except for the mention of P[r]oklaïs.

3   Alexander did not in fact get anywhere near the Ganges,
but had to turn back when he reached the Gurdaspur district
not far from Lahore. From here he went to the mouth of the
Indus, and thence his fleet went by sea to the head of the
Persian Gulf, while he travelled by land.

Chapter 48

1   In the time of Aśoka (3rd century B.C.) Ozēnē was the headquarters of a prince. It was not visited by the coast traders.

2   The meanings of Kattubourinē and Patropapigē are unknown; for Kabalitē McCrindle suggested a connexion with the Kabolitai, the people of Kabul, mentioned by Ptolemy (*see:* McCrindle, *Commerce*, pp. 123–4).

Chapter 50

1   The Greek word is κροκόττας, *krokottas*; this was thought to be a 'mixture of dog and wolf . . . but we do not believe those who say that it can imitate the human voice' (Agatharkhidēs v, 77). This animal was probably a hyaena; the Nandi of Kenya say that hyaenas talk to each other like people (G. W. B. Huntingford, *Nandi of Kenya*, London, 1953, p. 137). Pliny also mentions a belief that hyaenas can talk (*Nat. Hist.* VIII, 44).

Chapter 51

1   Paithana and Tagara were not visited by the coast traders.

2   αἰγιαλόν, *aigialon*, 'beach, strand', used as if it was a place name. It is uncertain to what part of the coast the term refers, unless it is to the Tamil coast in the south.

Chapter 53

1   The word αἰγιδίων, *aigidiōn*, though rendered Aigidioi, suggests the Greek αἰγιδίων, 'of the young goats'.

2 The word Καινειτῶν, *kaineitōn*, could be a genitive form of a native name rendered into Greek letters.

Chapter 54

1 The river is the Periyar.

2 This 'river' is probably lake Vembanad, though the *place* is beside a river which enters the lake.

Chapter 55

1 The king of Tundis, and the ruler of the Pāndya kingdom in which was Nelkunda.

2 See chapter 40.

Chapter 56

1 i.e. to Limurikē.

2 κοττaναρικὴ, *kottanarikē*, 'from Kottanara', the district called in ancient Tamil literature Kuṭṭam round Kottayam and Quilon (Kollam), Pliny's Cottonara and Ptolemy's Κοττιάρα, *Kottiara*. This area was known as the 'pepper coast'.

3 It is somewhat strange that beryl, βήρυλλος, is not mentioned in the *PME*, for both Pliny and Ptolemy refer to the beryl trade from the Tamil country.

Chapter 57

1 This is the only mention by name of a specific person as the discoverer of the use of the south-west monsoon—that is, from

the Greek or Egyptian point of view, for of course it was known to the Indians and Arabs long before. The only other references to Hippalos are two in Pliny and one in Ptolemy. Pliny says that 'from Syagros a promontory of Arabia they go to Patale [near the mouth of the Indus] with the wind Favonius [west wind] which there they call Hippalus', and further on in the same chapter, 'from Ocelis they go to Muziris in forty days with the wind called Hippalus' (*Nat. Hist.* VI, 26). Ptolemy says that east of five unidentifiable islands beyond Arōmata 'the sea is called Hippados or Hippalon, and on the east joins the Indian ocean' (*Geog.* IV, 7, 41). The alternative form suggests not only that his source was not clearly written (as in the case of several other names), i.e. *ΙΠΠΑΔΟΣ/ΙΠΠΑΛΟΝ*, but also that the name conveyed nothing particular to him. Beyond the fact that Hippalos was on the high seas by Pliny's time, nothing else is known about him. A marginal gloss at the beginning of this chapter says 'about Hippalos a very good navigator'.

2   On navigation in the Erythraean Sea, Pliny has the following remarks:

'They begin to sail in mid-summer before the rising of the Dog Star [i.e. before the end of July] or immediately after its rising, and come, on about the thirtieth day, to Ocelis in Arabia, or to Cane in the Incense-country. There is a third port called Muza, to which the Indian navigators do not come, except traders in Arabian incense and perfumes.' And further on, 'From India they sail back at the beginning of the Egyptian month of Tybi, our December, or the Egyptian Mechiris, within the sixth day, which is at our Ides of January. Thus it comes about that they return in the same year. They sail from India also with the south-east wind (Vulturnus), and when they have entered the Red Sea (Rubrum Mare), with the south-west (Africus) or south wind (Auster).'

(*Nat. Hist.* VI, 26). [On the monsoons see further in Appendix 4 on Shipping.]

Chapter 58

1   There is a lacuna in the MS, which has ἄλλη παρήκε <ι> χώρα τη . . . κης ἡ παραλία λεγομένη, for which Müller suggested τῆ<s ὑπὸ πανδίονι 'Ινδι>κῆς (Geog. p. clxiv). Paralia, though meaning 'coast land' in Greek, might be an Indian name, i.e. Parali, an old name for Travancore. See McCrindle, Commerce, pp. 139–40.

2   The MS has an unknown word βριάριον which was perhaps an unsuccessful attempt by a copyist to correct an illegible word. Stuck's emendation to φρούριον makes sense.

3   ἡ θεός (hē theos), 'the goddess' (masc. theos with fem. article). The name Komar, Komarei, in the next chapter, is the Indian word kumārī, 'young girl', a name of the goddess Durgā the consort of Śiva, who had a temple in the neighbourhood of Cape Comorin (Hobson-Jobson, p. 238). Monthly bathing in honour of Durgā was still practised here in the 19th century (McCrindle, Commerce, pp. 139–40). This goddess was originally a South Indian female demon called Koṟṟavai, 'victorious' (Smith, Early History, p. 457).

Chapter 59

1   This is another very corrupt passage. The reading of the MS is ἐν ἑνὶ τόπῳ τερονειτε παρ' αὐτὴν τῆς ἠπιοδώρου συλλέγομενον πινικόν. Müller corrected it to ἐν ἑνὶ <τούτῳ τῷ> τόπῳ <ἐν οὐδενὶ δὲ ἑ>τέρῳ ὠνεῖται τὸ παρ' αὐτὴν τῆς ἠπιοδώρου συλλεγόμενον πινικόν. Though a somewhat arbitrary emendation, at least the word ὠνεῖται may have been intended by the author. McCrindle translated it 'in this single place are obtained the pearls collected near the island of Ēpiodōros'. The word 'island' does not occur in the text, and the supposed name may be taken as the genitive of the adjective ἠπιόδωρος meaning

'bountiful'. The passage is, however, in such a mess that any translation is little more than guess-work.

Chapter 60

1, 2 On these boats, see below, p. 163.

3 i.e. Kamara, Podoukē, and Sōpatma where these two types of craft were found.

Chapter 61

1 The text is rather corrupt here, but this is what it seems to mean.

2 The distance to Africa is nearly 1600 miles, whereas the length of Ceylon is not much more than 200 miles.

Chapter 62

1 γένος ἀνθρώπων ἐκτεθλιμμένων τὴν ῥῖνα. Frisk (Le Périple, p. 120) quotes Apollodōros for the meaning of ἐκθλιβεῖν, who, referring to the Amazons, wrote Τοὺς μὲν δεξιοὺς μαστοὺς ἐξέθλιβον, 'they squeezed out their right breasts', i.e. destroyed them. The Kirradai are, it is suggested in Hobson-Jobson (p. 203), the Kirāta, a forest people living to the E and NE of Bengal.

Chapter 63

1 On this, see MacDowall and Wilson, Num. Chron. 7 ser., x (1970), 230, though they do not explain the word.

Chapter 64

1   Ancient writers often used the names of unknown countries for their capital cities as well.

2   Ptolemy, using the form *Σῖναι* Sinai, has also 'the natives of Sērikē (*Σηρική*) (VII, 5).

3   This sentence reveals the depth of the ignorance in antiquity concerning the extent of the world beyond India. Pontus was the ancient name for a country in the NE of Asia Minor, so called because it was on the coast of the Pontus Euxinus, the Black Sea; and Lake Maiōtis (*λίμνη Μαιῶτις*) was the Sea of Azov, the great inlet on the north side of the Black Sea. The Caspian Sea (*Κασπία θάλασσα*) is some 400 miles east of the Black Sea, which is some 3500 miles from Burma.

Chapter 65

1   The name Sēsatai, *Σησάται*, is correctly written thus, not Bēsatai, *Βησάται*, as in some MSS of Ptolemy, the best of which has Saēsadas, *Σαησάδας* (accusative); Pliny has Sosaeadae. This, of course, does not help us to find out who they were; the author's description suggests people of Mongol stock.

2   The buyers.

NOTE ON PLACE-NAME ENDINGS IN -*IS*, -*OU*, -*ŌN*

1   Of names ending in *ις*, *Μούζιρις*, (53), and *Ὄκηλις* (25) are given in only one form, presumably the nominative. *Τύνδις* (53) however occurs also in the genitive *Τύνδεως* (54). *Ποκλαΐς* (47) on the other hand occurs only in the genitive *Ποκλαΐδος*;[1] but Pliny's form Peucolais shows that the nominative is *Ποκλαις*.

[1] *Προκλαΐδος* in the MS.

2 νῆσοι Ἀλαλαίου λεγόμεναι (4), ἡ Μούνδου (9), νῆσος ἡ Διοσκουρίδου καλουμένη (30), ἡ Ἀπολόγου (35), χώραν λεγομένην Ἀργαλου (59), Ἀκαβαρου (52), and νῆσος λεγομένη παλαι σιμούνδου (61) are clearly uninflected and neuter in form (even though the article is feminine), i.e. Μούνδου is not a genitive form of Μούνδος nor Ἀπολόγου of Ἀπόλογος. On the other hand, in ἐν τῇ Διδώρου λεγομένῃ νήσῳ (4) and νῆσος ἡ Διοδώρου (25) the words appear to be genuine personal names in the genitive.

3 In νῆσοι ἡ τῶν Αἰγιδίων (53) the word might be the genitive plural of the Greek αἰγιδίον 'young goat'; or it might not be. In πυραλάων νήσων (15) the first word may be a genitive plural from an unknown nominative form; καινειτῶν (53) may be from nominative καινειταί.

APPENDIX I

The Topography of the *Periplus*

1. *The start of the journey and the ancient canals*

'When you sail from Hērōöpolis along Trōglodutikē,' said Strabō, 'you come to the town of Philōtera, called after the sister of Ptolemy' (XVI. 6, 5). This town was founded for Ptolemy II Philadelphos (282–45 B.C.) by Saturos as a base for elephant-hunting in Trōglodutikē, and was near Old Qosseir not far from Muos Hormos. Hērōöpolis was near the north end of the Bitter Lakes in the Suez Canal area, and Strabō's statement *seems* to show that as late as his time (he died *c.* A.D. 20) it was possible to go by boat from the Nile to the Red Sea through a canal.[1] The first attempt to build a canal to the Red Sea is generally attributed to Nekhō II in the 5th century B.C.; but 'the ruins on its banks show that it already existed in the time of Rameses II, and that the statement of Aristotle, Strabo, and Pliny, who ascribe its commencement at least to Sesostris, is founded on fact'.[2]

Whoever really began the work, there seems little doubt that, the original canal not having progressed very far from its starting point a little above Bubastis, it was continued by the Persians under Darius Hystaspes in the 6th century B.C., thus making an attribution to Nekhō II out of the question. In the 6th century the canal reached the Bitter Lakes, where the work

[1] But other evidence suggests that this was not so, and that by 'Hērōöpolis' he meant no more than the western arm of the Red Sea, often known as the Hērōöpolite Gulf.

[2] Sir J. Gardner Wilkinson in Rawlinson's *Herodotus* (4 ed., London, 1880), II, 158.

MAP 2. Sketch map of the Arsinoē Canal

was suspended on account of political troubles, and it became choked with sand. About 274 B.C. Ptolemy II Philadelphos reconstructed it and took it to Arsinoë, a village at the south end of the Bitter Lakes, but still not to the Red Sea. At length, about A.D. 106, the emperor Trajan had a new canal cut, this time from a different starting point, near the town of Babylon opposite Memphis, taking it more or less parallel with the Nile through Hēliopolis and Vicus Iudaeorum (Tell el Yahudieh) to Thou, where it joined the earlier canal, and turned east through Hērōöpolis and Serapium, going thence through the Bitter Lakes to Arsinoë, with a cut joining the latter with Klusma (Suez) on the Red Sea. This canal was accompanied by a road, on which the Antonine Itinerary gives the following stations:[1]

Babylonia	mpm XII
Heliu (Hēliopolis)	mpm XII
Scenas Veteranorum	mpm XXII
Vico Iudaeorum	mpm XII
Thou	mpm XII
Hero (Hērōöpolis)	mpm XXIIII
Serapium	mpm XVIII
Clysmo	mpm L

Trajan began his canal much higher up-stream than the earlier one, so that the fresh water which filled it could be used to irrigate the land through which it passed; and here there were in fact three lines of communication: the Nile, the canal, and the road just described. This canal was still working seven hundred years after Trajan's day.[2]

At the head of the Gulf of Suez was the port of Klusma ('the beach'), at or near the modern Suez. This port is not mentioned in the *PME*, but a few miles north of it was the village or town of Arsinoë, where were textile works producing what the *PME* calls Arsinoïtic robes and cloaks, and probably much of the other clothing exported to the Red Sea and Indian Ocean ports.

[1] Wesseling, *Vetera Romanorum Itineraria*, Amsterdam, 1735, pp. 169–71.
[2] *Dictionary of Greek and Roman Geography*, art. Nilus, by W. B. Donne.

Whether or not the canal was working as far as Arsinoē when the *PME* was written, the trading voyages described by our author did not start from Klusma. They began at Muos Hormos, some 300 miles south of Klusma, and opposite the town of Koptos on the Nile, which was connected with Muos Hormos by a road equipped with watering-places (*hudreumata*) at intervals along the hundred miles or so between the two towns; the names of the stations have not been recorded. At the time when the *PME* was written trade goods were probably sent by canal from Arsinoē to the Nile and thence by boat to Koptos, from which they went overland by camel (Pliny, *Nat. Hist.* VI, 26) to Muos Hormos and the next point of departure, Berenikē (written Bernikē in the *PME*), which was also connected with Koptos by a road with ten watering-places which are named in the Antonine Itinerary, the distance being about 240 miles. The stations were:[1]

A Copto Berenicen usque	mpm CCLVIII sic
Poeniconon	mpm XXIIII
Didime	mpm XXIIII
Afrodito	mpm XX
Compasi	mpm XXII
Iouis	mpm XXIII
Aristonis	mpm XXV
Falacro	mpm XXV
Apollonos	mpm XXIII
Cabalsi	mpm XXVII
Cenon Hydreuma	mpm XXVII
Berenicen	mpm XVIII

The last name but one is καινὸν ὕδρευμα, 'new watering-place'. Berenice was roughly opposite Syēnē (Aswan).

Ships, however, had sailed southwards from the north end of the Red Sea long before the 1st century A.D. Built on the model of the Nile boats, the Egyptian ships were often single-masted, with one sail and no hold, the cargo being simply piled on the

[1] Wesseling, p. 172.

deck. Such were the ships that queen Hatshepsut sent down the Red Sea to Punt about 1500 B.C. There was, in fact, a continuous movement of Egyptian shipping in the Red Sea, though not beyond Cape Gardafui, if as far; and there is no indication that they attempted to sail along the south coast of Arabia.

2. *Summary of the routes*

The *PME* contains 66 chapters, of which 18 relate to Africa (1–18), 18 to Arabia (19–36), 27 to India (37–63), and the last three to China and the unknown lands beyond India. From the topographical aspect it may be divided into two sections: (1) the route along the west coast of the Red Sea, continuing round Gardafui and thence to a point on the East African coast more or less opposite Zanzibar. (2) Having started with Muos Hormos in chapter 1, the author then goes back to Bernikē in chapter 19, and takes the second route, across the Red Sea to Leukē Kōmē, thence working along the west coast of Arabia into the Indian Ocean, and onwards to India, always keeping to the coast, and not including the Persian Gulf.

A number of the marts or trading-places, *emporia*, have a classifying adjective attached to them. There are four such adjectives:

(1) ἐμπόρια ἀποδεδειγμένα (*emporia apodedeigmena*), which may be translated 'appointed or customary marts'.
(2) ἐμπόρια νόμιμα (*emporia nomima*), 'established marts'.
(3) ἐμπόρια ἔνθεσμα (*emporia enthesma*), 'legal marts'.
(4) ἐμπόρια τοπικὰ (*emporia topika*), 'local marts'.

In the first category are put Muos Hormos, Bernikē, and Moskha. In the second are Adouli, Mouza, and Apologou. In the third is Kalliena city, though this was before the book was written. In the fourth, Kalliena re-classified, Akabarou,

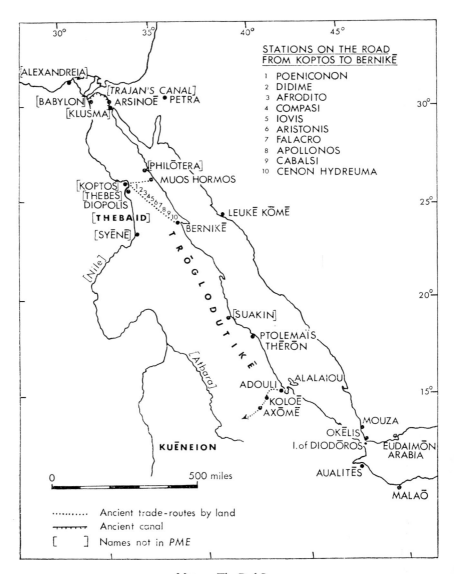

MAP 3. The Red Sea

Souppara, Sēmulla, Mandagora, Palaipatmai, Melizeigara, Toparon, and Erannoboas. No category is assigned to the rest, which were possibly all 'local' (*topika*). The first seem to have been under the control of officials appointed by the king or paramount ruler of the country. The second consisted of ports recognised as official marts for the hinterland they served. The third may have been under the direct control of the local ruler, while the last were under the control of local chiefs. It is curious that Leukē Kōmē, at which there were both a collector of customs and a garrison, is not assigned to any category.

(1) *Summary of the African section*

From Muos Hormos the trader went along the Red Sea coast, past Bernikē which lay on the right hand, the next place mentioned being Ptolemaïs of the Huntings. Then came the mart of Adouli, the port of the Aksumite kingdom, and the terminus of the ivory route from Kuēneion (Sennar) far in the interior. The coastlands with their hinterland between Adouli and Bernikē were known as Trōglodutikē, 'the land of the Troglodytes'; and although there was little of the ordinary trade here, it was one of the main areas where elephants had been hunted by the Ptolemies for purposes of war. This part of the coast was known also as Barbaria, 'the land of the Berbers'. Trōglodutikē extended as far as Cape Gardafui (near Opōnē), and in what is now northern Somaliland there was a region known as 'the other Barbaria'.

After Adouli there were no marts till the Straits of Bab al mandab had been passed, soon after which came in succession the marts of Aualitēs (Zeyla), Malaō (Berbera), Moundou (Heis), Mosullon (Bandar Kasim or B. Ziada), Akannai (Bandar Alula), and the Mart of Spices (Arōmatōn emporion, Olok). Then, after doubling Cape Gardafui, came a place of shelter called Tabai and the mart of Opōnē (near Ras Hafun). All these places exported ivory, tortoiseshell, spices, and incense.

Beyond Opōnē, sailing south-west along the African coast, there was a somewhat featureless stretch extending for 1100 or 1200 miles called the coast of Azania, to the island of Menouthias (Zanzibar or Pemba) and the coast town beyond it called Rhapta. This was the last African mart, and the limit of the author's knowledge. From it were exported ivory, tortoiseshell, and coconut.

(2) Summary of the Arabian and Indian sections

The eastern route began at Leukē Kōmē (Yanbu' al-bahr) on the Arabian coast opposite Bernikē. For nearly 900 miles from here there were no marts, the first being Mouza (Maushij) lying a little way inside the Straits and north of the island of Diodōros (Perim), with Okēlis (Sheikh Sa'id) on the mainland opposite Perim. Turning eastwards along the Arabian coast there followed the marts of Eudaimōn Arabia (Aden), Kanē (Hisn Ghurab), and Moskha beyond Suagros (Ras Fartak). Inland from Mouza were the capital cities of Sauē and Saphar; and above Kanē was Saubatha.

Beyond Kanē there was only one mart, Moskha, where the Sakhalitic incense was loaded from the land behind the bay of Sakhalitēs and Cape Suagros. It may be the modern Salala. After the mention of Suagros, the author makes a digression to describe the island of Dioskouridou (Socotra), which was on the trade route since it produced much tortoiseshell. Then no more harbours are named till Omana inside the Persian Gulf is reached, where the route crosses to the Asiatic continent—to the country of the Parsidai (Persians), the first mart being Hōraia, with an inland city of uncertain name behind it. Ships then sailed along the low-lying coast of Skuthia, through which flows the river Sinthos (Indus) into the Erythraean Sea; at one of its mouths, beside the sea, was the mart of Barbarikon or Barbarikē, and behind it the inland metropolis of Skuthia called Minnagar (Mandasor). From the Sinthos the trader went past the hitherto unexplored gulf of Eirinon (the Rann of Kutch) and a dangerous bay called Barakē (gulf of Kutch) where it was difficult and unsafe to anchor. No trade is recorded here. Then came the bay of Barugaza (Cambay) into which flowed the river Lamnaios (Narbada); behind the bay was Ariakē, with Surastrēnē (Kathiawar) and Abēria (Gujarat) on the west side of the bay, and Barugaza itself (Broach) on the east side. This region is called the beginning of the kingdom of Manbanos and of the whole of India (chap. 41). Far inland were the Arakhōsioi of Kandahar, the Aratrioi of the Panjab, and the Gandaraoi of Gandhara, in which was the city of Taxila, and the mart of Poklaïs (miswritten Proklaïs in the *PME*), the modern Charsadda, through which came spices to Barugaza. Trade goods came to Barugaza also through Ozēnē (Ujjain, NE of Broach). After Barugaza the central part of India began, called Dakhinabadēs, 'the south land', a region rather larger than the modern Deccan, where, inland, on and south of the Godavari river, were two important trading towns called Paithana and Tagara.

Returning to the coast, the local marts listed after Barugaza are Akabarou, Souppara (Sōpara), Kalliena (Kalyana in Bombay harbour), Sēmulla (Chaul), Mandagora (Bankot), Palaipatmai (Dabhol), Melizeigara (Jaigarh), Buzantion (Vijayadurg), and two which appear to have been called Toparon and Erannoboas. Then comes Limurikē, the corrupt *PME* form of Damirikē, 'the Tamil country'—the Travancore coast and the ancient kingdom of Kerala. The marts here were Naoura (Cannanore), Tundis (Tanor), Mouziris (Cranganore), and Nelkunda (Kottayam). Tundis was in the kingdom of Kerala, Nelkunda in the adjoining kingdom of Pandion. In this region was Bakarē (Vaikkarai), the landing-place for Nelkunda, and then Komar or Komarei (Cape Comorin at the southern end of India). Sailing along the east coast from here the trader came to Kolkhoi (Korkai) and Argalou (Uraiyur, inland), still in the kingdom of Pandion. Then came Podoukē (Arikamedu near

Pondicherry) and Sōpatma (near Madras) in the Chola kingdom. From here the author digresses to the island of Palaisimoundou or Taprobanē (Ceylon), the size of which he greatly overestimates. Then came Masalia (Masulipatam) and finally, with no intermediate harbours, the mouths of the Ganges where there was a town of the same name. Beyond this to the east was Khrusē, 'the golden land', and, far beyond to the north, the land of Thina from which came silk.

It will be noticed that the author's knowledge of the African coast, of the Arabian coast to Kanē, and of the Indian coast from the Indus to Madras is fairly comprehensive, but that thereafter it is rather sketchy, suggesting that, at least in his day, there was little trade in that region handled by people like himself.

3. *Local topography*

Prefixed numerals are those of the chapters.

I. THE AFRICAN COAST TO RHAPTA

1 MUOS HORMOS [Μυὸς ὅρμος] 'the Egyptian harbour'. The name means Mussel Harbour; according to Agatharkhidēs it was later called 'Aphroditē's Harbour', but however this may be, it was obviously still called Muos Hormos in the 1st century A.D. The site was near Qosseir on the Red Sea coast, at the modern Abu sharm al-qibli, about 300 miles south of Suez. Trade goods were brought to and from Koptos along a road equipped with watering-places, the distance from Muos Hormos to Koptos being about 100 miles.

1 BERNIKĒ [Βερνίκη] The proper name was Berenikē, and the place was so called after the mother of the founder, Ptolemy II Philadelphos. The town was important from its earliest days, and under the Roman Empire it was

controlled by a special prefect known as the Praefectus Berenicidis. The site is inside a bay known in both ancient and modern times as Foul Bay [Strabō XVI. 4, 5, ἀκάθαρτος κόλπος]; the distance given by the *PME* from Muos Hormos is approximately correct, being about 200 miles. At the modern Umm el ketef the 'ruins are still perceptible, even to the arrangement of the streets, and in the centre is a small Egyptian temple adorned with hieroglyphics and bas-reliefs of Greek workmanship. Opposite to the town is a very fine natural harbour . . . though the bar is now impassable at low water' (McCrindle, *Commerce*, p. 42). It was connected with Koptos, to and from which goods were brought (as in the case of Muos Hormos) by a road about 240 miles long. (See above, sect. 2.)

2   MEROĒ [Μερόη] The capital of the ancient kingdom of Meroē on the Nile.

3   PTOLEMAÏS OF THE HUNTINGS [πτολεμαῒς ἡ τῶν θηρῶν]. The distance given by the *PME* in stades from the Moskho-phagoi—not, it will be noted, from Berenikē—is more or less correct for the distance between Berenikē and Aqiq, with which Ptolemaïs may be identified. On the other hand, Suakin, about 150 miles north of Aqiq, is a possible candidate, and from it there was an ancient caravan road to Berber on the Nile; this would invalidate the *PME* distance from Berenikē, though it is not an insuperable difficulty. Perhaps one day someone will investigate both places.

4   ADOULI [῎Αδουλι] This was for many centuries the only harbour possessed by Ethiopia. It lies twenty miles inside the Gulf of Zula. It is said by the *PME* to be twenty stades from the sea; this fits the position of the ancient site, which is just north of the river Haddas and about four kilometres

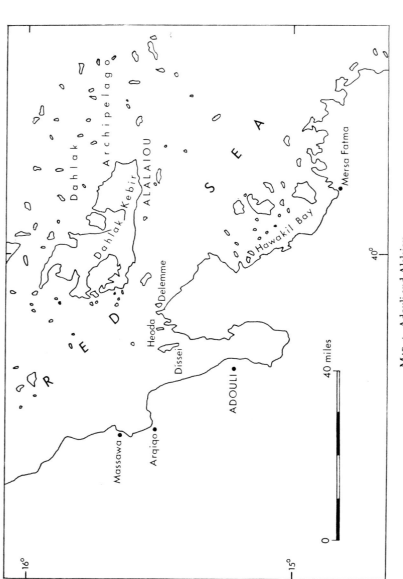

MAP 4. Adouli and Alalaiou

from Zula. It must have been a fair-sized place, judging by
the extent of the ruins, some of which go back to pre-
Christian days. Kosmas Indikopleustēs discovered here the
celebrated Monumentum Adulitanum, a Ptolemaïc throne
with on it a Greek inscription recording the conquests of a
king of Aksum whose name is missing (it may have been
Afilas of the late 3rd century A.D.), and a tablet containing
a record in Greek of Ptolemy III Euergetēs I (247–21 B.C.)
which mentions his use of elephants in war. This monument
has disappeared, and we are dependent on Kosmas for the
inscriptions.

4 OREINĒ ['Ορεινή] The position of this island is difficult to
fix, since there is no island which can properly be described
as near the mainland on both sides. The island now called
Dissei is, however, probably the place, being about
twenty-five miles from the south end of the bay; it is five
miles wide and at most eight miles long; and between
three and eight miles from the mainland.

4 THE ISLAND OF DIDŌROS [Διδώρου νῆσος] This is another
puzzle, for the only island accessible on foot from the
mainland can hardly be said to be 'right inside' the bay;
this is Delemme (ND 372 HFU) which at certain times can
be reached on foot from the mainland (H. de Monfreid,
Les Secrets de la Mer Rouge, Paris, 1932, p. 96). But it lies
outside the Gulf of Zula. On the name Didōros, Frisk
(*Le Périple*, p. 105) remarks that this form, instead of
Diodōros, is attested, and he refers to Josephus, *Antiquities
of the Jews*, 1. 241.

4 KOLOĒ [Κολόη] This is the modern Qohayto, over 7000 feet
above sea level, and about four miles north-east of Addi
Qayeh (ND 372 HFM). It is about 50 miles from Adouli
and 90 from Aksum. There are extensive ruins, including

houses and temples built of stone, and a stone dam 219 feet long and 74 feet high which recalls those in the Yemen of the same (pre-Christian) period (*see:* J. T. Bent, *Sacred City of the Ethiopians*, London, 1893, pp. 215–30; Dainelli and Marinelli, 'Le prime notizie sulle rovine de Cohaito', *Boll. Soc. Afric.*, anno XXVII, fasc. 3, 4, 1908).

4   THE METROPOLIS CALLED THE AXŌMITE [*Τὴν μητρόπολιν τὸν Ἀξωμίτην λεγόμενον*] This is the city of Aksum, the ancient capital of Ethiopia, but in the first century A.D. the capital of a small kingdom little bigger than the modern province of Tigrē, but stretching to Adouli.

4   KUĒNEION [*Κυηνείου*] Probably the Sennar region on the Nile south of Meroē, and some 350 miles west of Aksum.

4   ALALAIOU ISLANDS ['Ἀλαλαίου νῆσοι] These are the islands of the Dahlak archipelago, rather than those in Hawakil Bay.

4   GREAT SANDBANK [*ἄμμος πολλὴ κεχυμένη*] This is in Hawakil Bay, north of Mersa Fatma. On the opsian stone see Note 1 to chapter 5. The modern name of the next bay is Hanfila, which may represent the name *Antiphilos'* Port mentioned by Strabō (*Geog.*, XVI. 4, 9).

7   AUALITĒS ['Ἀναλίτης] This is Zeyla, a town and roadstead south of the Gulf of Tajurra. In the Middle Ages it became the port of entry to southern Ethiopia for the Moslem traders. Burton noted that no craft larger than a canoe can ride near Zeyla because of the coral reef.

7   On OKELIS and MOUZA see under chapters 21 and 26.

8   MALAŌ [*Μαλαώ*] The identification of Malaō with Berbera, 120 miles south-east of Zeyla, is put beyond doubt by the

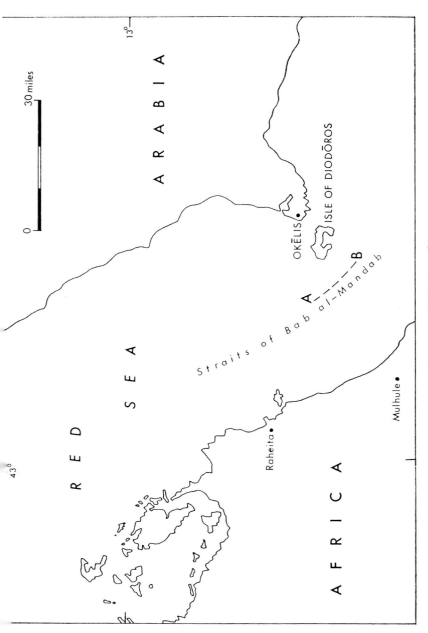

MAP 5. The Straits of Bab al-mandab

RED SEA

ARABIA

AFRICA

13°

43°

30 miles

0

OKĒLIS

ISLE OF DIODŌROS

Straits of Bab al-Mandab

A

B

Raheita

Mulhule

D2

description in the *PME* of a harbour sheltered by a projection running out from the east. The word used for 'projection' is ἀκρωτήριον, which means 'promontory', and although the projection is only a few feet above the sea, the end of it is still called the *ras*, 'headland'. The projection is a narrow spit about 3000 yards long. The place lies on the shore of a flat plain very little raised above sea-level, with mountains rising to over 2000 feet about five miles inland. Berbera was visited by Burton in 1855. He quotes from Lieut. Cruttenden of the Indian Navy who, writing in 1848, says that before four martello towers were built by the Governor of Zeyla at that time to house a garrison, there was no town and no life of any kind there between April and November; but when the monsoon changed people came to trade, and a vast temporary town of huts arose which lasted only for the period of the 'fair' (R. F. Burton, *First Footsteps in East Africa*, London, 1856, pp. 407–8). This shows that ruins need not necessarily be expected on the sites of pre-Islamic East African trading centres; and indeed there is nothing ancient visible at Berbera.

9   MOUNDOU [Μούνδου] There are two possible sites for this place: (1) Heis, 140 miles ENE of Berbera, (2) Mait or Bandar Harshau, forty miles east of Heis. The latter is perhaps the more likely on account of the island of Mait, although it is some ten miles from the mainland.

10   MOSULLON [Μόσυλλον] Possibly Bandar Kasim, where there is an anchorage, 160 miles ENE of Heis, and 120 miles east of Mait. B. Kasim is called Bosaso by the Somali.

11   NEILOPTOLEMAIOU [Νειλοπτολεμαίου], TAPATĒGĒ [Ταπατηγη] THE LITTLE LAUREL GROVE [δαφνῶνα μικρὸν], CAPE ELEPHAS ['Ελέφας]. *Neiloptolemaiou* is probably the result of a

copyist's error, though it is perhaps worth noting that an anonymous Cosmography (probably of the 6th century A.D., printed in Alexander Riese's *Geographi Latini Minores*, II, Heilbronn, 1878, 12) says that 'the river Nile which comes from the shore at the beginning of the Red Sea is seen to emerge at the place called Mossylon Mart; thence it flows west and makes in the middle of itself the island of Meroe'. This, however, may be no more than an echo of the *PME*. *Tapatēgē*, which clearly puzzled the scribe, for he gave it no accent, has been variously interpreted as τὰ πατήγη (ta patēgē), 'the breakers' (Letronne), τάπα πηγή (tapa pēgē), 'the spring of Tapa', and γάζα πηγή (gaza pēgē), 'the spring of Gaza' (Müller), the last perhaps suggested by the *oppidum Gaza* of Pliny (*Nat. Hist.* VI, 34) although it is on the wrong side of Mosullon. *Cape Elephas* is undoubtedly the modern Ras Filuk (in which *fil* means elephant) 100 miles NE of Bandar Kasim, which from certain aspects does suggest an elephant. Whether there was a *Little Laurel Grove* is uncertain, and there may be confusion here with the large laurel grove called AKANNAI [ἀκάνναι] which was perhaps Bandar Alula 120 miles NE of Bandar Kasim.

12   After Bandar Alula the coast turns ESE to Cape Gardafui (Ptolemy's Cape of Spices), and after that south to Ras Hafun. The MART OF SPICES ['Αρωμάτων ἐμπόριον] is perhaps the present small village of Olok one mile west of Cape Gardafui and thirty miles east of Alula. Some ruins here are comparatively recent (Georges Révoil, *La Vallée du Darror*, Paris, 1882, pp. 40–42). The precipitous headland which is the eastern end of the Barbarian mainland is given no name in the *PME*, but it is the modern Ras Asir or Aser, known to Europeans from the 17th century as Cape Gardafui. (Portuguese forms from 1516 to 1553 are Guoardaffuy, Guardafun, Guardafuny, and Guardafu.)

Müller gives Ras Jardafun as an alternative name for Ras Shenagef, which is about twelve miles south of Gardafui. This name might contain the Arabic *jarid*, 'barren, bare of vegetation'.

12 TABAI [*Τάβαι*] Probably Tohen, at the mouth of a small river, five miles south of Gardafui lighthouse (Faro Crispi).

13 OPŌNĒ ['*Οπώνη*] This name has descended from the ancient Egyptian name for the region, Pun-t, and still survives in Ras Hafun. The cape here is a somewhat oddly shaped projection of land about eighty miles south of Gardafui.

15 From Ras Hafun the coast trends to the south-west, and there are some 700 miles of rather dreary featureless land, divided by the author of the *PME* into the Lesser and Greater Bluffs of Azania [*μικρὰ ἀπόκοπα καὶ μέγαλα τῆς Ἀζανίας*, mikra apokopa kai megala tēs Azanias], which are the 200-mile stretch from Hafun to Eil at the mouth of the Nogal, anchorages being few, and Bandar Beila and Eil the most suitable. From the Bluffs extended southwards the Lesser and Greater Strands [*αἰγιαλὸς καὶ μικρὸς καὶ μέγας* aigialos kai mikros kai megas], which perhaps ended at Mogadishu. In all, this stretch is said to have comprised twelve courses, and in it there was no trade and nothing to attract traders except perhaps the need to put in for repairs or refuge from storms. Not only is the coast and the land behind it dreary and inhospitable—to all but the Somali— but it is also for long stretches badly supplied with water. From Hafun to Eil the 1/1,000,000 map NC 39, NB 39, NA 38, shows a dozen seasonal water-holes on the coast and two or three permanent ones in 190 miles. From Eil to Obbia in a stretch of 200 miles there are shown 29 permanent water-holes, and from Obbia to Meregh, in a 90-mile stretch, thirteen permanent and six seasonal

water-holes. From Meregh to Mogadishu (190 miles) the first fourteen are seasonal and only the last four are permanent.

Then come the courses of Azania [οἱ τῆς 'Αζανίας δρόμοι, hoi tēs Azanias dromoi] of which the first is Sarapiōn's and the second Nikōn's [Σαραπίωνος, Νίκωνος]; the first may be Mogadishu, and the second Brava (Barawa), 100 miles further south. There is nothing in either older than the end of the 7th century A.D. Next are seven more courses, with roadsteads separated by rivers and 'stations', each course being a day's run, as far as the Puralaōn Islands and The Channel. Starting from Brava, these courses might be the following:

1. Brava to Makasi well: 60 miles. No river; water-hole.
2. Makasi to El Dere: 40 miles. No river; water-hole.
3. El Dere to Kismayu: 40 miles. Mouth of Juba river.
4. Kismayu to Salama: 45 miles. Rivers Salama and Anole.
5. Salama to Burikao: 40 miles. River Kolbio and creek.
6. Burikao to Kiamboni: 40 miles. No river.
7. Kiamboni to Kwaihu: 40 miles. No river; water-holes.

At Burikao (Bur Kavo, Bur Gao) is a small port (once known as Port Durnford) at the mouth of a creek. Here in 1913 Captain C. W. Haywood, then Political Officer at Kismayu, made some slight investigations in a walled enclosure where, according to his statement, his men discovered a number of coins; 'there were coins of Ptolemy III, IV, and V, third and first century B.C.; Roman coins (Alexandria) of Nero, Trajan, Hadrian, and Antonius [sic] Pius, Maximin, Antioch and Constantinople; as well as many of Constantine XI and XII [sic], together with Mamelukes of Egypt, and Egypt under the Turks' (Geog. J., LXXXV (1935), pp. 59–64). The coins were preserved, but 'an urn shaped very like a Greek amphora', which was also found, was smashed on the return voyage and the fragments thrown away. An earlier account by

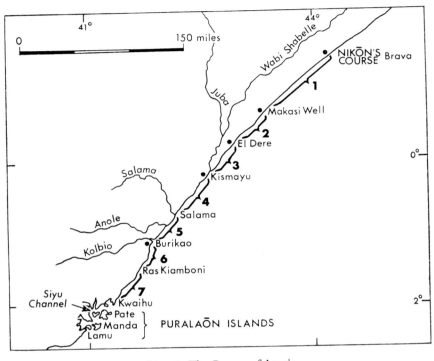

MAP 6. The Courses of Azania

Haywood, *To the mysterious Lorian swamp* (London, 1927) differs greatly from his later version and does not mention the coins. However, coins said to be from Bur Kavo were shown to Harold Mattingly who identified them (*Num. Chron.*, ser. 5, XII (1932), 175); his list differs from Haywood's in specifying Maximin II, Licinius, Constantine I and II and Constans, but no subsequent Byzantine emperor. Such ruins as exist at Bur Kavo are centuries later than the time of the *PME*, and the ancient name of the place is unknown. The coins cannot have been buried before the sixteenth century. Grottanelli (*Pescatori dell' Oceano Indiano* (Roma, 1955), pp. 385–87) remarked on the discrepancies and inaccuracies of Haywood's accounts and Mr Neville Chittick even expresses a doubt as to whether the coins really came from Bur Kavo (*Azania*, IV (1969), 129–30).

Then come the PURALAŌN ISLANDS [πυραλάων νῆσων]; this name appears to be in the genitive case, but if so the nominative is unknown. These are probably the islands of Pate, Manda, and Lamu, The Channel being the Siyu channel between Pate and Manda and the mainland.

After two courses of a day and night along the Ausineitic coast is the island of MENOUTHIAS [Μενουθίας]. The text says that this is two courses 'from The Channel'. If the channel is the Siyu channel, the distance from it to Pemba is about 200 miles and to Zanzibar 300 miles, though both islands are some thirty to forty miles from the nearest point of the mainland, which is roughly the 300 stades of the text. If we accept the sailing distance of the *PME*, Menouthias should be Pemba, though Zanzibar is often claimed for it. The only other candidate is Mafya Island, chosen principally because of the old-fashioned and corrupt Portuguese form Monfia; but this is ninety miles south of Zanzibar and less than fifteen miles from the mainland. The statement in the *PME* that there are in

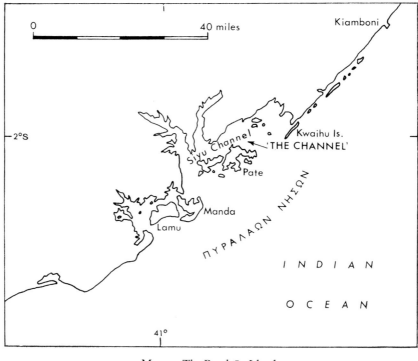

MAP 7. The Puralaōn Islands

Menouthias 'crocodiles which hurt no man' doubtless
refers to the giant water-lizards called *kenge* in Swahili,
which are harmless, and could be mistaken by sailors for
crocodiles. This rules out one of the objections made to
identifying Menouthias with Zanzibar, and of course
applies equally to Pemba, which also has *kenge*.

16 RHAPTA [τὰ ῥάπτα λεγόμενα] This was the last mart on the
coast of Azania, after which 'the land curves round to the
west' (chap. 18). Much ingenuity has been expended in
trying to fix the site of this place, without much success.
Ptolemy in the 2nd century A.D. has three positions here:

> Mouth of river Rhaptos ῾Ράπτος πόταμος (masc.).
> Rhapta metropolis of Barbaria a little way back from the
> sea[1] ῾Ράπτα μητρόπολις (fem.).
> Rhapton cape ῾Ράπτον ἀκρωτήριον (neut.).

There are five possible sites for Rhapta: (1) Tanga, at the
mouth of two small rivers Mkulumuzi and Sigi, with a
good harbour; (2) Pangani, at the mouth of the Ruvu
river; (3) Msasani, about three miles north of Dar es
salaam—or even Dar es salaam itself; (4) Kisiju, about
sixty miles (measured along the coast) south of Kisiju;
(5) somewhere in the Rufiji delta. The first two, of which
Pangani is probably the favourite, are much too close to
Zanzibar and Pemba, for the text says quite unmistakably
ἀφ᾽ ἧ μετὰ δύο δρόμους τῆς ἠπείρου τὸ τελευταιότατον τῆς
᾽Αζανίας ἐμπόριον κεῖται, τὰ ῾Ράπτα λεγόμενα, 'from which
[Menouthias] after two courses of the mainland lies the
last mart of Azania called Rhapta' (chap. 16). I must admit,
with some reluctance, that this indicates that Rhapta must
be sought further south than Pangani. Of the three
southern sites, Msasani has no river, and therefore Kisiju

[1] Note that it is not the *PME* which says this, but Ptolemy, and he was never
near the place, though Diogenēs and Theophilos who are quoted by his
predecessor Marinos of Tyre, undoubtedly knew it.

and Rufiji are the most likely candidates. Dr Gervase Mathew indeed has suggested that it probably 'lies lost in the Rufiji delta' (*History of East Africa*, p. 97).

II. THE ARABIAN COAST TO OMANA[1]

19 BERNIKĒ. See above.

19 LEUKĒ KŌMĒ [Λευκὴ κώμη] 'white village', distant about 200 miles from Bernikē, and possibly the modern Yanbuʻ al-bahr. From Leukē Kōmē to Petra the capital of the Nabataeans ran a road, the distance being some 500 miles.

20 BURNT ISLAND [Κατακεκαυμένη νῆσος] Identified by McCrindle with Zebayir, an island till recently volcanic, about 120 miles NW of Mouza.

21 MOUZA [Μούζα; Ptolemy has Μοῦσα and Μούζα ἐμπόριον] Usually identified with the modern Mauzaʻ, about twenty-five miles north of Mokha, which has replaced it as a port, since it is now not on the sea. It was under the rule of Kholaibos. However, Professor R. B. Serjeant, who has visited the sites, considers it to be Maushij on the coast, locally pronounced Moshi.

22, 23 SAUĒ [Σαυὴ perhaps the Σαβάτ of Ptolemy] the town of Kholaibos, was between Mouza and SAPHAR [Σαφάρ, Ptolemy Σαπφάρα μητρόπολις] the town of Kharibaēl king of the Homēritai and Sabaïtai. Sauē was three days' journey from Mouza, and was probably the modern Udain, which is about fifty miles from Mouza. Saphar, nine days from Sauē, was near Yerim, ninety miles NE of Mouza. These two places were not visited by traders from the coast.

[1] Ptolemy's forms are given when they differ from those of the *PME*.

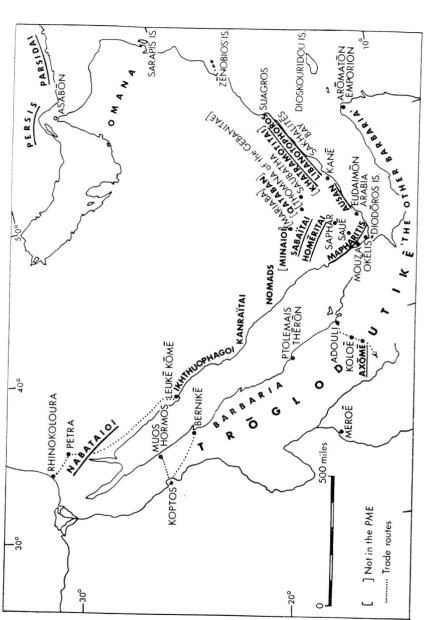

MAP 8. States and kingdoms in Africa and Arabia known to the Author of the *Periplus*

PERSIS PARSIDAI
ASABÔN
OMANA
SARAPIS IS.
ZĒNOBIOS IS.
SUAGROS
DIOSKOURIDOU IS.
SAKHALITĒS
SAKHALITAI
[LIBANOTOPHOROS]
[KHATRAMOTITAI]
[TOMNA of the GEBANITAE]
[SAUBATHA]
[CATABAN]
[MARABA]
[MINAIOI]
SABAÏTAI
HOMĒRITAI
MAPHARITIS
AUSAN
SAPHAR
SAUĒ
MOUZA
OKĒLIS
ARŌMATŌN EMPORION
KANĒ
EUDAIMŌN ARABIA
DIODŌROS IS.
'THE OTHER BARBARIA'
UTIKĒ
TRŌGLODUTIKĒ
BARBARIA
ADOULI
KOLOĒ
AXŌMĒ
MEROĒ
PTOLEMAIS THĒRŌN
NOMADS
KANRAÏTAI
IKHTHUOPHAGOI
LEUKĒ KŌMĒ
NABATAIOI
PETRA
RHINOKOLOURA
MUOS HORMOS
BERNIKĒ
KOPTOS

10°
5°
40°
30°

[ ] Not in the PME
.... Trade routes

500 miles
0

30°
20°
30°

25 THE ISLAND OF DIODŌROS [Διοδώρου νῆσος] This is the island of Perim in the Straits of Bab al-mandab, 'the gate of lamentation', known to some of the English navigators of the 17th and 18th centuries as 'the Babbs' or 'the Babe' (see: Hobson-Jobson, p. 43).

25 OKĒLIS ["Οκηλις] The village of Sheikh Saʿid on the Arabian mainland opposite Perim, from which it is distant about four miles. It was in the territory of Kholaibos.

26 EUDAIMŌN ARABIA ['Ευδαίμων 'Αραβία, 'Arabia Felix'; Ptolemy 'Αραβίας ἐμπόριον and ἡ 'Αραβία τὸ ἐμπόριον]. This was the name usually given to Aden by the Greek geographers, though Pliny has a form Athana, and Philostorgios in the 5th century A.D. has 'Αδάνη Adanē. Its importance increased when it became a coaling station for ships going to India even before the opening of the Suez Canal, and it is still famous for its ancient tanks or reservoirs.

27 KANĒ [Κανή] Hisn Ghurab, lat. 14° 19′ N, long. 48° 19′ E (McCrindle), the projecting headland which is the Ras al-ʿUsēde of the 1/1,000,000 map (ND 39), written Ras-al-Asidah by McCrindle. In the indented bay between this and Barraqa Island are two islands called Halania and Sikha, the first of which may be the TROULLAS [Τρουλλάς] of the PME, and the second the ISLAND OF BIRDS [νῆσος τῶν ὀρνέων], 'which is covered with the dung of birds' (McCrindle). Here, at the foot of a 'square mountain' there were in the early 19th century ruins of houses and towers (J. R. Wellsted, Travels in Arabia, London, 1838, II, 421–6). Mukalla some eighty miles to the east has superseded Kanē.

27 SAUBATHA [Σαυβαθά; Ptolemy Σάββαθα] This, like Sauē and

Saphar, was not a place visited by men who traded at the coast. It was the capital of Eleazos ruler of the Atramitai of the Hadramaut. It lay about 120 miles inland to the NW of Kanē, and is represented by the modern Shabwa, at an altitude of over 1000 metres. The statement that incense was brought to it by water is difficult to understand.

29 SAKHALITĒS BAY [Σαχαλίτης]. The stretch of coast between Kanē and Suagros, especially the part which includes Mukalla and Shihr.

30 SUAGROS [Σύαγρος] Ras Fartak, about 550 miles ENE of Aden.

30 DIOSKOURIDOU [Διοσκουρίδου; Ptolemy Διοσκορίδους νῆσος] This is the island of Socotra, which is not really half way between Suagros and the Cape of Spices, but in fact 150 miles from the Cape and some 250 miles from Suagros. The name is not Greek, as might be thought, but represents the Sanskrit *dvīpa sukhadhara*, 'island of bliss'. The inhabitants seem always to have been a mixed people. Some of them at one period were Christians, converted, it was said, by St Thomas in A.D. 52 while on his way to India. Abu Zaid Hassan, an Arab geographer of the 10th century, said that in his time most of the inhabitants of Socotra were Christians (Guillain, *Documents sur l'histoire, la géographie et le commerce de l'Afrique Orientale*, Paris, 1856, p. 189); but by the beginning of the 16th century Christianity had almost disappeared, leaving little trace but stone crosses at which Alvares said people worshipped (Beckingham and Huntingford, *Prester John*, 1, 43). However, a group of people was found here by St Francis Xavier in 1542, claiming to be descended from the converts made by St Thomas (Smith, *Early History of India*, p. 261).

32 MOSKHA [*Μόσχα*] The 'bay which cuts deep into the mainland of Omana' after passing Suagros is probably that now called Qamar, and Moskha lay beyond this bay, being possibly the modern Salala.

33 ASIKHŌNOS [*'Ασίχωνος*] Here, McCrindle suggested that the mountain range is Subaha, and that the cape is Ras Hasik, where there was a roadstead called Hasik and a village of Arab fishermen in the 14th century (Gibb, *Ibn Battuta*, II, 391). The fishermen on this coast to-day are the Bautahara.

33 ISLANDS OF ZĒNOBIOS [*Ζηνοβίου νῆσοι*]. These are probably the group of five islands known as Kuria Muria, which do in fact lie in a row; their names are Jubaylah, Hallaniya, Sawda or Suda, Hasikiya, and Gharzaut. The Greek name may have been taken from a tribe called Beni Jenabi (McCrindle, *Commerce*, p. 99).

33 ISLAND OF SARAPIS [*Σαράπιδος νῆσοι*] Masira, a large island 250 miles north-east of the Kuria Muria group and from 7 to 10 miles from the mainland. The *PME* has exaggerated its size. It was still inhabited by fish-eaters in the time of Ibn Battuta.

34 KALAIOU ISLANDS [*Καλαίου νῆσοι*]. After leaving Masira the first islands to be encountered near the coast are beyond Muscat after doubling the cape called Ras al-hadd (the Rosalgat of European writers). Westwards from Muscat are the islands (or groups of islands) called Fahal, Daimaniyat, Jaz Jun, and Suadi, which must be the Kalaiou Islands.

35 KALON [*Κάλον*] Unless this 'mountain' is the unnamed projection near Billah close to Suadi, it is difficult to place

it. McCrindle, following General Miles (*J.R.A.S.*, n.s. x (1878), 168), identified it with Jebel Lahrim or Sha'am, the highest peak on the Musandam promontory, which however is a long way from Muscat, and Asabōn is named as another mountain, at the entrance to the Persian Gulf. McCrindle also quotes a suggestion by General Miles that, since the MS reading for καλαίου in chapter 35 is παπίου (the former being an emendation by Fabricius accepted by Frisk) the latter may be the correct name and derived from the Arabic *bāb*, 'gate', implying nearness to the entrance to the Persian Gulf (*Commerce*, p. 101–2). But this seems doubtful.

35   ASABŌN ['Aσαβῶν] This is the cape at the entrance to the Persian Gulf proper, now called Cape Musandam which is actually on an island. McCrindle derives the Greek form from a tribe called Beni Asab.

35   HEIGHT OF SEMIRAMIS [Σεμιράμεως ὑψηλόν], for which Ptolemy has an alternative name Στρόγγυλος Strongulos, a Greek word meaning 'round'. This might be Larak Island, 40 miles N of Cape Musandam in the middle of the entrance to the Persian Gulf.

35   APOLOGOU [ἡ Ἀπολογου] A place at the head of the Persian Gulf, which, although it is called an established mart, does not seem to have been a place where people like the author of the *PME* traded. It is represented by the town of Al-Ubulla near Basra, now sixty miles from the head of the Gulf, though the site has not been identified on the ground (G. le Strange, *Lands of the Eastern Caliphate*, Cambridge, 1930, p. 19). It was at one time frequented by traders from India.

35   PASINOU KHARAX [Πασίνου χάραξ] Written Kharax

Spasinou by other writers, it was the chief town of the district of Kharakēnē in Susiana, originally founded by Alexander the Great, who called it Alexandreia. After it had been destroyed by floods a new town was built by Pasinēs son of Sogdonaios the chief of the Arabs of that area, whence its later name 'fort of Pasinēs'. It is now represented by large fortifications at Jebel Khiyabar SE of the Tigris-Euphrates confluence near Qurna (J. Hansman, *Iranica Antiqua* VII (1967), pp. 21–7). (I owe this reference to Dr Bivar.)

36   OMANA ["Ομανα, "Ομμανα] It seems clear that there were two places known to the author of the *PME* (or so written in the MSS) as Omana/Ommana. The first, in chapter 32 was clearly in Arabia, and is now represented by Oman. The second, in chapters 27 and 36 is written Ommana and Omana, and is called 'another mart of Persis' and was on the coast of Persia. It has been variously placed near Cape Jask, some 150 miles E of the nearest point of Arabia (Vincent); at Bandar Tank, about 220 miles E of Jask (Mannert); and at Ormara, some 300 miles E of Bandar Tank (suggested in a letter from Sir Laurence Kirwan).

From here the route crosses the Persian Gulf to the land of the Parsidai, India, and the Far East.

III. THE COASTS OF PERSIA AND INDIA

37   BAY OF THE GEDRŌSIANS [κόλπος τῶν Γεδρωσῶν] This was perhaps the bay which extends from Cape Guadel to Cape Monze on the coast of Baluchistan, the ancient Gedrōsia. The Parsidai may be the same as the Pasirees of Arrian (*Indika* XXVI). Müller conjectured Terabdōn, in which he was followed by McCrindle and Frisk; Gedrōsians seems better.

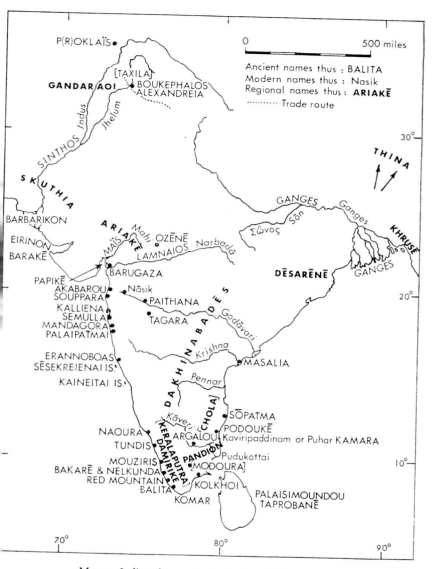

MAP 9. India as known to the Author of the *Periplus*

37 HŌRAIA ['Ωραία] This lay on the inner side of the mouth of a river which may be the Purali or the Habb.

37 RHAMBAKIA ['Ραμβακία] There is a lacuna in the MS here, and Mannert conjectured Rhambakia, a place which occurs in Arrian's *Anabasis* (VI. 21), the position of which is not known, except that it was a village of the Ōreitai, a people whose country reached the coast. Their name may be connected with Hōraia (above) in spite of the difference of vowel—*ai–ei*; and their country may be 'the other kingdom' referred to at the beginning of chapter 37.

38 SINTHOS [Σίνθος] The river Indus, Sanskrit *sindhu*, 'the sea', Hellenized as 'Ινδός, from which comes the *Latin* form India. (*Hobson-Jobson*, pp. 433–4.)

38 SKUTHIA [Σκυθία] Scythia, the name applied by the Greeks to the country of the Śaka.

40 BARBARIKON [Βαρβαρικόν] written BARBARIKĒ [Βαρβαρική] in chapter 39. Owing to the changes that have taken place in the area of the delta of the Indus, it is unlikely that even the land on which Barbarikon stood still exists, or the 'small island' off it. If Barbarikon was in the Indus delta, goods carried up the Indus to the king—presumably of Skuthia—cannot have gone to Minnagara by river, if the latter is Mandasor. In the time of Aśoka (250 B.C.) the coast line was to the north of the Indus delta, and what is now the Rann of Kutch was sea (Smith, *Early History*, p. 245).

40 EIRINON ['Ειρινόν] The Rann of Kutch (Kachch, Cutch), from Hind. *ran*, Sanskt. *irina*, 'salt-swamp', a great extent of waste-land and swamp, often under water, which has taken the place of the bay which formerly existed at the

mouth of the Indus. The text of the *PME* suggests that it was still under water in the 1st century. The area 'is no longer covered with water except during the monsoon, when it is flooded by sea water or by rains and inundated rivers. At other seasons it is not even a marsh, for its bed is hard, dry, and sandy; a mere saline waste almost entirely devoid of herbage, and frequented but by one quadruped —the wild ass' (McCrindle, *Commerce*, p. 111).

40 BARAKĒ [Βαράκη] This, it is suggested in *Hobson-Jobson* (p. 334), is the later Dwarka (Dvaraka), at the NW end of the peninsula of Kathiawar, a sacred place of pilgrimage. It is called Bharraky in 'an old Persian map'. Barakē, however, would seem to be the Gulf of Kutch, in which there are in fact seven islands along its south coast, Dwarka being on the south side of the entrance to the Gulf. It appears from the text that ships entered Barakē only if they were driven into it by storms.

41 BARUGAZA. See below, chapter 43.

41 ARIAKĒ ['Αριακῆ] The country behind Barugaza and Gujarat.

41 ABĒRIA ['Αβηρία] The part of Gujarat north of Broach and Kathiawar, called Abhīra by the Indians (McCrindle, *Commerce*, p. 114).

41 SURASTRĒNĒ [Συραστρήνη, Ptolemy Συραστρά] The Kathiawar peninsula, the ancient Indian Saurashtra, a name (later) represented by Sorath, but sometimes written Surath (and not to be confused with Surat on the opposite side of the Gulf of Cambay) one of the political districts of the peninsula under British rule (*Hobson-Jobson*, p. 876).

41 MINNAGARA [Μιννανάρα, written Μιννανάρ in chapter 38; Ptolemy, Μιναγάρα] The capital of Surastrēnē, identified with a place called Mandasor, some eighty miles NW of Ozēnē (Ujjain) (Smith, *Early History*, p. 221).

41 ASTAKAPRA ['Ασтакάπра] The Indian name of this was Hastakavapra, now Hathab near Bhavnagar nearly opposite Broach (McCrindle, *Commerce*, p. 115).

41 PAPIKĒ [Παπικῆ] This must have been close to Astakapra, possibly opposite the modern town of Dehej on the Barugaza side of the Gulf of Cambay.

42 THE OTHER BAY is undoubtedly the Gulf of Cambay, and the island called BAIŌNĒS [Βαιώνης νῆσος] is identified in *Hobson-Jobson* with the island of Peram or Piram.

42 MAÏS [Μάϊς] A large river which discharges into the upper part of the Gulf of Cambay, and is difficult to cross; the modern name is Mahi (*Hobson-Jobson*, p. 536).

42 LAMNAIOS [Λαμναῖος, Ptolemy Νάμαδος Namados] The river Narbada, which flows into the Gulf of Cambay, and is the river of Barugaza. (The form with L is one of the curious substitutions of L for another letter which occur in the *PME*, as in Limurikē for Damirikē. The explanation *may* be due to a misreading by a copyist of Greek Δ for Λ (as is undoubtedly the case in some of Ptolemy's names, e.g. 'Laphninē or Daphninē'), though *Limurikē* occurs several times in the *PME*). The river name is Sanskrit Narmadā, 'causing delight' (*Hobson-Jobson*, p. 623).

43 BARUGAZA [Βαρυγάζα] The original name of this place was Bharukacha, reduced to the modern Broach. It was an important trading station at the mouth of the Narbada, in

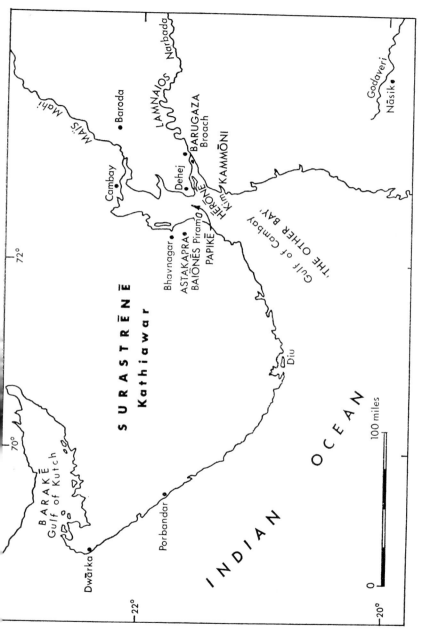

MAP 10. The Gulf of Cambay

Ariakē and the territory of king Manbanos (Nahapāna).
Ariakē produced iron and steel as well as cotton cloth;
and murrhine ware was made at Barugaza. (*See:* Glossary
of Exports and Imports.) Idrisi says that 'the Indians excel
in the art of ironworking, and of making alloys which
produce the soft iron known as "Indian iron"''. They have
factories in which are made the most highly prized swords
in the world' (Guillain, *Documents*, p. 225).

43 HĒRŌNĒ ['Ηρώνη] A shoal opposite Kammōni. This might
be part of the reef on the south side of the mouth of the
Narbada.

43 KAMMŌNI [Καμμωνὶ] A village on the south side of the
mouth of the Narbada; perhaps represented by the name
which appears as Kim on the 1 : 1,000,000 map NF 43.

47 PROKLAÏS [Προκλαΐς] This should be written Poklaïs
Ποκλαΐς, for it occurs everywhere else without R:
Πευκελαῶτις Arrian; Πευκολαίτις Strabō; Peucolais,
Peucolitae, Pliny; all these forms represent the Indian
name Puṣkalāvatī. The site of this place is now called
Charsadda, about 25 miles NNE of Peshawar; it was an
important city in the time of Alexander the Great. It was
not, however, visited by the traders from Egypt, being
nearly a thousand miles from Barugaza.

47 BOUKEPHALOS ALEXANDREIA [Βουκέφαλος ᾿Αλεξάνδρεια].
Ptolemy has Βουκεφάλη. This town was built by Alexander
in memory of his beloved horse Boukephalos (Bucephalus)
which died here, near a ferry over the Jhelum river on the
high road from the west to the interior of India, whence
the town became of great commercial importance. The
site is marked by a large mound west of the modern town

of Jhelum (Jihlam), about 150 miles SE of Peshawar (Smith, *Early History*, p. 75).

47 LIMURIKĒ. See chapter 42 above, under Lamnaios, and chapter 53, where it refers to the Tamil coast.

48 OZĒNE [Ὀζήνη] Another inland city, the modern Ujjain, a very ancient place, and the meridian from which the early Hindu astronomers calculated the longitudes of their system (*Hobson-Jobson*, p. 637). It is seventy miles N of the Narbada, and some 200 miles E of Barugaza.

50 DAKHINABADĒS [Δαχιναβάδης] The Deccan, Sanskrit *Dakṣiṇāpatha*, 'southern region'. The term has been taken to cover the whole of India south of the Narbada, though generally excluding the Tamil and Malabar coast.

51 PAITHANA [Παίθανα] Paithan on the Godavari river, one of the great inland marts, about 180 miles E of Souppara on the W coast.

51 TAGARA [Ταγάρα] Another great inland mart, about 100 miles SSE of Paithan, now Ter (1 : 1,000,000 map NE 43 Thair).

52 AKABAROU [Ἀκαβαρου without accent] After the digression in chapters 47–51 to inland places, we now return to the west coast of Limurikē. Akabarou was a 'local' mart; Frisk suggested that it may be a place called Khabirun by Idrisi (*Le Périple*, p. 117).

52 SOUPPARA [Σούππαρα, Ptolemy Σουπάρα] This is the 'local' mart now called Sopara near Vasai (Bassein) about thirty miles N of Bombay.

52 KALLIENA [Καλλίένα] Kalyana on a river which enters the gulf of Bombay, from which place it is distant about thirty-three miles.

53 SĒMULLA [Σήμυλλα], now Chaul, twenty miles S of Bombay, a Portuguese station in the 16th century. Ptolemy has Σίμυλλα 'called by the natives Τίμουλα', with which may be compared Tseimwal, the Konkani form.

53 MANDAGORA [Μανδαγόρα] The modern Bankot, about seventy miles south of Bombay, at the mouth of the Savitri river; though, alternatively, the site may be at Mandangad, a little S of Bankot (Smith, Early History, p. 226).

53 PALAIPATMAI [Παλαιπάτμαι] The modern Dabhol or Dabul on the river Anjanwel or Vashishti (Vishishti), 100 miles S of Bombay. Described by Barbosa as 'a good harbour' (M. L. Dames, The Book of Duarte Barbosa, Hakluyt Society, London, I (1918), p. 165).

53 MELIZEIGARA [Μελιζειγάρα] The next mart S of Palaipatmai, at the mouth of the Jaygad river, for which Smith suggests Jaigarh, twenty miles S of Dabhol.

53 BUZANTION [Βυζάντιον] For this McCrindle suggests Vijayadurg (Visadrog) fifty miles S of Jaigarh, at the mouth of a river.

53 TOPARON and ERANNOBOAS. These occur in a corrupt passage in the MS, which has τοπαρον καὶ τύραννος βοας (sic). For the first, McCrindle suggests Togaron, which he identifies with Devagadh (Devgarh); this appears to be the Jamsanda of the International 1 : 1,000,000 Map, Sheet

NE 43 at the mouth of a river. The second may be Malvan, some forty miles S of Vijayadurg. As for the name, all that can be said is that 'Εραννοβόας (Erranoboas) occurs in both Arrian and Pliny, though Pliny's Erranoboam was a river in Bengal.

53 SĒSEKREIENAI ISLANDS [Σησεκρείεναι νῆσοι] Possibly the Vengurla Rocks in the group known as the Burnt Islands, about twenty-five miles S of Malvan (McCrindle, *Commerce*, pp. 129–30).

53 AIGIDIŌN ISLAND [ἡ τῶν 'Αιγιδίων νῆσος] Possibly the island called Anjediva or Anchediva, where there was good water. Several writers, from Ibn Battuta (1345) to Correa (1561) have described it, and all mention the stone-built reservoirs there (*Hobson-Jobson*, pp. 28–9). It is a little S of Karwar fifty miles S of Goa. [On the name, see note 1 to chapter 53.]

53 KAINEITŌN ISLAND [Καινειτῶν νῆσος] Possibly Oyster Rock, W of the roadstead of Karwar; or it might be the Island of St George. [On the name, see note 2 to chapter 53.]

53 WHITE ISLAND [Λευκὴ νῆσος] Perhaps Hog Island or Pigeon Island, both about fifty miles S of Karwar.

53 NAOURA [Νάουρα] Cannanore (Kannanur), some 220 miles S of Karwar. The Portuguese embassy to Ethiopia came to Cannanore in 1520 on its way from Cochin, and Alvares records that supplies of a palm wine called *urrachas* were taken on there (Beckingham and Huntingford, *Prester John*, I, 41); this was arrack, distilled from fermented palm sap. McCrindle, however, puts Naoura at Honavar at the mouth of the river Sharavati, forty miles S of Karwar.

53 TUNDIS [*Τύνδις*] This may be the modern Tanor, about seventy-five miles S of Cannanore (*Hobson-Jobson*, p. 900). It was once a small kingdom.

53 LIMURIKĒ [*Λιμυρικὴ*] At Naoura and Tundis begins the region called Limurikē by the *PME*. This form is clearly wrong, and should be *Δαμυρικὴ* Damurikē, the Damirikē of Ptolemy (*see:* Lamnaios in chapter 42 above). It is 'a good transliteration of Tamilakam', the Tamil country (Smith, *Early History*, p. 457). The term included the ancient kingdom of Chera or Kerala which existed in the time of Aśoka (mid-3rd century B.C.) with its old capital at Vanji or Karur up the Periyar river, and about twenty-eight miles ENE of Cochin (Smith, *op. cit.*, pp. 468–9).

53 MOUZIRIS [*Μούζιρις*] Cranganore, about 125 miles S of Cannanore, one of the earliest Jewish and Christian settlements in India, but decayed by the time the Portuguese first came there (*Hobson-Jobson*, p. 272). On the evidence of the Peutinger Table there was a temple of Augustus here (Smith, *Early History*, p. 463). Pliny (*Nat. Hist.* VI, 26) says 'Thence from Ocelis with the wind Hippalus they sail in forty days to Muziris the first emporium of India, not to be sought on account of the pirates in the neighbourhood'.

54 NELKUNDA [*Νελκύνδα*] This is Kottayam about fifty miles S of Cranganore. The town of Nelkunda was about twelve miles from the sea and about five miles from the lake called Vembanad; the landing-place for it was Bakarē, mentioned in the next chapter. It belonged to the Pāndya (Pandion) kingdom.

55 BAKARĒ [*Βακαρή*] The modern Vaikkarai, the landing-place on the sea-coast for Nelkunda (Smith, *Early History*, p.

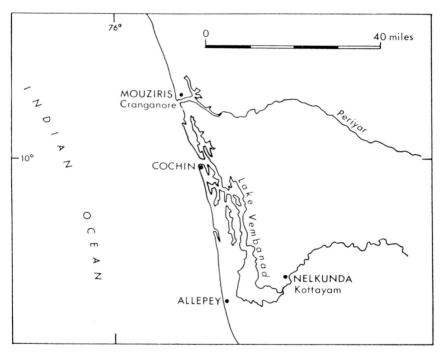

MAP 11. Mouziris and Nelkunda

468). Pliny has: 'another more useful port belonging to the people of Nelcyndon, which is called Bacare. Pandion rules there' (*Nat. Hist.* VI, 26).

58 RED MOUNTAIN [τὸ πυρρὸν ὄρος] Red Cliffs is the name given in modern times to the steep coast below Quilon, the town in Kerala called Kollam in Tamil (*Hobson-Jobson*, pp. 751, 758).

58 BALITA [Βάλιτα] Perhaps Trivandrum; or else Manpalli, a little NW of Anjenga, which is about twenty miles N of Trivandrum (McCrindle, *Commerce*, p. 140).

58 KOMAR [Κομάρ. Ptolemy has Κομαρία. In the next chapter it is written Κομαρεὶ Komarei]. Cape Comorin, the southernmost point of India. See note to this chapter.

59 KOLKHOI [Κόλχοι] Near Tutikorin, at the mouth of the Tamraparni river in Tinnevelly. Originally there were two ports here, one called Cael (Kayal), the other Kolkai or Korkai; the latter is the equivalent of the Greek form. Both ceased to function as ports through the gradual elevation of the coast. Kolkhoi was the early capital of the Pāndya kingdom.

59 ARGALOU ['Αργαλου without accent]. The modern Uraiyur or Old Trichinopoly, the capital of the Chola kingdom, from which comes the name Cholamandalam (Coromandel) denoting the coast and interior from Nellore onwards.

60 KAMARA [Καμάρα] The ancient port of the Chola kingdom, called Kaviripaddinam or Puhar, now buried under sand (Smith, *Early History*, p. 462).

60 PODOUKĒ [Ποδούκη] This is possibly Arikamedu, a place about two miles from Pondicherry, where Roman pottery and other remains were found in 1937. Excavations made between 1944 and 1949 showed that it was the site of an Iron Age settlement which became a trading station to which goods of Roman manufacture were imported during the first half of the 1st century A.D. ((1) Sir Mortimer Wheeler, *Rome beyond the Imperial Frontiers* (London, 1954), pp. 129, 141–50, and (2) F. R. Allchin, art. Arikamedu, in L. Cottrell (ed.), *Concise Encyclopaedia of Archaeology* (London, 1970).)

60 SŌPATMA [Σωπάτμα] Possibly the forerunner of Madras, sited (as I suggest with some diffidence) at Saidapat at the end of a creek on the southern outskirts of Madras.

61 PALAISIMOUNDOU [Παλαισιμούνδου] The island of Ceylon, which according to the author of the *PME* was so large that it nearly reached the opposite coast of Azania. He was slightly confused by the geographical position of the island; and he seems also to be in error when he says that the old name was Ταπροβάνη Taprobanē (Sanskrit Tāmraparṇī), for this was the name commonly used by Europeans from the time of Strabō to that of Ptolemy; whatever it really meant, the Greeks seem to have interpreted the first name as πάλαι Σιμούνδου, 'formerly Simoundou', even if both names were in use in the 2nd century A.D. Ptolemy has 'the island of Taprobanē, called formerly Simoundou (ἡ πάλαι Σιμούνδου καλουμένη) now Salikē'. Pliny has a town Palaesimondo and a river Palaesimundum.

62 MASALIA [Μασαλία, Ptolemy Μαισωλία] Masulipatam, between the Kistna and Godavari rivers.

62 DĒSARĒNĒ [Δησαρήνη] Possibly the region occupied by the modern state of Orissa. Müller altered the spelling to Dōsarēnē Δωσαρήνη, perhaps influenced by the river-name Δωσάρων Dōsarōn, which Ptolemy says flows into the Gangetic Gulf.

63 GANGES [Γάγγης] Applied to both the river Ganges and to a town; the site of the latter is unknown. Ptolemy has Γάγγη Gangē for the town and Γάγγης Gangēs for the river. The river is called Ganga on the Indian Government maps.

63 KHRUSĒ [Χρυσῆ] This term probably includes not only Burma but also south-east Asia as a whole, while the 'inland city called Khrusē' may even have been Sumatra. Pliny, in a slightly confused passage says that 'outside the mouth of the *Indus* are Chryse and Argyre [i.e. Golden and Silvered], productive of metals, as I believe' (*Nat. Hist.* VI, 23). The latter name is the 'Αργυρῆ Argurē, of Ptolemy, referring to the modern Arakan, the western part of Burma (*see: Hobson-Jobson*, p. 34).

64 THINA [θῖνα, θῖνος] Though called a great inland city, this word really refers to the *country* of China as a whole; it occurs in the *PME* only in the accusative and genitive cases, and the supposed nominative, θίς This, is speculative. Ptolemy has οἱ Σῖναι for the people.

66 The unexplored and unknown lands are those beyond, i.e. north of Burma and China, from which stories of the cold of winter had penetrated vaguely into the known world.

CORRELATION OF SPELLINGS OF MODERN FORMS OF SOME INDIAN PLACE-NAMES

McCrindle	1: 1M. Map[1]	IGTM[1]	Hobson-Jobson	Smith
Angediva	Anjidiv		⎰Anjadwa ⎱Anjediva	
Anjenga	Anjengo		⎰Anjenga ⎱Anjengo	
Bankut	Bānkot			
Bharoch	Broach	Broach	Broach	Bharoch
	Cannanore	Cannanore		
Chaul ⎱ Chenval ⎰	Chaul		⎰Chaul ⎱Choul	
Debal	Cranganur Dābhol		Cranganore Dabul	
	Jaigarh	Jaigarh		
Jaygaḍh	Jaygad			
Kalyana	Kalyān	Kalyān	Kalyān	Kalyan
Kaveripattam				Kaviripadanam
Khambat	Cambay	Cambay	Cambay	
Kolkei				Korkai
	Kottayam	Kottayam		
Kumari	Comorin	Comorin	Comorin	Comorin
Mahi	Mahi	Mahi	Mahi	Mahi
Mâlwan	Mālvan	Mālvan		
Masulipatam	Masulipatnam	Masulipatam	Masulipatam	
Narmadâ	Narbada	Narmada	Nerbudda	Narmadā
Paithana	Paithan	Paithan		
Peram	Piram			
Puduchêri	Pondichéry	Pondicherry	Puduchcheri	
Ran of Kachch	Rann of Cutch	Rann of Kutch	Runn of Cutch	Ran of Cutch
Supârâ			Supara	Sopāra
Ujjain ⎱ Ujjayini ⎰	Ujjain	Ujjain	Ujjain ⎱ Ujjayanī ⎰	Ujjain
Vasai	Bassein	Bassein	Bassein	
Vijayadrug	Vijaydurg	Vijayadurg		
Vingorla	Vengurla	Vengurla		

[1] For these maps, see pp. 203–4 below.

APPENDIX 2

The Products of the Erythraean Area

THE products recorded in the *PME* consist of two main groups:
(1) Animal: tortoiseshell, ivory, and rhinoceros horn. (2) Plant:
'arōmata', i.e. spices, fragrant gums, incense, spikenard, kasia,
malabathron, aloes, cinnabar, etc. (3) Less in quantity were
precious stones, cloth, skins, silk, purple dye, indian ink (or
indigo), murrhine ware, ghi, sesame oil, corn, wine, rice, and
sugar. These were exported both to places in the Erythraean
area and to Egypt and southern Europe. They were obtained
largely, if not entirely, by exchange of things which the local
people could not make or produce themselves. Thus, to the
ports on the north Somali coast were brought for exchange
with arōmata, ivory, and tortoiseshell such things as clothing,
glassware, cups and bowls, tin, iron, gold and silver, precious
stones, corn, wine, and unripe olives, as well as a little money,
not for trade but as presents to the natives. Money, in fact, does
not seem to have been used for buying goods, but only for
gifts, except that in certain civilised places where coinage was
in normal circulation, like Barugaza and the Tamil coast,
money was imported, sometimes in large quantities.

Many of the goods used for exchange probably came from
Egypt, though some came from Barugaza and Ariakē, and
others from Mouza, and Omana; the latter exported its own
make of sewn boats to other parts of Arabia. There seem in fact
to have been four main sources of supply for these exchange
goods: Egypt, and especially the clothing factory at Arsinoē;
Mouza, where there seems to have been a factory for making
tools and weapons; Omana; and Barugaza, to which were sent

products from places far inland for export. A certain amount came from the Mediterranean area, like the Laodikean and Italian wines, and possibly, though it nowhere says so, manufactured things from Rome.

Of the animal products, the largest quantity was in the form of tortoiseshell, which came from the Red Sea coast (Adouli), the Somali coast, the East African coast (Rhapta), Socotra, the south Arabian coast, the Tamil coast, Ceylon, and Khrusē. The author of the *PME* names four types of tortoise which he calls land tortoise, mountain tortoise, true tortoise, and white tortoise. McCrindle in his translation defines 'true' tortoise as the marine variety, though I know not on what grounds. All that can be said here is that the *OED* lists four types of tortoise: land tortoise, order *Testudinidae*; marsh tortoise, order *Emydae* (Greek ἐμύς *emus*, fresh water tortoise); river tortoise, order *Trionychidae* ('three-nailed', because only three of the five toes have nails); and marine tortoise, order *Chelonidae*, also called turtles. Tortoiseshell was much in demand in civilised countries for making various articles of furniture and ornaments.

Ivory came from the Red Sea coast, the Somali coast, the East African coast (Rhapta), and from Barugaza, the Tamil coast, and the East Indian coast (Dēsarēnē). In the ivory trade there are two sorts of ivory, soft and hard; the latter is more brittle than the soft. Ivory from East Africa is of the soft kind, and when the author of the *PME* says that the ivory from the Rhapta area is inferior to that from Adouli, he may have meant that the Rhapta ivory was hard. In his time, as now, much of the African ivory may have gone to India, which uses about half the world's supply of ivory. Europe of course uses (or used) a good deal, and it is said that hard ivory is preferred there, while India likes the soft kind.[1]

[1] See: G. S. P. Freeman-Grenville, *The medieval history of the coast of Tanganyika*, London, 1962, p. 25, from which have been taken these facts about ivory.

Rhinoceros horn was exported only from Africa—Adouli and Rhapta. It is possible that much of it went to India.

Plant products, 'arōmata' in general, came mainly from the north Somali coast (Aualitēs to Opōnē) with some from the south Arabian coast (especially the Sakhalitic frankincense from Moskha), Socotra, the north-west Indian coast, the Tamil coast (especially pepper), the Ganges region, and China. Their distribution may be summarised thus:

(1) Exports from the north Somali coast

Aualitēs: arōmata, and a little myrrh, some of it sent across to Okēlis and Mouza; possibly most of it went in fact to Arabia for re-export.

Malaō: myrrh, incense, hard kasia, douaka, kankamon, and makeir, all apparently sent to Arabia.

Moundou: the same as from Malaō, plus some fragrant gums.

Mosullon: much kasia, fragrant gums and spices, and incense.

Akannai: incense.

Arōmatōn Emporion: kasia, gizeir, asuphē, magla, motō, and incense.

Opōnē: kasia, spices, and motō. This was the last place in Africa from which arōmata were exported, or indeed where they were grown. It is probable that most of the Somaliland arōmata were sent over to Arabia and re-exported to Egypt, though the author does not actually say so.

(2) Exports from Arabia and Socotra

Mouza: myrrh and staktē.

Kanē: incense and aloes; incense exported to Omana.

Moskha: Sakhalitic incense.

Socotra: cinnabar.

(3) *Exports from the Indian coast*

Hōraia: bdella.

Barbarikon: kostos, bdella, lukion, spikenard; and, imported, storax and incense.

Barugaza: spikenard, kostos, bdella, myrrh, lukion, pepper.

Tamil coast: pepper (a great deal), malabathron, spikenard.

Ganges: malabathron, spikenard.

China: malabathron.

As a supplement to the *PME*, some passages from Pliny's IXth and XIIth books are printed, in translation, below.

PLINY, Book IX

The Indian Ocean produces tortoises (*testudines*)[1] of such a size that a single shell is enough to form a hut to live in, and the inhabitants of the islands in the Red Sea use them as boats. They are caught in many ways, but chiefly when carried out to sea in the warm hours before midday. They float on the surface with their backs out of water, and the pleasure of breathing freely so lulls them into forgetfulness that their shells are dried by the sun's heat and thus they cannot sink, but float aimlessly, an easy prey to the hunter. They feed at night; when they have eaten enough they return in the morning and sleep on the surface of the water. The noise of their snoring betrays them to the fishermen who swim up quietly and capture them, three men taking one tortoise between them: two men turn the creature on to its back, and the third puts a noose round it, and thus it is pulled to the shore.

Tortoises have no teeth, but instead jaws with sharp edges, the upper shutting on the lower like the lid of a box. They feed

----

[1] These are clearly turtles (order Chelonidae).

on shell-fish, for their jaws are so strong that they can break stones with them. They come out on land and lay eggs like birds' eggs, up to a hundred in number; they bury them in the ground out of the reach of water, cover them with sand, and smooth it with their breasts; they sit on them at night. The eggs are hatched after a year. The female flees from the male till he puts some sort of herb on his unwilling partner. In the Troglodyte country there are tortoises with horns like lyres, but moveable, which they use as oars when swimming. This kind is called *chelyon*; it has a valuable shell, but is rare, because the Tortoise-eaters are afraid of the sharp rocks among which they live; and the Troglodytes whose coast they visit account them sacred.

PLINY, Book XII

Macir is brought from India; it has a large root with a reddish cortex, but I am ignorant of its nature. The cortex is made into a decoction with honey as a remedy for dysentery.

Arabia produces saccharon (sugar), but that from India is preferred. It is a kind of honey collected in canes, white like gum, easily bitten, and much used in medicine.

Incense was formerly cut once a year when required for sale. Now the demand for it necessitates a second cutting. The first and natural time is about the rising of the Dog Star [towards the end of July], when the heat is greatest, and the plant seems to the harvester to be full of sap and the bark very soft. The sap is set free by a blow and no bark is removed: a liquid oozes out. This drops out and hardens, and is caught sometimes on a frame covered with palm leaves, sometimes on the ground, which is cleared and beaten hard. What sticks to the tree is removed with a knife, but is mixed with bits of bark. The woods are divided into tracts by the collectors; nobody guards the trees which are cut, for nobody steals from his neighbours. It is otherwise at Alexandria, where the incense is manufactured, for there the factories cannot be sufficiently guarded. The workmen's loincloths are sealed by the manufacturer [to prevent them from taking incense away in them]; but they cover their heads with a cloth [to hide what they steal] and are sent out naked. How much less is our honesty with its attendant penalties than the simple faith of the forest! In the autumn the produce of the summer cutting is collected. This is white, and the purest. The second harvest is in the spring, when they collect what has oozed from the incisions made in the winter. This is red, and not to be compared with the first harvest. The autumn produce is called carphiatum; that of the spring, dathiatum.

Myrrh is said to grow in the same woods as incense; but it is found in many places in Arabia. It is carried to the islands in the Red Sea and the Sabaeans even seek it by crossing to the Troglodyte country. There is also a cultivated variety which is much preferred to the wild. It responds to forking and trenching, and is better when the root is exposed.

The tree grows to a height of seven and a half feet. It has thorns and a hard twisted stem, thicker than the incense tree.

Myrrh also is cut twice a year, at the same times as incense, but is taken from the roots up to such branches as can be cut. Before being cut the trees exude as it were by sweating a kind of oil called stacte. . . . There are several kinds of myrrh: first, the Troglodytic, of the forest; second, the Minaean, including the aromatic; third, the Dianitic; fourth, the mixed kind; fifth, the Sembracene, from near the Sabaean kingdom; sixth, the Dusaritic. . . . The Troglodytic is esteemed for its richness, for although it is dirtier to look at, it is sharper and stronger. . . . The Troglodytic is sold in lumps at sixteen denarii; and what is called odoraria, at fourteen denarii.

Cinnamon or casia grows near the Troglodytes who, buying it from their neighbours, carry it over the sea in boats which have no means of steering or propulsion; these voyages are made mostly in midwinter when the south-east (sic) wind blows. Keeping close to the shore they unload at Ocelis, the port of the Gebanitae, after rounding cape Argeste. The voyage occupies a long time; some return after five years, and others die there. In return they bring back glassware, brass, clothes, brooches, armlets, and necklaces; this trade depends to a great extent, therefore, on female whims. The cinnamon is a shrub which grows to a height of three feet, though the smallest may be only a few inches high; it is four fingers thick, and at the ground is woody like a withered plant. When growing it has no smell; the leaf is like marjoram. It prefers dry conditions, and yields but little when there is much rain; it is deciduous. Sometimes it grows on the plains, but usually in dense thickets, where it is difficult to collect. It can be harvested only with God's permission; by this some understand Juppiter, though the Arabians call him Assabinus. This permission is obtained by the sacrifice of fifty-four oxen, goats, and sheep, and must not be done before sunrise or after sunset. The priest cuts the twigs with a spear and puts some aside for God; the collectors put the rest together in heaps. . . . The best part is the thin twigs, of about a palm's length [three inches], and the worst is that nearest to the roots, because that has the least bark, and the bark is what is preferred. . . . Some say that there are two kinds of cinnamon, white and black. . . . The produce belongs entirely to the king of the Gebanitae, who sells it by his own orders. It used to be sold at a thousand denarii a pound, but the price has been raised to fifteen hundred denarii, owing, it is said, to the destruction of the woods by the savages.

Casia is also a shrub and grows near the cinnamon country; but in the hills it has more branches and a thinner bark, which unlike cinnamon is stripped off. The shrub is four and a half feet in height, and of three colours. When it first shoots, it is white for the height of a foot, then for six inches it becomes red, and above that turns black. This last is the most valuable part, then the red, while the white is valueless.

Near where casia and cinnamon grow are to be found cancamum and tarum, which are brought through the Nabataeans to the Troglodytes.

GLOSSARY OF EXPORTS AND IMPORTS

E= Export. I= Import. * Native names and words of uncertain meaning. Numerals= chapter numbers. (Case-endings as in the text.)

I. CLOTHING MATERIAL

Belts περιζώματα I 6, I 14.
Blankets λώδικες I 24.
Brocades, Damasks πολύμιτα I 39, I 56.

Cloaks ἀβόλλαι I 24.
Cloaks, Arsinoïtic σάγοι I 8. The Roman *sagus* was a rectangular mantle made of coarse material. These and other textiles exported from Egypt were made in a factory at Arsinoē near Klusma (Suez).
Cloaks, cloth ἱματίων ἀβόλλαι I 6.
Cloaks, coloured ἀβόλλαι χρωμάτινοι I 6.
Cloth, assorted ὀθόνιον παντοῖον E 49; twice it is called simply ὀθόνιον, I 24, I 32. The word is used for cotton cloth of various kinds, which was imported into a number of African ports in large quantities. It was the equivalent of the modern cotton cloth originally made in America and latterly in India, known all over East Africa as *amerikani*.
Cloth, barbaric unfulled ἱμάτια βαρβαρικὰ ἄγναφα I 6. ἱμάτια here seems to mean 'cloth' rather than 'clothing', made for the Barbaroi or Berbers. [ἄγναφα means 'unfulled', 'undressed'; it is a late form of ἄγναπτος, and occurs also in the New Testament (Matthew 9, 16; Mark 2, 21).]

Cloth, broad (Indian), called monakhē ὀθόνιον, ἡ μοναχὴ I 14, I 6.

Cloth, coarse Indian called sagmatogēnē ὀθόνιον ἰνδικὸν τὸ πλατύτερον ἡ λεγομένη μοναχὴ καὶ σαγματογῆναι I 6 (in 14 σαγματογήνη).

Cloth, Chinese ὀθόνιον σιρικὸν E 39, E 56, E 64.

Cloth, common Indian ὀθονίων ἰνδικῶν τῶν χυδαίωνE 41, E 48, E 51.

Cloth, cotton ὀθόνιον I 24, I 32.

Cloth, Indian cotton ὀθόνιον ἰνδικὸν I 31.

Cloth, mallow- μολόχινα, μολόχιναι, μολόχινον I 6, E 48, E 49. Clothing made of mallow-fibre, a species of *Hibiscus* belonging to the genus *Malvaceae*.

Cloth, purple πορφύρα I 24.

Clothing ἱματισμὸς I 24. General term for clothing as opposed to *othonion*, cloth not made up. The adjective σκοτουλᾶτος, from the Latin *scutulatus*, means 'with a check pattern'.

Clothing, Arabian ἱματισμὸς ἀραβικὸς I 28. Clothing made in their own style for Arabs, without sleeves.

Clothing, Arabian sleeved ἱματισμὸς ἀραβικὸς χειριδωτός I 24.

Clothing, barbaric, miscellaneous ἱμάτια βαρβαρικὰ σύμμικτα I 7. Clothing made for the Barbaroi or Berbers.

Clothing, local ἱματισμὸς ἐντόπιος E 36. Made in local styles.

Clothing, unlined ἱματισμὸς ἁπλοῦς. I 28, I, 39, I 49, I 56. The adjective means 'single', but it is to be translated 'unlined'. I have discussed this with a practical textile expert, M. Guy Catois of the Paris firm of Tissus Berguy, who agrees with me in this.

Damask. See Brocades.

Flax-cloth καρπάσου E 41.

Garments γαυνάκαι I 6. The word occurs twice in chapter 6, the first time with the adjective ἁπλοῖ, 'unlined'. The word spelt with initial κ, occurs, e.g. in Aristophanēs, *Wasps* 1137; Liddell and Scott define it as 'a thick Persian garment or rug'; perhaps it was a skin garment. McCrindle translates it 'frieze' (*Commerce*, p. 39).

Girdles, damask πολύμιται ζῶναι I 49.

Linen λέντια I 6. A word borrowed from Latin *lintea*, and used elsewhere mainly in the New Testament and ecclesiastical writers, and in Nonnos (late; in the form λύντεον).

Mantles, fringed δικρόσσια I 6.

Muslin σινδόνες, σινδόναι I 6, E 61, E 62. 'The land of Masalia, where much muslin is produced' (chap. 62). The word *muslin* is derived from the town of Mosul in Mesopotamia where muslin was formerly made, according to the *O.E.D.* But what about Masalia as the *origin* of the name?

Muslin, Argaritid σινδόνες αἱ ἀργαρίτιδες E 59. Muslin from Argalou.

Muslin, assorted σινδόνων παντοῖα E 51.

Muslin, Gangitic σινδόνες αἱ γαγγιτικαὶ E 63. Muslin from the region near the mouths of the Ganges.

Muslin, Indian σινδόνες ἰνδικαὶ E 48.

Robes, Arsinoïtic ἀρσινοϊτικαὶ στολαὶ I 6.

Sashes, striped ζῶναι σκιωταὶ I 24.

Silk σηρικὸν E 49.

Silk, raw ἔριον E 64.

Skins, Chinese σιρικὰ δέρματα E 39.

Tunics χιτῶνες I 7.

Yarn, Chinese [silk] νῆμα σιρικὸν E 39, E 49, E 64.

II. VEGETABLE PRODUCTS

A. Exports

Aloes ἀλόη 28. Aromatic wood.

Asuphe★ ἀσυφη cinnamon 12. Common cinnamon. *See* Kasia.

Bdella★ βδέλλα 37, 39, 48, 49. Fragrant gum which exudes from the plant bdellion, *balsamodendron mukul*; the *PME* spelling is erroneous. [βδέλλα really means 'leech'.] Pliny (*Nat. Hist.* XII, 9): 'The most celebrated bdellium comes from Bactriana. It is a black tree, of the size of an olive, with strong leaves, and fruit like wild fig. The gum is called *brochon* by some, and *malacham* and *maldacon* by others. It is black and lumpy.'

Cinnabar κιννάβαρι ἰνδικὸν 30. 'Dragon's blood', a dye obtained from the sap of a tree, vermilion or bright red in colour, and formerly got from the Dragon-tree, *dracaena draco*, *pterocarpus draco*, and *croton draco*; and also from the fruit of a palm, *calamus draco*. The *dracaena* grows also in the Canary Islands.

Cinnamon. *See* Kasia, Asuphe, Gizeir, Magla, Motō.

Coconut ναργίλιος/ναύπλιος 17. The MS has ναύπλιος; but since this word is virtually unknown (see note to chapter 17) Müller conjectured ναργίλιος, which makes sense, since it could be the Greek form of a word meaning coconut, e.g. Arabic *nārjīl*, Persian *nārgīl*. Coconut may have been exported in the form of copra, the dried kernel of the nut, an industry which still flourishes at Pangani and elsewhere on the East African coast, and produces a smell which nearly rivals that of drying shark-flesh.

Corn σῖτος 37, 41. Wheat; any cereal.

Dates φοῖνιξ, φοίνικα 36, 37. Dates, product of the palm called *phoenix dactylifera*.

Douaka* δουακα 8. Fine cinnamon. *See* Kasia.

Frankincense λίβανος 12, 27, 28, 32. Produced from trees of the *Boswellia* species, two of which grow in Somaliland: *Boswellia Frereana*, called *yehar* in Somali, and *B. Carteri*; *yehar* yields the better quality incense. The latter is called *loban maidi*, the inferior, *loban dakar*, which the Indian traders called *isas* (R. E. Drake-Brockman, *British Somaliland*, London, 1912, pp. 256–7).

Frankincense from beyond the straits λίβανος ὁ περατικὸς 8, 10, 11. The second word appears to mean here 'from beyond the straits', i.e. the Horn of Africa, which is beyond the straits of Bab al-Mandab from Egypt.

Frankincense, Sakhalitic λ. σαχαλιτίκος 32. From Southern Arabia.

Ghi βούτυρον 41. Also written ghee; butter clarified by boiling.

Gizeir* γιζειρ 12 [cinnamon] Fine cinnamon. *See* Kasia.

Gum, fragrant εὐωδία 10. From trees *Balanites* sp. and *Commiphora* sp.

Gum, fragrant μοκροτου 9. 10. θυμίαμα τὸ λεγόμενον μοκροτου, 'fragrant gum called m.'. This was used as incense, and may have been derived from a species of *Boswellia* called *mohor* in Somali.

Indikon melan [ἰνδικὸν μέλαν] 39. *See* note to chapter 39.

Kankamon Κάγκαμον 8. Described by Dioskoridēs (*Materia Medica* I. 63) as the sap of an Arabian tree (*Amyris kataf*). Dalecamp in a note to Pliny, *Nat. Hist.* XII, 20 (Frankfort, 1608) says, I know not on what authority, that 'it is called *anime* in Spanish'; for this word, Cassell's *Spanish Dict.* gives 'locust-tree; its resin'.

Kasia κασία 8, 10, 12, 13. This is the general term for cinnamon in the *PME* instead of κιννάμωμον, *Laurus cinnamomum*, of which there were three grades: 1st. gizeir and duaka; 2nd. motō and magla; 3rd. asuphē. Drake-Brockman (pp. 5–9) says that cinnamon is not found in Somaliland. If he is right, it could be that cinnamon in Somaliland was wiped out by some disease, just as coffee in Ceylon was wiped out by a disease called *hemileia vastatrix*. This spread to East Africa, but was controlled by spraying, a thing unknown in ancient times. For further evidence, *see below*, p. 169. Pliny says that it was exported from the Troglodyte country in boats to Okēlis in Arabia, and the *PME* says that great quantities were exported from Malaō, Moundou, Mosullon, and Opōnē. (But cf. also the evidence of Strabō, *see below*, p. 169.)

Kostos κόστος 39, 48. A root used as a spice, like pepper.

Lukion λυκιον 39, 49. Liddell and Scott: 'A Lycian kind of thorn, elsewhere πυξάκανθα [box-thorn], Dioscoridēs I, 132'. Also a medicinal liquor drawn from it.

Magla★ μαγλα [cinnamon] 12. *See* Kasia.

Makeir μάκειρ 8. A plant with a large root said by Galen to come from India (*De Fac. Simp. Med.* VII). Pliny also says that it comes from India, and that the red cortex of the root was made into a decoction with honey as a remedy for dysentery (*Nat. Hist.* XII, 16). However, it was exported from Malaō to Arabia.

Malabathron μαλάβαθρον 56, 63, 65. An aromatic leaf, the dried leaf of some species of cinnamon, called *tamāla-pattra* in Sanskrit, whence the hellenized form by which it is commonly known, and possibly also the word πέτροι used in chapter 65. It was at one time confused with *folium indicum*, 'Indian leaf' (Dioskoridēs *Mat. Med.* I, 11). That it was also

used to make unguents or perfumes is clear from Horace:
coronatus nitentes
malabathro Syrio capillos   (*Od.* ii, 7, 7)
and from Pliny, who says 'Syria produces malabathrum, a
tree with convoluted leaves from which oil is extracted for
ointment. The best, however, comes from India' (*Nat. Hist.*
xii, 26). (But it is not betel leaf (*see: Hobson-Jobson*, 543).)
Mokrotou. *See* Gum.
Motō★ μοτώ 12, 13. Second grade cinnamon. *See* Kasia.
Myrrh σμύρνα 7, 8, 10, 24. A gum resin produced by the tree
balsamodendron myrrha. This grows in Somaliland where it is
called *malmal*; the tree is *didin*. There are two main varieties:
guban malmal, from a bush not more than four or five feet
high which grows in the hot, dry maritime plain; and *ogo
malmal*, which grows in the interior. Myrrh was used as an
ointment under the name of *staktē* (q.v.) and it was one of
the ingredients of the 'royal ointment' of the Parthian kings
which contained also nard, cinnamon, storax, honey, wine,
and ladanum, the last being a gum-resin from plants of the
genus *Cistus*.

Pepper πέπερι, πίπερι 49, 56. Pepper. There are three kinds of
pepper: long pepper (as in chapter 49), black pepper, and
white pepper. The first comes from the plants *piper officinarum*
and *piper longum*, the others from *piper nigrum*. Long pepper
is the spike of the fruit picked unripe, and white is black
pepper with its dark covering removed, making it less
'peppery'. Pliny recognised *piper longum*, *piper candidum*, and
piper nigrum; he says that long pepper was adulterated with
mustard (*Nat. Hist.* xii, 14).

Rice ὄρυζα 37, 41. Rice.

Sesame oil ἔλαιον σησάμινον 41. Oil produced from the seeds

of sesame or simsim, originally grown in India, the plant *sesamum indicum*.

Spices ἄρωμα, ἀρώματα 7, 10, 12, 13. General term for sweet-smelling spices.

Spikenard νάρδος 39, 48, 49, 56, 63. Derived from the rhizoma of *nardostachys jatamansi*, and used in making ointment as an aromatic.

Staktē στακτή 24. The oil that comes from fresh myrrh. It was of two kinds: Abeiraian and Minaian, the latter from the land of the Minaioi north of the Sabaïtai.

Wine οἶνος 37, 38.

B. Imports

Corn πυρός 28. Wheat. It is not clear whether any difference is intended by the use of σῖτος in some places, and πυρός once.

Corn σῖτος 7, 14, 17, 24, 31, 32, 56. Wheat; any grain.

Ebony, sticks of φαλάγγων ἐβενίνων 36.

Frankincense λίβανος 36, 39.

Ghi βούτυρον 14. Butter boiled and clarified.

Kuperos* κύπερος 24. An aromatic plant of the order Cyperaceae, said by Hērodotos (*Hist.*, IV. 71) to have been used by the Scythians for embalming their kings. It was also used in medicine (Pliny, *Nat. Hist.* XXI, 18).

Lac λάκκος χρωμάτινος 6. A red incrustation formed on certain trees by an insect, *coccus lacca*, and used as a dye.

Oil ἔλαιον 6, 32. Perhaps olive oil.

Olives, unripe χυλὸς ὄμφακος 7. This came from Diospolis, a town in Lower Egypt.

Perfume μύρον 24, 49.

Rice ὄρυζα 14, 31.

Saffron κρόκος 24. Used as a dye.

Sakkhari σάκχαρι 14. Sugar; though apparently the sugar was not extracted as it is nowadays. The *PME* says that the cane was from India, though Pliny (*Nat. Hist.* XII, 8) says that it was also produced in Arabia, but that the Indian was preferred.

Sesame oil ἔλαιον σησάμινον 14.

Shisham beams φαλάγγων σησαμίνων 36. A hard wood, *dalbergia sissoo*, used for furniture, boat-building, etc.

Storax στύραξ 28, 39, 49. Storax, a fragrant gum-resin grown in Somaliland and Arabia.

Wine οἶνος 6, 7, 17, 24, 28, 39, 49, 56.

III. IVORY, HORN, AND SHELL

Exports

Ivory ἐλέφας 3, 6, 7, 10, 16, 17, 49, 56, 62.

Rhinoceros ῥινόκερως 6, 17. Rhinoceros horn was much esteemed as an aphrodisiac.

Tortoiseshell, Tortoise χελώνη, χελωνάρια 3, 4, 6, 7, 10, 13, 16, 17, 30, 31, 33, 56, 61, 63.

Tortoise, land χ·χερσαίαν 3, 30.

Tortoise, mountain χ·ὀρεινὴν 15, 30.

Tortoise shell, true χ·ἀληθινὴν 3, 30.

Tortoise, white χ·λευκὴν 30.

IV. HARDWARE

Imports

Adzes σκέπαρνα 6.

Awls ὀπήτια 17.

Axes πελύκια 6, 17.

Copper χαλκὸς 28, 36, 49, 56.

Copper, objects made of χαλκουργήματα 24.

Coral κοράλλιον 28, 39, 49, 56.

Glass, crude ὕελος ἀργὴ 49, 56.

Glassware λιθίας ὑαλῆς 6, 7, 17; ὑαλᾶ σκεύη 39.

Gold χρυσὸς 36.

Gold, objects of χρυσουργήματα 6, 24.

Iron, Indian σίδηρος 6, 8, 10.

Lead μόλυβος, μόλιβος 49, 56.

Meliephtha khalka* μελιέφθα χαλκὰ 6, 8. Literally 'copper cooked in honey', and possibly meaning sheets of ductile or soft copper.

Murrhine* μουρρίνης, μορρίνης 48. In chap. 6, 'imitation m.'. A material of uncertain nature. Pliny says (*Nat. Hist.* xxxIII, 2) 'murrhine and crystalline material are dug from the same earth; their value is due to their fragility'. Murrhine vases came from Barugaza, and an imitation was made at Diospolis in Egypt. The true murrhine was possibly a red and white agate; 'all vases of Agate were afterwards included under the name; all that was required being that the material should be clouded with various colours, and not present the regular stratification of the Onyx. In fact, they were exactly the same as the Agate vases still imported from India, where the manufacture seems to be even yet going on, though in a languishing manner' (C. W. King, *The Natural History, ancient and modern, of Precious Stones and Gems* (London, 1865), p. 242).

Ōrokhalkos★ ὠρόχαλκος 6. Other Greek writers use the form ὀρείχαλκος oreikhalkos. This was a copper alloy, though its composition seems to have varied at different times. A sample from Halki near Constantinople (one of the islands called Dēmonnēsoi by the Greeks, from which the Pseudo-Aristotelian tract known as 'De Mirabilibus Auscultationibus', sect. 58, says oreikhalkos came) proved to be a copper alloy; and it appears that the early alloy was formed of copper and silver, and that later zinc was substituted for silver (O. Davies, 'ὀρειχαλκος,' *Man*, XXIX (1929), 36–7).

Sailyards κεράτων 36. Timber for carrying the sail.
Sandal wood ξύλον σαντάλινον 46. A fragrant wood, *Santalum* sp., of which *Santalum album* comes from the Malabar coast.
Silver, objects of ἀργυρώματα 6, 24, 28, 39, 49; σκεύη ἀργυρᾶ 10.
Spears λόγχη 17.
Steel, Indian στόμωμα 6.
Swords μάχαιραι 6; μαχαίρια 17.

Timber baulks δοκῶν 36.
Tin κασσίτερος 7, 28, 49, 56.

V. PRECIOUS STONES

E= Export; I= Import

Diamonds ἀδάμας E 56.

Khrusolithos χρυσόλιθος I 39, 56. Possibly topaz.

Lapislazuli σάπφειρος E 39.

Pearls μαργαρίτης E 56.

Pearls πινικὸν E 35, 36, 59, 61, 63. 'Whitish silk spun by the πίννα and woven' (Liddell and Scott, *Greek-English Lexicon*), the *pinna* being a kind of mussel. But the word is used in the *PME* for pearls; chap. 35 πινικίου κόγχου, 36 πινικὸν. Precious stones λιθία διαφανὴς E 56, 61; λιθία I 10. Precious stones in general.

Sapphire ὑάκινθος E 56.

Turquoise καλλεανὸς λίθος E 39. [The *PME* form of καλλάϊνος.]

VI. MISCELLANEOUS

E = Export; I = Import

Antimony στῖμι I 49, 56. Latin *stibium*, Arabic *kuḥl*. Powdered antimony used by women for staining their eyelids.

Boats, sewn ῥαπτὰ πλοιάρια τὰ λεγόμενα μαδαράτε E 36.

Clover, sweet μελίλωτον I 49. 'Honey-lotus', a sweet clover, formerly used in parts of Europe for making poultices.
Cups, drinking πότηρια I 6, I 8.

Girls παρθένοι I 49.

Horses ἵπποι I 24, I 28, I 39.

Madarate* μαδαράτε. *See* Boats, sewn. Arabic *muddara'at*, 'fastened with palm-fibres' (Eduard Glaser, *Skizze der Geschichte und Geographie Arabiens* (Berlin, 1890), p. 190; Frisk, *Le Périple*, p. 114).

Marble λύγδος E 24. McCrindle translates it 'alabaster' (*Commerce*, p. 82).

Melilōtos. *See* Clover.

Money χρῆμα I 24, I 28, I 39.

Money δηνάριον I 6, I 49.

Money, gold and silver δηνάριον χρυσοῦν καὶ ἀργυροῦν I 8.

Musicians μουσικὰ I 49. Translated 'musicians' on the strength of Strabō's μουσικὰ παιδισκάρια (*Geog.*, I, 3, 4), rather than musical instruments'.

Pack-mules ἡμίονοι νωτηγοὶ I 24.

Slaves σώματα E 8, E 36.
Slaves, female σώματα θηλυκὰ I 31.
Slaves δουλικὰ E 13.
Statues ἀνδριάντες I 28.

It will be noticed that there are more references to the export from the coasts of the Erythraean Sea of spices, incense, fragrant gums, ivory, and tortoiseshell, than to any other type of export. These may be broken down roughly thus:

spices in general: Africa, 4 references
cinnamon: Africa, 13
fragrant gums in general: Africa, 7
incense: from Africa, 4, from Arabia, 5

Total number of references: 33

ivory: from Africa, 5; from India, 3
tortoiseshell: from Africa,[1] 6; from Arabia, 1; from Socotra, 1; from India and Ceylon, 2

Total number of references: 18

Very little is said about the final destination of these products; no doubt most of them went to Egypt and Rome. Certainly some spices were sent across to Arabia from the Somali coast, but these were probably absorbed in the Arabian exports. It is

[1] Although the *PME* says that tortoises are found in Menouthias, it does not say that the shell was exported from that island.

stated in chapter 13 that most of the slaves from Opōnē were sent to Egypt. There was a certain amount of local exchange, like incense from Kanē to Omana (chapter 36); from Omana sewn boats were sent to (southern) Arabia, and pearls to Barugaza and Arabia, as well as other things including slaves (chapter 36). See also chapters 49, 51.

It is somewhat curious that no mention is made in the *PME* of beads as articles of trade. None of the objects listed can be interpreted as 'beads', unless they were included in the term λιθίας ὑαλῆς 'glassware' (chapters 6, 7, 17). I mention this because beads, especially glass beads, have been imported to East Africa for centuries, and glass beads made at Brahmagiri in S. India were in use from as early as the 2nd century B.C. and may have been exported to Africa (or even copied there). It is not that there is a lack of beads in Eastern Africa; what is strange is that the *PME* has nothing to say about them.

The Ethnology and History of the Area Covered by the *Periplus*

1(a). *The African Coast*

No identifiable tribal names are given in the *PME*, and very few clues to what sort of people the inhabitants were; different tribal groups are designated in a manner which does no more than indicate some outstanding characteristic, in Agatharkhidēs, Strabō, and the *PME*, and it is only in the last that any indication is given of their position. Between Berenikē and Ptolemaïs lived the Ikhthuophagoi or Fish-eaters, on the coast; behind them inland were the Barbaroi (Berbers), the Agriophagoi or Wild animal-eaters, and the Moskhophagoi or Plant-eaters; these were under the rule of 'chiefs', κατὰ τυραννίδα. After the Moskhophagoi was Ptolemaïs of the Huntings, and the people along this stretch of the coast were the Barbaroi, who were the ancestors of the Hamitic Saho, a pastoral people; and south of Adouli, the eastern side of Ethiopia, mainly stark desert, is the land of the 'Afar or Danakil, another Hamitic people, who extend southwards as far as Djibouti. Eastward, from here to Cape Gardafui, in the 'Horn of Africa', was what the *PME* calls 'the other Barbaria', the land of the Somali, also Hamites, whose ancestors were probably here, under a different name, in the 1st century and even earlier. The whole of this region was under tribal chiefs (*see:* chapter 14, p. 29 above).

Both Agatharkhidēs and Strabō end their catalogues of 'tribes' with the Trōglodutai (Trōglodytes), who are mentioned as if they were a distinct people; but neither say where they

143

lived, except that it is clear that they inhabited north-east Africa, for the west coast of the Red Sea from Adouli to Gardafui was called Trōglodutikē. It is somewhat strange that this name does not occur in the *PME*, though it is found in Ptolemy, who says that 'the coastlands [of Africa] along the Arabian and Aualitic or Abalitic gulfs are generally called Trōglodutikē as far as Mount Elephas' (*Geog.*, IV. 7, 27). The accounts of these people given by Agatharkhidēs and Strabō are clearly no invention, since they mention certain customs which exist at the present day among some of the pastoral peoples of the interior of Eastern Africa. Strabō, whose description seems to have been borrowed from Agatharkhidēs, thus describes them:

> The Trōglodytes lead a pastoral life. They have many despotic chiefs; their women and children are common property, except those of the chief; and those who lie with a chief's wife are fined a sheep. The women carefully paint their eyebrows with antimony, and they wear shells hung round their necks as amulets against the evil eye. The men fight over the grazing grounds, first with fists, then with stones, and then wounds are inflicted with arrows and swords; but when their quarrels become really dangerous the women intervene, and by soothing the fighters restore peace. They live on meat and bone broken up together, wrapped in skin and then cooked. They call the cooks 'Unclean'. They drink blood mixed with milk. The ordinary people drink water in which the plant paliurus[1] has been soaked; the chiefs drink honey and water, the honey being pressed from some kind of flower. They have a winter, when the monsoon blows and rain falls; the rest of the year is summer. They go naked or clad in skins, and carry clubs. They not only mutilate their bodies, but some are circumcised like the Egyptians. . . . Some of the Trōglodytes bury their dead, binding the neck to the feet with cords of paliurus fibre; then they cover the body with stones, laughing and joking till the face is hidden; then they put a goat's horn on top of the cairn and depart. They travel by night and fasten bells to the necks

[1] *Rhamnus paliurus* L.

144

of the male stock so that the noise may scare wild beasts. (xvi. 4, 17.)[1]

Four remarkable things may be noted in this passage:

(1) Drinking blood mixed with milk, a practice of the Nandi and Masai of Kenya, the Karamojong of Uganda, the Iraqw group of Tanzania, and the Bari, Didinga, and the Murle of the southern Sudan.

(2) Circumcision, a practice ultimately due to Hamitic influence, and not practised by the Nilotic peoples, but by the Nandi and the Masai.

(3) The erection of mounds of stone over the body is found in Ethiopia among the Galla, and in the southern Sudan among the Bongo, Moro, and Zande, sometimes with an upright stone or wooden post planted in the mound, and sometimes with a Y-shaped post representing horns at the side. Further south the custom occurs among the Masai, and stone cairns of unknown date are found in many places in the highlands of Kenya.

(4) More remarkable still is the custom of laughing at a funeral. The Nandi used to bury a very old person with no show of sorrow and with laughter and talking, for, they said, 'He has now arrived where he expected to arrive a long while ago.'[2]

The Greeks thought that the name Trōglodutai meant 'cave-dwellers', as if it were derived from the Greek words τρώγλη (trōglē), 'hole or cave', and δύται (dutai), 'divers or creepers', i.e. 'people who crept into holes'. From this comes the English 'troglodyte'. (The word was applied to the wren by Linnaeus, who called it, poor bird, *Troglodytes troglodytes troglodytes*.) There is evidence, however, to show that the Greek word is due to a misconception. Pliny cites Juba[3] as writing the word

---

[1] Agatharkhidēs' account (from Bk. V, chap. 61) will be found on pp. 189–90 below.

[2] A. C. Hollis, *The Nandi* (Oxford, 1909), p. 72; cf. also Huntingford, *The Nandi of Kenya* (London, 1953), p. 148.

[3] King of Mauritania, d. A.D. 19, a learned man who wrote on Africa and Arabia, though all his works are now lost except in quotations.

without L, and a 10th century MS of 'Extracts from Strabo's Geography'[1] says that in Book XVI, iv. 55 Strabō wrote Trōgodutai without the L, although all the existing texts have the L. Moreover, in Greek inscriptions referring to the Red Sea, the word is written without L.[2] It is quite understandable that an L should have crept in, making a word that had a meaning for the Greeks. What it really means is anyone's guess. Stripped of the Greek termination *dutēs* it yields a root TRG suggestive of the name Targi, plural Tuareg, the veiled people of the Sahara, though its etymology is unknown. It has been suggested that this word is akin to the Arabic *tawāriq*, sing. *tāriqa*, 'tribe'.

Although the *PME* does not mention the name Trōgodutai, it does refer to peoples near Berenikē, and Adouli, and along the coast as far as the Spice Mart near Gardafui as Barbaroi, and calls the country Barbaria, which we should translate 'Berbers' rather than 'Barbarians'.[3] These Berbers would seem to be the same as the Trōgodutai, that is, people of Hamitic stock whose descendants still inhabit north-east Africa. The author of the *PME* clearly had some knowledge and experience of these Berbers and their habits. Those living round Aualitēs, for instance, are described as 'more disorderly' (ἀτακτότεροι), while those in the next district, Malaō, were 'more peaceful' (εἰρηνικώτεροι), and those in the Moundou area 'more stubborn' (σκληρότεροι). The natives of the Rhapta region, on the other hand, who are given no ethnic name, are described as having large bodies and piratical habits. The existence of pirates in the Indian Ocean has been doubted, for example by Dr Freeman-Grenville, who says that the phrase does not occur in Müller's text, and asks, if there were pirates, on whom did they prey?[4] But sea-robbers (Swahili *haramia*) have existed everywhere at all times since there have been ships, and there is

---

[1] Heidelberg 398, printed in Müller, GGM. II, 629.

[2] Dittenberger, O.G.I.S. I, nos. 70, 71, quoted on p. 172.

[3] See note 1 to chapter 2.

[4] *Medieval history of the coast of Tanganyika* (London, 1962), p. 26, *n.* 1. On pirates, see note 1 to chapter 16.

in fact evidence for them from both Pliny in ancient, and de Monfreid in modern times. The former writes of Arabs called Ascitae who went to sea on inflated skins and practised piracy (*piraticam exercent*), using poisoned arrows;[1] and de Monfreid came across pirates in the Gulf of Aden.

But who these people of Rhapta were, we do not know. It is certain that they did not speak a Bantu language, since the 1st century A.D. is too early for Bantu-speakers to have reached the East African coast, and the theory that the Bantu originated in the east coast area of Africa is without foundation.[2] Possibly survivors of the 1st century inhabitants may be found in the Lake Eyasi district, some 300 miles inland from Rhapta, where now live a few tribes of unknown ethnic affinities—the Iraqw, Gorowa, Alawa, and Burungi. There are also people of Hottentot type, known as Sandawe, in the same area, who speak a click-language. The Hadza Bushmen in the same area also may be ruled out, since they have not 'large bodies', their average stature being 5 ft. 3 ins. (men) and 4 ft. 11 ins. (women) (see Huntingford, *The Southern Nilo-Hamites*, p. 132).

As to the organisation of these peoples, both Agatharkhidēs and Strabō describe the Trōglodytes as being under despotic chiefs; the *PME* says that the Barbaroi were under chiefs, and adds that from the end of Zōskalēs' territory there were no paramount rulers, but that each 'place' (*topos*) and market (as in the Rhapta district) was under its own chief. Only in the case of the Red Sea section is there anything more definite—the mention of Zōskalēs in chapter 5, of whom it is said 'Zōskalēs rules these parts from the Moskhophagoi to the other Barbaria'. It is certain that Zōskalēs was not king of Aksum (on the meaning of the Greek word translated 'rules' see note 2 to chapter 5), and it is equally certain that his authority did not

---

[1] *Nat. Hist.* VI, 35.

[2] This is not the place to discuss the origin of the Bantu, but anyone who is interested is referred to the present writer's chapter in Oliver and Mathew, *History of East Africa*, pp. 80–93.

stretch as far as the text suggests, if 'the other Barbaria' is, as it would appear, the coast south of Bab al mandab. Zōskalēs was in fact probably the forerunner of the *bāḥrnagāsh*, 'sea-king', who in later times ruled the northern coast province of Ethiopia under the king of Ethiopia. The statement that each place was under its own chief probably means no more than that the local chief claimed dues from the traders. As ruler of Adoulis, Zōskalēs would have paid the customs dues, or part of them, as his tribute to the king of Aksum; Kosmas Indikopleustēs in the 6th century A.D. found a customs-house (τελώνιον, telōnion) there, of which he drew a picture.

It may be added that even at this early period, part at least of the East African coast was under some kind of foreign domination, as we can see from chapters 15 and 16 of the *PME*. In chapter 15 the coast between the Puralaōn Islands and the island of Menouthias is called the Ausineitic coast. This, it is true, depends upon Müller's emendation of the meaningless παρ' αὐτὴν τὴν δύσιν ειτενηδιωνμενουθεσιας ἀπαντᾷ νῆσος of the MS to παρ' αὐτὴν τὴν αὐσινείτην ἠιόνα μενουθ[εσ]ιὰς 'along the Ausineitic coast (ἠιόνα) the island of Menouthias is encountered'. This emendation is likely to be correct, and thus implies that the small state of Ausan east of Mouza had exercised some influence on this section of the coast. Ausan, which was flourishing as early as the 7th century B.C., later became part of the Homērite or Himyaritic kingdom.

In chapter 16 we are told that the Rhapta district is ruled by the Mopharitic chief (τύραννος), 'according to an ancient agreement by which it comes under the kingdom which has become first in Arabia'. This kingdom appears to have been that of Kholaibos, whose capital Sauē is said in chapter 22 to be in Mapharitis (Maʿafir). Rhapta was therefore tributary to Kholaibos through the chief of Mouza, which was a manufacturing place, as we see from chapter 17.[1] Being a tributary

[1] Chapter 31 however says that Azania was under Kharibael and the Mapharitic chief. This must be a mistake for Kholaibos.

town, Rhapta must have been quite an important place, and Ptolemy calls it a metropolis, a term which he does not apply to any other place on the East African coast. (In the *PME* the term metropolis is applied only to Meroē, Aksum, Saphar, Saubatha, and Minnagar, none of which is likely to have been visited by traders like the author of the *PME*.)

1(b). *On Zōskalēs and the kingdom of Aksum*

The only kingdom in the whole East African area was that of Aksum, which later developed into the kingdom of Ethiopia. Aksum is about 140 miles inland from Adouli and at an altitude of more than 6000 ft. The 'half-way house' between the two places was Koloē (Qohayto), the collecting place for the ivory from the Sudan (Kuēneion). It is noteworthy that the only exports from the Aksumite area mentioned in the *PME* are tortoiseshell, ivory, and rhinoceros horn, though many products of civilisation—glass, clothing, metals, and gold and silver objects (the latter made for the king in 'the shapes of the country') were imported to Aksum. In the 4th century A.D. the kingdom of Aksum appears, from epigraphic evidence, to have consisted of the city itself and the surrounding country, and three sub-kingdoms: Gabaz (which included Adouli), Aguēzāt or Gazē immediately east of Aksum, and Saranē next to Aguēzāt. In the first century it was probably much the same. The man named Zōskalēs who 'ruled these parts' was certainly not king of Aksum, but rather the tributary king (*negus* in Ethiopic) of Gabaz, and the forerunner of the *Bāḥrnagāsh* ('Sea king'), the governor of the coast province of later times. Zōskalēs has often been identified with one Haqlē or ZaHaqlē of Conti Rossini's king-list C,[1] though this name is found only in this list. But these lists are most untrustworthy, and there is nothing in the *PME* to suggest that Zōskalēs was king of

---

[1] B.L. MSS Orient. 817, 821.

Aksum. In the 6th century Kosmas Indikopleustēs names Asbās as the ruler (ἄρχων, arkhōn) of Adouli.[1]

2. Arabia

'Native tribes' mentioned in the *PME* as inhabiting the coast of Arabia are the Ikhthuophagoi south of Leukē Kōmē, the 'scoundrelly' Kanraïtai, and, thence to Mouza, more civilized 'nomadic' people who owned camels. Along the south coast, beyond Aden, are other Ikhthuophagoi and Nomads. All these were 'Arabs' of one kind or another. The northern, south-western, and southern parts of Arabia, however, were divided into states or kingdoms, of which a few only seem to have been known to the author of the *PME*. The most northerly kingdom was that of the Nabataioi, the port of which in the south was Leukē Kōmē, about 450 miles from Petra the capital of 'Malikhas', king of the Nabataioi, with which it was connected by road. The Nabataioi, though a pastoral people with camels and sheep, were traders in the sense that the *arōmata* from southern Arabia which were unloaded at Leukē Kōmē and sent overland to Petra, were distributed by them to the Mediterranean area through the town of Rhinokoloura (El-'Arish, about 120 miles from Petra) even as late as the time of the *PME*, though by then the trade was beginning to be diverted to Egypt.

The remaining kingdoms mentioned by the *PME* were far down in the south of the peninsula, where there was enough fertile and productive land for kingdoms to flourish and send their products to various ports on the coast. The first to be named is Mapharitis, the ruler of which, Kholaibos (who is called τύραννος), had his capital at Sauē three days inland from the roadstead and mart of Mouza. This state had control over part of the East African coast.[2]

[1] Huntingford, 'Three notes on early Ethiopian geography', *Folia Orientalia*, xv (1974), pp. 198–9.
[2] Chapter 16; *see above*, p. 30.

Nine days' journey from Sauē was Saphar the capital of Kharibaēl king (βασιλεὺς) of the Homēritai (Himyarites) and Sabaïtai or Sabaeans. These tribes are merely given a mention, though Kharibaēl ruled not only over them but also over the old kingdom of Ausan, which formed part of the area known as Qataban, the people of which were the Katabanoi or Gebanitae whose chief town was Thomna[1] or Tamna.[2] Kharibaēl's kingdom included Eudaimōn Arabia (Aden).

Next to this kingdom, on the east, was that of Eleazos (Ili-azz) king the Khatramōtitai, the people of the Hadramaut, part of whose country the *PME* calls Libanōtophoros. The capital was at Saubatha, and the king's jurisdiction or rights to tribute extended from Kanē to Ras Fartak, and included the island of Dioskouridou (Socotra) which lies off the Horn of Africa. The kingdom of Eleazos seems to have been especially productive of incense, and Pliny has something to say about it:

The capital of the kingdom of the Atramitae is Sabota, on a high hill, from which the incense-producing country, called Sapa [var. Sariba] is distant eight stages (*mansiones*). It faces east, and on all sides is unapproachable on account of rocks, and on the right because of inaccessible cliffs. The woods are 20 *skhoinoi* (120 miles) in breadth, and half that in width. . . . The trees are indigenous and grow on the slopes of high hills running down to the plain. The soil is said to be clayey, with little water, what there is being full of nitre. . . . The incense when collected is carried on camels to Sabota, where one gate is open for its reception. To diverge from the route is a capital offence. There the priests take for their god, whom they call Sabin, a tax of a tenth on the volume, not on the weight. Before this is taken it may not be sold; and thus public expenses are paid. . . . It may be taken out only through the land of the Gebanitae, whose king also taxes it; his capital is Thomna.[3]

[1] *Nat. Hist.* VI, 32.   [2] Strabō, *Geog.*, XVI, 4, 2.
[3] *Nat. Hist.* XII, 14.

In past times the people of the Hadramaut had a reputation for hardness and determination. Burton quotes a proverb about them: 'if you meet a viper and a Hazrami, spare the viper', and he tells a story about a Hazrami who, 'flying from his fellow-countrymen, reached a town upon the confines of China. He was about to take refuge in a mosque, but entering, he stumbled over the threshold. "Ya Amud el Din"—"O Pillar of the Faith" exclaimed a voice from the darkness, calling upon the patron saint of Hazramaut to save a Moslem from falling. "May the Pillar of the Faith break thy head," exclaimed the unpatriotic traveller, at once rising to resume his vain peregrinations.'[1]

The country of Eleazos came to an end somewhere to the east of Suagros (Ras Fartak); the last civilized harbour was Moskha (Salala) which received the incense from the Sakhalitic region of Libanōtophoros. After this the coast was, at least nominally, under the domination of what the *PME* calls Persis (τῆς Περσίδος), the country which lay on the north side of the Persian Gulf opposite Arabia, though the part of Arabia between Suagros and the Persian Gulf was called Omana, a name which survives to this day. The personal knowledge of the author may have extended as far as the mountains which he calls Asabōn, the modern Cape Musandam, 500 miles from the inner end of the Persian Gulf, where he mentions the established mart called Apologou near Pasinou Kharax, though he says no more about it, unless the statement in chapter 36, that ships come to 'both these Persian marts' means to Omana and Apologou, a mart called Omana being near Asabōn, and described as a mart of Persis, though in Arabia. Though perhaps only nominally under Persia, in the time of Darius the Great Omana was included in the 8th satrapy of his empire.

Here the Arabian section of the itinerary ends, and it crosses over the Persian Gulf into Asia.

[1] *First Footsteps in East Africa* (London, 1856), p. 32.

3. *The Coast of India*

The first part of Asia named is the Bay of the Gedrōsians, which may be the great bay which curves round the Musandam peninsula and on the north shore of which is the modern Bandar 'Abbas. Then came a great river with an entry for ships and the mart of Hōraia, inland from which, seven days from the sea, was a kingdom called Rhambakia. The river may have been the Purali or the Habb, though the site of the mart is unknown. In this area lived the Ōreitai (who may be connected with Hōraia), who were defeated with great loss in a battle with Leonnatos, one of Alexander the Great's officers, in 325 B.C.

After this comes India properly so called, beginning with the coast parts of Skuthia (Scythia) and the river Sinthos (Indus). Skuthia was the name by which the author of the *PME* knew the lower Indus Valley; it was in fact a normal Greek term for an Indo-Scythian (Indo-Parthian, as Smith calls it) or Śaka kingdom founded originally in the north-west of the sub-continent by Maues or Mauas who became ruler of the western Panjab about 98–5 B.C., which lasted till the beginning of the Christian era. To its rulers it was known as Śakastan. The statement in the *PME* (chap. 38) that the country was ruled by Parthians who were 'continually expelling each other' suggests that there were 'petty Parthian principalities', as Smith calls them, among whom may have been such men as Sasan, Sapedanes, and Satavastra, said to be named on coins found in a hoard at Tando Muhammad Khan in Sind.[1]

Next to Skuthia (*PME* 41) was the Bay of Barugaza, the mainland of the country of Ariakē, and the beginning of the kingdom of Manbanos. Continuous with Skuthia was the inland region called Abēria, and the part of the coast called Surastrēnē, which included what is now Gujarat, Saurashtra, and

---

[1] Personal communication to the editor from Dr Bivar; *see also* MacDowall and Wilson, *Num. Chron.* 7 ser. X (1970) 231.

Kathiawar. The two kings whose 'ancient coins stamped with Greek letters' were still current in Barugaza (*PME* 41) are named as Apollodotos and Menander. Both are much earlier than the time of the *PME*. Apollodotos was the predecessor but one of Menander; they were rulers of the Indo-Greek (or as Bivar prefers, Indo-Bactrian) kingdom the capital of which was Charsadda (Poklaïs). Menander invaded the Indus delta and the Kathiawar region, though his occupation was short-lived. Manbanos was the Kṣaharāta ruler Nahapāna who occurs *c.* A.D. 115–25 and was defeated by the Andhra king Saraganēs (Gautamīputra Śrī Śātakarṇī) about 125. Nahapāna's capital was possibly Nāsik, or even Barugaza. To the NE of Nāsik on the other side of the Narbada river was the ancient city of Ujjain, the Ozēnē of the *PME*, which says it was formerly a seat of government, that is, of the Chastana line, *c.* 100–20, which was eventually driven out by Nahapāna.[1] There was also, far to the north, the capital of Menander already mentioned, which the *PME* calls Proklaïs (a miswriting for Poklaïs), another collecting centre for northern trade goods, including spices which were sent to Ozēnē. Charsadda, NNE of Peshawar, has been excavated by Sir Mortimer Wheeler. In this region, too, were the Gandaraoi, the people of Gandhara, whose country may have included the ancient kingdom of Taxila which was excavated by Sir John Marshall. In Gandhara there was a famous school of art, sometimes called 'Graeco-Buddhist' 'because the forms of art were applied to Buddhist subjects with considerable artistic success. Images of Buddha appear in the likeness of Apollo, the Yaksha Kuvera is posed in the fashion of the Phidian Zeus, and so on.'[2] But although there are undoubted Classical influences in it, Roman as well as Greek, 'it is nowadays unfashionable to emphasize the Greek element at the expense of the others (Iranian, Buddhist, Hindu, etc.) as Vincent Smith was inclined to do' (Bivar, personal com-

[1] MacDowall, 'Early western satraps', *Num. Chron.*, 7 ser. IV (1964) 278.
[2] Smith, *Early History*, 136.

munication, 29 March 1975). This country had been part of the 10th satrapy of the empire of Darius and Xerxes and included Arakhōsia (Kandahar).[1]

Central India was known to our author as Dakhinabadēs, the Deccan or 'southern region'. In it were the marts of Paithana and Tagara SE of Barugaza on and near the Godavari river. This region included the coast marts of Akabarou, Souppara, and Kalliena, which were under kings of the Āndhra dynasty. The *PME* mentions one of these by the name of Saraganēs, the Gautamīputra Śri Śātakarṇī who defeated Manbanos (Nahapāna) about 125. This Śātakarṇī survived till about 130. Sandanēs seems to be a military title rather than a personal name, and occurs on an Indo-Sassanian coin in the form *ΣΑΝΔΑΝΟ*, and the person so denominated in the *PME* was probably an Indo-Scythian (Śaka) official.[2] Smith adds that the Śaka satraps certainly endeavoured to divert trade from Barugaza, and that other sea ports under their control were Sēmulla, Mandagora, Palaipatmai, Melizeigara, and Buzantion.[3]

The next state was that called in the *PME* the kingdom of Kēprobotos, which stretched from Naoura (Cannanore) to Cape Comorin. This was the region which the *PME* called erroneously Limurikē, a mistake for Damirikē, 'the Tamil country'.[4] Kēprobotos is an error for something like Kērobotros (Frisk), which would be the Greek form of a name like Keralaputra, Kailobothras being another Hellenized form; Pliny has Celebothras. This was the Dravidian kingdom of Keralaputra (also known as Kerala and Chera), the ancient capital of which was Vanji or Karur up the Periyar river about twenty-eight miles NNE of Cochin. It had existed from the time of Aśoka in the middle of the 3rd century B.C.[5]

Next to Keralaputra, after Cape Comorin, was the kingdom

[1] Smith, *Early History*, 40.
[2] As suggested by Smith, *Early History*, 1924, p. 266; Bivar, personal communication, 1975.
[3] Cf. also MacDowall, *Num. Chron.*, 7 ser. IV (1964) 278.
[4] Smith, *op. cit.*, p. 457.   [5] *Ibid.*, pp. 468–9.

of Pandion, the Indian Pāndya, the early capital of which was Kolkhoi (Kolkai, Korkai). This, by native tradition, was the cradle of South Indian civilization, and the home of the three brothers who founded the three Dravidian kingdoms of Pāndya, Keralaputra, and Chola. The capital, Kolkhoi, decayed as a port through changes of the coast-line, and it would seem that even in the 1st century A.D. it was no longer a port, for the *PME* mentions it only as a place where pearl-diving was carried on.[1] Pliny does not mention Kolkhoi, but speaks of the inland town of Modusa in Pandion's kingdom,[2] the Modoura of Ptolemy.[3] This place is now called Madura, and is about 150 miles from Cochin and more than 100 from Korkai. It is not mentioned in the *PME*. The author of the *PME* says that pepper is grown in quantity only in the kingdom of Pandion; he calls the pepper Kottonaric, κοττοναρικὴ, from the district of Kottonara, from which according to Pliny[4] it was sent in wooden boats (*monoxylis lintribus* = dug-out boats) to Bakarē. Kottonara represents the ancient Tamil name Kuttam, in the Quilon area.[5]

The third Dravidian kingdom, along the eastern side of India, was called Chola, whence Cholamandalam, anglicized as Coromandel, and extended northwards to Nellore, with its capital at Uraiyur or Old Trichinopoly, the Argalou of the *PME*. Its port of Kaviripaddinam or Puhar is now buried under sand; it was the Kamara of the *PME*. The kingdom was in decline by the 2nd or 3rd century A.D.[6]

Of the political condition of the rest of the Indian coast to the Ganges the *PME* has nothing to say. Ceylon is mentioned, and on the mainland Masalia (Masulipatam); then nothing till Dēsarēnē or Dōsarēnē is reached, probably the modern Orissa. After this the Ganges river and city, and beyond, vaguely, Khrusē (Burma) and Thina (China). In this remoter region we

[1] Chapter 59: *see above*, p. 53.   [2] *Nat. Hist.* VI, 26.
[3] *Geog.*, VII, 1, 89.   [4] *Nat. Hist.* VI, 26.
[5] Smith, *op. cit.*, p. 476.   [6] *Ibid.*, p. 465.

get a few ethnic names—Kirradai, Bargusoi, Hippioprosōpoi (*sic*='horse-faces'), 'who are said to be cannibals', and last of all the Sēsatai who brought malabathrum from the remotest parts. None of these is identifiable.[1]

[1] On the Kirradai see note 1 to chapter 62.

APPENDIX 4

Shipping

FOREIGN traders in the Erythraean Sea—Greeks and Egyptians—doubtless used, in the 1st century A.D., Egyptian ships, and Greek-owned ships of Mediterranean *type* may have sailed from Muos Hormos and Leukē Kōmē.; though on this the book gives no information. Fig. 6 shows a typical Egyptian ship of the kind used for the voyage to Punt. Merchant ships had no hold, and the load was piled on deck.[1]

A great deal of the trade in the Erythraean Sea, however, must have been carried on in local ships, the shapes of which have probably varied little in the course of centuries. On this subject the *PME* does give a little information. It mentions the sewn boats and dug-outs of the East African coast, and the eastern ships which it calls *trappaga*, *kotumba*, *sangara*, and *kolandiophōnta*.

The sewn boats are first mentioned in the *PME*, and much later by Prokopios (6th century A.D.). The latter says that the ships used in the Erythraean and Indian seas 'are not covered with pitch or any other substance, and the planks are fastened together, not with nails, but with cords'.[2] It may be mentioned here that the plank-built ships of East Africa were caulked with cotton and grease, in Swahili *kutia pamba na mafuta yasingie maji*, 'application of cotton and fat that the water may not get in'. In the *PME* it is said that on Menouthias Island there are πλοιάρια ῥαπτὰ καὶ μονόξυλα (chapter 15) and that Rhapta gets its name from the afore-mentioned sewn boats, ἀπὸ τῶν

---

[1] Maspero, *Dawn of Civilisation*, p. 392.

[2] *On the Persian war*, I, 1923.

158

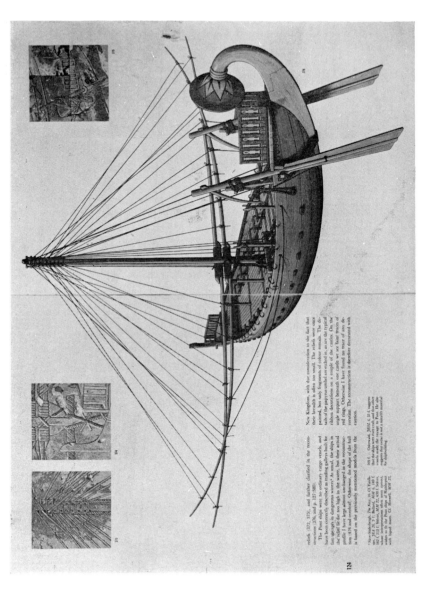

FIG. 6 Egyptian ship used for the voyage to Punt

reliefs 372, 373, and further clarified in the reconstructions (376, and p. 127-380).

The Punt ships were no ordinary cargo vessels, and have been correctly described as trading galleys built for sea approach in dangerous waters. As usual, the ships in the relief lie far too high in the water, but their actual profile I have kept almost unchanged in the reconstruction: 41% stand overleaf. Otherwise, the shape of the hull is based on the previously mentioned models from the

New Kingdom, with due consideration to the fact that their breadth is often too small. The reliefs were once painted, but only fragments of colour remain. The details of the papyrus umbel were studied, as are the typical ribbon decorations on a couple of the castles. On the single support beneath one castle we see faint traces of red rings. Otherwise I have found no trace of any decoration. The reconstruction is therefore decorated with caution.

124

1

2

3

Fig. 7. *Galawa* at Dar es-salaam, 1926 (1, 2), attachment to boom and float; outrigger canoe, Zanzibar, 1926 (3)

προειρημένων ῥαπτῶν πλοιαρίων. These boats were used in Menouthias for fishing and catching turtles. The four words which describe them mean literally 'small-boats sewn and of-a-single-piece-of-wood'. But it is not clear whether the expression refers to one or two kinds of boat, for both 'sewn boats' and 'boats made of a single piece of wood' have been made on the coast for centuries. Müller interpreted the expression as meaning a dug-out canoe with the sides raised by planks fastened with cords made of [coconut] palm-fibre. But since in Greek μονόξυλον is used also for a boat made from one piece of wood, i.e. a dug-out canoe, the words of the *PME* may be interpreted in one of two ways: (1) 'dug-out canoes with their sides raised by boards sewn to them', or (2) 'small boats with their planks sewn together, *and* dug-out canoes made from one piece of wood'. The second is possibly the correct explanation, because both types are found on the coast. The dug-out canoe type is represented, on the East African coast, by the *mtumbwi*, a canoe with no outrigger and big enough to be furnished when necessary with a small mast and sail. It is often made from the stem of the mango tree; further north, Grottanelli says that one of the favourite trees is that called *mchondoo* in KiBajuni, *mtondoo* in Swahili (*Calophyllum inophyllum*).[1] The *galawa* is a smaller dug-out canoe, with a sail and outriggers. The *PME* text may refer to either of these types. The fact that it does not mention outriggers (*matengo* in Swahili) is not necessarily decisive either way.

The sewn boat type is more difficult. The word used, πλοιάριον, is a diminutive; such as would suit a vessel used for catching fish and turtles. But it is possible that the niceties of Greek terminations did not trouble the author of the *PME*. It is generally assumed that he was referring to the East African coast ship called *mtepe*, in recent times built at Pate, Lamu, and other places north of Mombasa. It has a very long projecting prow, an upright mast, and a large square matting sail. Steere's

[1] Grottanelli, *Pescatori*, 1955, p. 190.

FIG. 8. East African sewn boat, *mtepe*

description is: they 'are sharp at the bows and stern, with a head shaped to imitate a camel's head, ornamented with painting and tassels and little streamers. They . . . have always a white streamer or pennant at the mast-head: their planking is sewn together, and they are broad and shallow'.[1] In addition to being sewn, the planks are pegged with wood. The *mtepe* is a fairly large ship and can carry up to twenty tons.

Other East Coast boats are built of planks, and are mentioned here because their prototypes at least were certainly sailing the Erythraean Sea 2000 years ago. The names are all Swahili.

Bedeni: a ship with a perpendicular cutwater or else simply a piece of board forming a prow, a sharp stern, and a high rudder-head. The mast is upright, not slanting as in some ships. Of Arabian origin.

---

[1] *Handbook of the Swahili Language* (London, 1884) *s.v. Mtepe.*

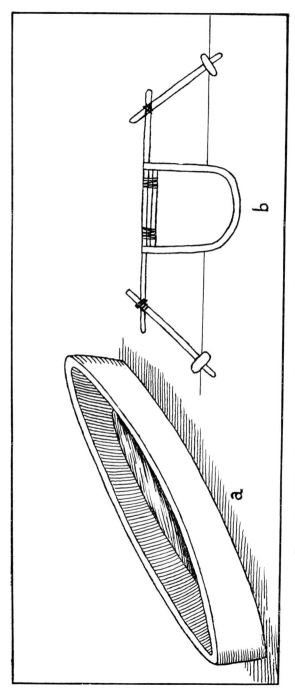

Fig. 9. East African dug-out canoes: (a) *mtumbwi* type; (b) outrigger with *galawa* type

Awesia: a ship like the *bedeni,* but with only a perpendicular cutwater.

Bágala: the 'buggalow' of Europeans. A large ship with a square stern, high poop, and a very long prow; furnished with a small mizzen-mast. This type was formerly used by Indian traders who came to Berbera from Bahrein and elsewhere.

Batela: a ship with a square stern, small quarter-deck, and sail. Smaller than a *bágala.*

Gangi: of the *bágala* type, but with a shorter prow and lower sail.

Dau: this type, with both stern and bow sharp, and a square matting sail, was used in Steere's day mostly for bringing firewood from the south end of Zanzibar to the town.[1]

Mashua: general term for a boat built of planks. Here may be mentioned the East Indian 'sewn boat' called *Masula,* made of planks sewn together and caulked with coir. This was in common use on the Coromandel coast, and the name, which is possibly the origin of the Swahili *mashua,* may be connected with Masulipatam on the East Indian coast.[2]

Eastern vessels mentioned by the *PME* with specific names are the following:

Madarate, μαδαράτε, sewn boats exported from Oman to Arabia. Glaser suggests that this is an Arabic word *muddara'at* meaning 'fastened with palm-fibre cord'. (Quoted by Frisk, p. 114.)

Trappaga Τράππαγα and *Kotumba* Κότυμβα (chapter 44). Both of these were fairly large ships, especially the *kotumba.* This last was identified with the modern *kotia,* thus described by Hornell: 'In appearance it approaches closely to the baggala type, being two-masted [unlike the East African variety], with poop, carved square stern, and quarters; usually with a rudder trunk. In size it runs generally under 200 tons. . . . Kotias are

[1] These descriptions are taken from Steere's *Handbook of the Swahili Language* and Madan's *Swahili-English Dictionary,* Oxford (1903).
[2] *Hobson-Jobson,* 1909, 602–3.

the oceanic tramps of Indian craft' (Hornell in *Mem. Asiat. Soc. Bengal*, VII (1920), p. 142). Lieut. Cruttenden of the Indian Navy writing in 1848 said that to Berbera 'the fat and wealthy Banian traders from Porebunder, Mandavie, and Bombay rolled across in their clumsy Kotias, and with a formidable array of empty ghee jars slung over the quarters of their vessels' (quoted in Burton, *First Footsteps*, pp. 408–9). (These Banyans were from Porbandar and Mandavi in Kutch.)

Sangara σάνγαρα (*sic*) (chapter 60): described as 'very large vessels made of single logs bound together'. This word passed into Portuguese as *jangada*, 'raft', the more recent Indian type consisting of two boats joined by a wooden platform, with a bamboo rail (*Hobson-Jobson*, p. 450).

Kolandiophōnta κολανδιοφωντα (no accent). These ships, according to Hornell (*loc. cit.*) 'must almost certainly have been two masted vessels with pointed ends and probably equipped with a stout outrigger, counterparts of the present-day Sinhalese *yatra-oruwa* (*yatra-dhoni* in Tamil), but unlike them steered by quarter oars, the rudder not being invented'. Burnell suggested for the origin of the name the Tamil *kulinta*, 'hollowed', and *oṭam*, 'boat' (*Hobson-Jobson*, p. 450). Christie, however, has recently suggested that the word is *k'un lun po*, the ships of the K'un lun people, who traded between India, China, and Ceylon (A. Christie, 'An obscure passage from the *Periplus*', *B.S.O.A.S.*, XIX (1957), 345–53).

Although he knew about the monsoons, the author of the *PME* does not say a great deal about seasonal navigation. His statements on this, in fact, may be summarised thus:

1. From Egypt to Ptolemaïs and Adouli ships sailed from January to September, the best time being September (chapter 6).

2. From Egypt to Opōnē (and presumably to Rhapta, though he does not say so) the best time was July (chapter 14).

3. From Egypt to Mouza the best time was September, but voyages could be made earlier (chapter 24).

4. Referring to Barbarikē in chapter 39, he says 'those who sail with the Indian winds put to sea about the month of July', that is with the SW monsoon.

5. From Egypt to Barugaza ships sail about July (chapter 49).

6. From Egypt to Limurikē the season is about July (chapter 56).

7. In chapter 57 he says that ships going to Barugaza and Skuthia sail clear of the land across the ocean with the SW monsoon.

He says nothing about the return journey, which was presumably made with the NE monsoon. The times of the monsoons are: south-west, from the end of March to September; north-east, from the end of November to February. On the Swahili coast there was a proverb:

> Kasikazi mja naswi,
> (The NE wind comes with fish)
> Kusi mja na mtama.
> (The SW wind comes with millet)

On the year's weather in general on the east coast of Africa, the Rev. W. E. Taylor has the following remarks in his *African Aphorisms* (London, 1891), no. 128:

The NE monsoon, called also Kasikazi and Musimu (i.e. *the* Monsoon), begins in November and lasts till February; the weather is hot and dry, and there is no rain. The favourable wind brings dhows from the Persian Gulf and Southern Arabia (Sheheri, Mkele or Makalla), mostly laden with salt fish to be exchanged for grain and other produce.

After the end of the NE monsoon comes a short period of calms (Maleleji, from ku-lala, to lie, and -ji, water), and the rains of the Mwaka fall, usually with a burst that keeps everyone in the house for a week or more.

The wind has now veered, and the SW monsoon, or Kusi, has begun, and the climate considerably alters. The air is oppressive and laden with moisture, and mildew corrupts everything. The land had been prepared for planting towards the end of the Kasikazi, and now all kinds of seeds are sown . . . and as the monsoon breaks earlier to the South, dhows may now be hurrying to the Northern coasts with the first-fruits of the Southern crops.

The latter part of the Kusi is called Demani, the 'Fair Winds' (from dema, the 'sheet' of a vessel). Dhows will now visit Arabia with the crops of the 'Mwaka'. This is about August, but *before* this, in July, there has been a scanty rain, called the 'Mchoo', Lesser Rains, with light winds springing up from the West, and a very damp and chilly air. This is the cold season, Kipupwe. *After* the Demani comes a period called 'Tanga Mbili' (two sailings?), the 'Variable Winds'—when the wind is so much altered that it allows vessels to sail North or South. The sea is frequently calm and oily in character (another period of the 'maleleji' above referred to).

The SW monsoon practically ends in September, and the interval between that and the NE is filled by the end of the Demani and the variable breezes. The Latter Rains ('Vuli') occur from about the end of the SW monsoon and into the beginning of October.

The normal year is as above, but some years seem to go quite contrary to experience. The beginning of the Kusi and its end are, it will be noticed, both just before the times when the sun is in zenith, March 4 and October 9.

APPENDIX 5

Elephant-Hunting

ALL along the hinterland of Trōglodutikē during the Ptolemaïc period an organized business of elephant-hunting was carried on by the Ptolemies; the *PME* refers to it in chapter 3. This business was not primarily for ivory, but for the collection of live elephants for use in war, and its administration was mainly in the hands of Greeks, some of whom seem to have made a previous but less respectable appearance in history. According to Agatharkhidēs, who flourished about 130 B.C., this business was started or perhaps reorganized by Ptolemy II Philadelphos (282–47 B.C.). Part of the Monumentum Adulitanum recorded by Kosmas was an inscription of his successor Ptolemy III Euergetēs I (247–21 B.C.) describing his conquests in Asia and his use of elephants in war; this inscription was as follows:

> The great king Ptolemy son of king Ptolemy
> and of queen Arsinoē, brother-sister deities, children of king
> Ptolemy and queen Berenikē, Saviour Deities,
> descended on the father's side from Hēraklēs son of Zeus and on
> 5 the mother's from Dionusos son of Zeus, having succeeded to his father's
> kingdom of Egypt, Libya, and Syria,
> and Phoenikē, and Kupros, and Lukia, and Karia, and the
> Kuklades Islands, led an army into Asia with
> infantry, cavalry, and naval forces
> 10 and elephants from Trōglodutikē and Aithiopia which his father
> and he first captured in these countries,
> and taking them to Egypt, trained them
> for military purposes. Having dominated on the Euphratēs
> all the country, and Kilikia, and Pamphulia, and Ionia, and the

166

15 Hellespont and Thrace, and all the forces in these countries, and having captured many Indian elephants; and all the kings in these places being subjected to him, he crossed the Euphratēs river; and Mesopotamia and Babylonia and Susiana and Persis and Media and all the rest as far as

20 Baktriana being brought under him, and searching for all the sacred things taken from Egypt under the Persians and carrying them back with the other treasure from the places to Egypt, he sent away the forces through the canalized rivers.

(Dittenberger, *Orientis Graeci Inscript. Select.*, I, 54)

The following notes may be made on this:

Line 1: Ptolemy is Ptolemy I Sōtēr (306–285 B.C.), often referred to as the son of Lagos.

Line 6: Libya here means Cyrenaica.

Line 6: The reference is to the war of Ptolemy III against Seleukos II Kallinikos king of Syria.

Line 16: Seleukos is known to have made use of elephants for warfare on a large scale. (Cf. Polubios v. 84, 6.)

Line 21: Jerome in his Commentary on Daniel says that Cambyses took from Egypt to Persia 2500 images of gods, which Euergetēs recovered during this campaign.

Line 23: It is not certain whether the phrase 'canalized rivers' refers to the canals of the Euphrates and Tigris or to canals connected with the Nile (Dittenberger thought the latter).

The elephant-hunting has been described by Agatharkhidēs and Strabō, and we cannot do better than quote their words:

AGATHARKHIDĒS

Ptolemy king of Egypt ordered the tribe called Elephant-hunters, by an edict, to refrain from killing elephants so that he himself might be able to take them alive; and he promised them great rewards for obedience. But not only could he not persuade them to obey, but they answered that they would not change their mode of subsistence for the whole kingdom of Egypt. (*On the Erythraean Sea*, V, 56.)

STRABŌ

When you sail from Hērōöpolis along Trōglodutikē you come to the town of Philōtera, called after the sister of Ptolemy II, and built by Saturos, who was sent to Trōglodutikē to supervise the elephant-hunting. Then you come to another Arsinoē. . . . Then comes the town of Muos Hormos, also called Aphroditē's Port, a large harbour with a very tortuous entrance. . . . Next you come to a bay called Foul Bay situated like Muos Hormos opposite the Thebaïd. This bay is called Foul because of the hidden rocks and frequent storms which make it dangerous. In the inner part of the bay is the town of Berenikē. . . .

Still further south is the town of Ptolemaïs[1] founded by Eumēdēs for the elephant-hunting. This man, being sent by Ptolemy Philadelphos to supervise the hunting, secretly fortified the peninsula with a ditch and wall, and by careful treatment gained the friendship of those who tried to hinder him. . . . Further on is the port of Saba[2] and the elephant-hunt of the same name. . . . Beyond, on the coast, are the Watch-towers of Dēmētrios and the Altars of Konōn . . . after which is the Harbour of Mēlinos, above which is the Fort of Koraos and the Hunt of Koraos, then another fort, and several hunts. Then comes the Port of Antiphilos.[3] . . . After this is the Sabaean town of Berenikē and a large town called Sabai;[4] then the Wood of Eumenēs, the city of Darada [or Daraba], and an elephant hunt called At the Water-hole.[5] Here live the Elephant-eaters, who hunt in the following way. When they see from the trees that a herd of elephants is coming through the forest, they do not straightway attack, but cautiously follow the stragglers who have got separated from the herd, and cut the tendons of their legs. Another way is to shoot them with arrows dipped in snake-poison. It takes three men to shoot: two hold the bow, while the third draws the string. Others make use of the trees against which the elephants are in the habit of resting, and approaching from the other side cut through the trunk so that when the elephant leans against it, the tree falls

168

and he falls with it; being unable to get up because his legs have a continuous, rigid bone, he can then be cut in pieces by the men who jump down from the trees. . . .

From the Port of Eumenēs to Deirē[6] and the Straits[7] . . . there are also several elephant-hunts and less known towns and islands along the coast... There is also an island called Philip's Island, above which is an elephant-hunt called the Hunt of Puthangelos; then comes the city and port of Arsinoē, and after them Deirē; above them is an elephant-hunt. After Deirē is the Spice-country, the first that produces myrrh; it is the land of the Ikhthuophagoi and Kreophagoi (Flesh-eaters), and it produces also the persea and Egyptian mulberry trees. Beyond it is the Hunt of Likhas. In many places there are tanks for rain-water; when they are dry the elephants dig water-holes with their trunks and tusks. On this coast, extending to the promontory of Putholaos are two great lakes;[8] one is salt and is called a sea; the other is sweet, and the home of hippopotamuses and crocodiles, with beds of papyrus round its edge, and the ibis is to be seen here. In the neighbourhood of the promontory of Putholaos the people do not mutilate their bodies. After this is the Incense Country, where there is a promontory covered with a sacred poplar grove. Inland there is a river-land called the River-land of Isis, and another called Nile,[9] both of which produce incense and myrrh. There is also a tank which is filled with water flowing down from the mountains. Then comes the Village of Leōn, and the Port of Puthangelos. The country beyond produces false kasia. Then come several river-lands in succession, where incense trees are produced, and several rivers occur as far as the Cinnamon Country; the river which bounds this country produces a great deal of the water-plant called phleōs.[10] Then comes another river, and the Port of Daphnē,[11] and a river-land called Apollō's, which produces incense, myrrh, and cinnamon; the latter flourishes most in the interior. After this is mount Elephas,[12] which juts out into the sea, and a channel, a large harbour, of Psugmos,* a watering-place called Of the Kunokephaloi, and finally the Headland of the South Wind,[13] the last cape on this coast. When you turn southwards here you enter the unknown, for we have no

* Lit. 'of cooling or drying'.

knowledge of any ports or other places beyond it. There are pillars and altars of Putholaos, and Likhas, and Puthangelos, and Leōn, and Kharimortos[14] along the known coast, extending from Deirē to the Headland of the South Wind, but the distance is not known. ('Geography', XVI, 4–14.)

NOTES ON THE EXTRACTS FROM STRABŌ

1 Ptolemaïs Thērōn.
2 Possibly Adouli, which is not otherwise mentioned by Strabō.
3 This may have been in Hanfila Bay, the modern name being possibly a corruption of Antiphilos.
4 Possibly Assab.
5 πρὸς τῷ φρέατι.
6 Probably Ras Dumeira, with the nearby village of Raheita.
7 Bab al mandab.
8 These two lakes may represent, first the inner part of the Bay of Tajurra, called Gubbet al kharab, which has a very narrow entrance, and second Lake Assal nearby, although the latter is salt not sweet.
9 This suggests the Neiloptolemaiou of the PME (chapter 11), beyond Bandar Kasim.
10 φλέως.
11 This suggests one of the Laurel Groves of the PME (chapter 11 : δαφνῶνα μικρὸν—δαφνῶνα μέγαν λεγόμενον 'Ακάνναι.
12 The Headland Elephas (Ras Filuk) of the PME (chapter 11).
13 Νότου κέρας. Ptolemy, who worked a century after Strabō, puts this south of Opōnē (Ras Hafun).
14 See below.

Strabō's account may be supplemented by two inscriptions:

1. Found at Edfu in Egypt, of the reign of Ptolemy IV (Dittenberger, O.G.I.S., I, no. 82):

To king Ptolemy and
queen Arsinoē, the deities
Philopatōr,[1] and to Sarapis and
Isis, Likhas son of Purrhos the Akarnanian,
sent as officer in charge[2]
of the elephant hunting
for the second time.

[1] θεοῖς φιλοπάτορσι, 'loving one's father', a name of Ptolemy IV.
[2] στρατηγός.

2. Provenance unknown; now in the British Museum. Of
the reign of Ptolemy IV (Dittenberger, *O.G.I.S.*, I, no. 86):

For king Ptolemy and
queen Arsinoē and their son Ptolemy,[1] the Philopatōr deities,
the children of Ptolemy and Berenikē the divine
benefactors,[2] to Arēs bringer of victory and good hunting,
Alexander son of Sundaios of Oroanda[3]
who was sent out as successor[4]
to Kharimortos the officer in charge of
the hunting of elephants, and
Apoasis son of Miorbollos of Etenna[5]
a subordinate commander, and the
soldiers in his unit.[6]

[1] Afterwards Ptolemy V Epiphanēs (205–181 B.C.).
[2] A name of Ptolemy III and VII, εὐεργέτης.
[3] A town of Pisidia in Asia Minor. Dittenberger reads *OPOANΔEYΣ* for
the *OPO ANNEYΣ* of the inscription.
[4] διάδοχος.
[5] This may have been in Pamphulia.
[6] On Kharimortos see below.

Two more inscriptions recall the dangers of the journey to
the Red Sea coast:

1. In a temple near Redesieh in the Thebaïd (Dittenberger,
no. 70):

To Pan who helps on the way,[1]
Saviour, Artemidōros
son of Apollōnios of Pergē,[2]
for a safe return from the Trōgodyte* country.

[1] εὔοδος.
[2] A town of Pamphulia.

2. In a temple near Redesieh (Dittenberger, no. 71):

Akestimos the Cretan
of Kourtōlia, to Pan who helps on the way,
for a safe return from the Trōgodyte* country.

Kharimortos was associated with Skopas, one of the leading generals of Aitolia (c. 220 B.C.) and is almost certainly the person to whom Polubios refers when he writes of Skopas 'taking for his partner the drunken ruffian Kharimortos and pillaging the palace' (History, XVIII, 55, 2).

Strabō gives two terms for elephant-hunts: κυνήγιον and θήρα. The hunt of Puthangelos, for example, is called a kunēgion, while the neighbouring hunt beyond Deirē is a thēra. It is not clear what the distinction is, if there is any; but possibly thēra refers to a regular hunting establishment (like Ptolemaïs Thērōn), while kunēgion means the area hunted over, under the control of a thēra.

* Note the spelling—without L.

The Mountain of the Moon

THE site of this enigmatic mountain is described by Ptolemy in relation to the site of Rhapta, although the *PME* does not mention it. Since it is the only distinct geographical feature in the interior of East Africa mentioned in classical antiquity, it merits discussion in an Appendix. Only in Ptolemy is anything like a detailed account to be found, for the other two writers in whose works it occurs merely make passing reference to it; these are Philostorgios in the 5th century A.D. and the unknown author of a nameless geographical fragment attributed to the 7th century printed with other *apospasmatia geographica* in Müller's *Claudii Ptolemaei Geographia*, I. ii, 776. There are statements in two books of Ptolemy's *Geographikē Huphēgēsis* which W. Desborough Cooley considered to be interpolations (*Claudius Ptolemy and the Nile*, London, 1854, pp. 77–98).

Omitting the latitudes and longitudes, which are guess-work, Ptolemy's statements are the following:

(1) Of the voyage between Arōmata and Rhapta, Marinos of Tyre says, 'Diogenēs, one of those who used to sail to India, turning back a second time, was driven from his course off Arōmata by north winds, and keeping Trōglodutikē on his right, after twenty-five days arrived at the swamps (*limnai*) from which the Nile rises, which are a little north of Cape Rhapton. Theophilos also, another of those who used to sail to Azania, put out from Rhapta with a southerly wind, and on the twentieth day came to Arōmata' (I. 7, 9).

(2) Marinos says that the voyage from Arōmata to the swamps from which the Nile rises is performed with a north wind, although Arōmata is a long way east of the Nile (I. 15, 10).

(3) We learn from traders who cross from Eudaimōn Arabia to Arōmata, Azania, and Rhapta that the voyage is not due south, but to the west and south; and that the swamps from which the Nile rises are not beside the sea, but a long way inland (I. 17, 6).

(4) After Sarapion's roadstead begins the bay leading to Rhapta, the passage of which takes three nights and days. At the beginning of it is the mart called Niki or Toniki. Beside Cape Rhapton is the river Rhaptos, and, a little way back from the sea, the metropolis of the same name (I. 17, 12).

[Niki or Toniki, i.e. το νικι, is perhaps Burikao. The time is an underestimate, the distance from Burikao (if it is Niki) being some 550 miles.]

(5) Beside it [Cape Prason, Ras Kimbiji or Cape Delgado] on the east lies an island called Menouthias. . . . The cannibal Ethiopians live round this bay; to the west of them extends the mountain of the moon, from which the swamps of the Nile, lying below it, receive the snow (IV. 8, 1/2).

Whether or not these passages were written in the 2nd century A.D. is not really important, though the fact that two informants of Ptolemy's predecessor Marinos are cited by name suggests that they are neither interpolations nor late.

Although it is now usual to speak of the mountains of the moon, the MSS of Ptolemy have τὸ τῆς σελήνης ὄρος, 'the mountain of the moon'. The word ὄρος can, it is true, mean 'mountain range', but in this case it is not necessary to look for a range. For it is inconceivable that a Graeco-Egyptian trader of the 2nd century A.D., whose vocation was the sea, should have got within reach of even rumours of such a range as Ruwenzori, with which the Mountains of the Moon are now commonly identified, a thousand miles and more from the coast, and not seen or even heard of by Europeans till the middle of the 19th century.

On the other hand, there is a snow–clad mountain, the summit of which is above the equatorial snow-line, called Kilimanjaro, within 350 miles of the Rufiji delta, and less than

200 from Pangani at the mouth of the Ruvu river which rises on the slopes of the mountain. (Mount Kenya is too far away and the intervening country too difficult to make it a likely candidate.) Rivers flow down all sides of Kilimanjaro, and there is a large area of swamp a few miles to the north—Lakes Amboselli, Engoni naibor, Nyiri, and Loginya. It is true that the rivers peter out before reaching the swamps, and that no river runs north from them. Nevertheless, the essential conditions are here for a foreign trader to have heard, at the coast, even if he never saw it, of a great snowy mountain from which rivers ran into lakes, and to have passed on his story till it finally reached a geographer working at Alexandria. Hence could have arisen the account of the Nile source which was current in classical antiquity. Many a modern traveller has made similar mistakes, as did Erhardt and Rebmann, who thought that Lakes Tanganyika and Nyasa were one vast lake, and Speke and Grant, who believed that Lakes Victoria Nyanza and Baringo were connected by a short channel.

My suggestion that Kilimanjaro was the Mountain of the Moon was made in 1940, and was subsequently ridiculed in J. Oliver Thomson's *History of Ancient Geography* published in 1948. Sir Harry Johnston had also suggested Kilimanjaro in 1911 (*The Opening up of Africa*, p. 110), and Dr Gervase Mathew made the same suggestion more recently (*History of East Africa*, 1963, pp. 96–7).

The occurrence of the tribal name BaNyamwezi, 'people of the moon', to the WSW of Kilimanjaro, is not to be taken as confirming any theories of identification, since this name is comparatively modern, and the moon-element in it (*mwezi*) has no reference to any mountain, but to the position of the rising or setting of the moon.

In opposition to the Kilimanjaro theory is the late Dr O. G. S. Crawford's suggestion that the mountains of the moon are to be sought in central Ethiopia, i.e. in the Mount Abuna Yosef area in Lāstā, which he identifies with a place called

Çiebelchamir on Fra Mauro's map of 1460. This, he says quite rightly, stands for Jebel Khamir, 'mountain of the Khamir', one of the central Agaw tribes. But 'at some early date' *khamir* having been turned into the Arabic *qamar*, 'moon',[1] we have 'mountain of the moon'. Fra Mauro says that the Nile rises in the provinces of 'Marora' and 'Salgu', and flows by the side of a very high mountain called Marora or Chamir. Since the Khamir country was Lāstā, his 'Nile' was either the Takkazi or Sellari. Marora and Salgu may represent Marora somewhere near Ṣelā Asfarē in Wadlā, and Ṣalgo somewhere in Angot, neither very important places. Crawford's identification of Marora with Marawa is impossible, for Marawa is the name of a Galla tribe, and the Galla had not arrived by the 15th century (O. G. S. Crawford, 'Some medieval theories about the Nile', *Geog. J.* cxiv (1949), pp. 17–19, 26; *Ethiopian Itineraries circa 1400–1524*, Hakluyt Soc., Cambridge, 1958, pp. 88, 197).

It may seem unreasonable to suggest Kilimanjaro instead of a place nearer the real Nile; but unreason may sometimes be right. Or perhaps there never was a mountain or mountains of the moon. The author of the article 'Lunae Montes' in the *Dictionary of Greek and Roman Geography*, W. Bodham Donne, went so far as to write 'their position is unknown, and if they have any real existence, they must be placed S. of the Equator' (II, 1857, p. 216).

---

[1] In Agaw the word for 'moon' is *arbā.*

Extracts from Agatharkhidēs
'On the Erythraean Sea'
as epitomised by Phōtios

1   PTOLEMY[1] who reigned in Egypt after the son of Lagos, was, according to Agatharkhidēs, the first to put the hunting of elephants and other large beasts on a proper basis, and to collect as it were under one central management what had been previously scattered owing to natural conditions. Yet it is true that before the age of the Ptolemies many are said to have trained elephants and used them in war, like Pōros the Indian who fought against Alexander, and others not a few. Ptolemy is perhaps then to be regarded as the first who made this into a business, either as the first of Alexander's successors, or as the first of the kings of Egypt.

2   The Erythraean Sea does not derive its name from the fact that the western mountains of the Arabian Gulf, struck by the piercing fiery rays of the sun, give out something like glowing coals, while on the eastern side mounds of sand and reddish earth make the water red in colour for many stades from the shore. Not for this reason, says Agatharkhidēs, is it called the Red Sea; for even if the navigable passage is narrow, with peaks and mounds overhanging it on each side of the gulf, the light falling from each side of the gulf is responsible for the sea being like the land, as all can see, though the cause is not known to all. Yet it is not from this that the sea has its name, though many before Agatharkhidēs thought so.

3   This then is the first reason that has been suggested, though

177

it is not the true one. A second, equally false, is that in those parts the rising sun strikes the sea, not with clear rays, as with us, but with blood-coloured rays, whence the beholder imagines that the sea is of this colour and that this is why it is called the Erythraean or Red Sea.

4   A third explanation comes from Argolis, which, says Agatharkhidēs, is great in its boldness but without proof. For the school of Deinias,[2] taking security from poetic licence, says that Perseus set out from Argos to Aithiopia (which was then called Kēphēnia) to free the daughter of Kēpheus,[3] and crossed thence to Persia, passing the name of one of his sons, to wit his son Eruthras, to the Persians, from which circumstance the name was given to the sea. Such is the unconsidered Argolic tale about the Erythraean Sea.

5   The fifth [sic] and true explanation is that which the author [Agatharkhidēs] learnt from a Persian. Boxos, he said, was his name; he had learnt to think and speak like a Greek, having left his own country and settled in Athens. What he said was this. There was a Persian, the son of Muozaios, named Eruthras, well known for his courage and wealth, who lived not far from the sea opposite two islands which are now inhabited, but were deserted in the time of the Median empire when Eruthras knew them. He was in the habit of living at Pasargadai[4] in winter, returning to his home in the spring for both pleasure and profit. His not inconsiderable herd of mares was one day attacked by lions which killed some of them. The rest, frightened by the sight, and tormented by the gadfly, rushed down to the shore and, there being at the time a strong wind blowing from the land, charged into the sea in their excitement, swimming along the shore till, their terror not abating, they were carried out by the force of the waves and scarcely reached the island in safety. One of the herdsmen, bolder than the rest, crossed with them, clinging to the shoulder first of one then of another. Eruthras,

therefore, seeking his lost mares, made a raft, being the first man in those parts to do such a thing. The raft was not large, but strongly made; and taking advantage of a favourable wind he put it to sea, and by the swift propulsion of the waves found both his horses and his herdsman. Much taken with the island, he built there a port in a suitable place, and brought over from the mainland people who were living in poor circumstances; after this he established other settlers in the remaining un-inhabited island. Such was his fame from these actions that this sea, so infinite in its extent, is still known in our day as the Erythraean Sea. The reasons for this name must be distinguished, for there is a great difference between saying ἐρυθρᾶ θάλατταν, 'sea of Eruthras, and θάλατταν ἐρυθρὰν, 'red sea'. The derivation from colour is false, while that from the name of a man who ruled there, as in the Persian explanation, is the true one.

9   India produces elephants as well as Libya[5] and the part of Aithiopia bordering on the territory of Thebes.

10   The Aithiopians use in warfare large spears and short javelins; the blades are formed of oblong stones lashed to the shaft with cord, sharpened to a point, and dipped in poison.

20   Agatharkhidēs says that Ptolemy collected five hundred horses from Greece for his war against the Aithiopians. Those that went in the front line and were exposed to danger, to the number of one hundred, he furnished with armour in the following way. He caused the horses and their riders to be dressed in felt garments, called *kasas*[6] in those parts, which completely enveloped the whole body except the eyes.

BOOK V

30   To the south of Egypt are four great races of mankind. First are the riverain peoples, who sow millet and sesame.

Second are the marsh-dwellers, who live on reeds and tender shoots. Third, the people who wander here and there without plan, feeding on meat and milk. Fourth are those who live by fishing on the sea-shore.

31 This race (the fourth) has neither towns nor districts, nor even the most rudimentary civilization; and it is also, as some say, the largest of races. Among the Autaioi[7] who are found everywhere in the islands subject to Persia there live the Ikhthuophagoi [Fish-eaters] who go stark naked, both men and women, and indulge in common procreation of children. They have an instinctive knowledge of pleasure and pain, but none of moral qualities.

32 The places nearest to the sea are devoid of all that might sustain life, as are also those adjacent to the great coasts. But the country inland offers good hunting; and the people are averse neither to fish nor to any kind of game. Their dwelling places are exposed to the blasts from the shore; and there are deep hollows, ravines, and narrow gorges with sloping paths to which, when it is convenient, they bring rough stones and fill up the hollows. When the tide comes in, which it does twice a day, the sea covers the whole ridge, bringing with it from the swirling waters a great many fish to the shore, which then remain there, seeking their food from these hollows and recesses. When the tide goes out, the water recedes through the stone filling of the hollows, but the fish, left inside, afford nourishment to the Ikhthuophagoi.

34 The whole catch of fish is thrown together on to the hot surface of the rocks at midday, and it is not long before the heat makes the flesh fall away from the bones, provided the heap is big enough and well stirred. The bones are collected into piles which from a distance look like enormous tumuli. Then the flesh is spread on the flat rocks, and after being mixed with

seeds of Christ-thorn is well trodden for a certain length of time; the admixture of this sticky matter, which seems to take the place of a condiment, makes the whole into a glutinous mass. At length, when it has been subjected to sufficient pressure from the feet, it is made into solid cakes and again exposed to the sun. The dried food thus obtained is eaten by all, who lie down to eat, according to appetite, and not by weight or measurement.

35 They take the following steps against sudden spells of cold weather which interrupt the fishing: travelling the whole length of the shore, they collect certain shells which are found there, of immense size, and so large in fact as to be unbelievable to those who have not seen them. In these they find compensation for the difficulties of the weather. Indeed they collect these shells even when they still have a stock of fish, and keep them in holes full of water, feeding them with freshly-gathered sea-weed and the heads of small fish; then when need compels them they turn them into food.

36 But if both sources of supply fail, they pick out bones from the bone-heaps which are still somewhat fresh and juicy; these are carried away and partly broken up on the rocks; then they gnaw them, for in their need they show the skill of the beasts that lurk in the bush.

37 Their drinking water is obtained in a still more remarkable way. For four days they have a holiday, with songs and merry-making, distracted by nothing on account of the ease with which their food is prepared. When the fifth day arrives, they go inland to a district lying at the foot of the mountains to get water, where are the rivers of the Nomads, who water their herds there.

38 They start in the evening, and when they reach the

watering-places of the Nomads, they stand round the water in a circle and then, kneeling with hands on the ground, they drink like cattle, not with one continuous draught, but with frequent pauses. When in this way they have filled their bellies with water like jars, they make their way back to the sea with difficulty.

39   On the next day, when they reach the sea, no one eats fish or anything else; but, being full to bursting point, they all lie about hardly able to breathe, like drunken men, though their affliction is due to weight and not to intoxication. The following day they return to the accustomed mode of feeding; and this they do throughout their whole lives, as the seasons revolve, no man among them devoting himself to any other kind of business. Because of the simplicity of their food they seldom fall ill.

40   In this way, then, live the Ikhthuophagoi, who have their habitations in the inlets and tortuous parts of the coast; and those who claim for themselves the outer shore thrive continually by fishing in this way. They have no need of moisture, for when they have eaten their succulent and practically raw fish, they do not require drink. And thus they bear with patience whatever fortune has sent them from the beginning.

41   Living in the place which we have described, they have not, as we have, any of that knowledge and experience of the greatest evils which are common to most of mankind. For they have no occasion to flee from the drawn sword with which a neighbour threatens; they are disturbed by no insults or injuries; unharmed, they bewail no adverse change of fortune; and should such by chance come to them from strangers, they gaze with intent face and many shakings and nods of the head, but they take not the slightest notice of the things which one man commonly does to another. Whence it seems to me that

they have no definite indication of knowledge, but that they regulate all their lives by custom, expressed in words, sounds, and imitative signs.

43   Part of the Ikhthuophagoi have caves for dwellings, facing not the south on account of the great heat, but the opposite direction. Others shelter under the ribs of fish which they cover with sea-weed; others again make use of the interlacing branches of olive trees as huts: this division of the people eats the fruit of the olive, which is very like chestnut.

44   The fourth division of the Ikhthuophagoi have the following kind of dwelling-place: an immense mound of sand like a mountain, collected during the course of many years, becomes hardened by the continual motion of the waves against it so that finally it differs in no way from any other kind of hard solid mass, on account of the hardening of the sand. In these mounds they make passages of the length of a man, and allow the upper part to harden so that it forms a roof; in the lower part they make oblong passages opening into one another, where they take their rest, the light being admitted to the inner parts which are exposed in some measure to the wind. And should the sea come in flood, they catch fish in the way which we have already described (chapter 32).

45   The dead are considered worthy of no further care, for their minds are not touched by pity, which is a product of thought. They are merely thrown out and lie on the shore till the movement of the tides carries them out to sea to be the food of fishes.

48   Not far from this group lives another of the same size, which lives in this manner: they get their food from whales which are cast up on the shore; and if this supply fails, as it often does, they make good the deficiency, even if with some

trouble and inconvenience, by preparing the cartilage from the bones and ribs of former catches. These then are the groups of the Ikhthuophagoi which are known to us; there are many more of which we are as yet ignorant.

50   After the country of the Ikhthuophagoi the Astabara river[8] flows down through Aithiopia and Libya at a distance from the Nile, and lower; and on that account, by joining its stream with the larger river, produces by its circuit the island of Meroē.[9] An inconsiderable horde of peoples inhabits both banks of this river. They break up the roots of reeds and after washing them clean break them up into small pieces on the rocks. When they have there reduced them to a smooth, sticky mass, they make lumps as big as small handfuls which are cooked in the sun and served up as food. These people are harassed by evils from which they cannot escape, such as the attacks of lions from the marshes; and about the time of the rising of the Dog-star[10] immense and irresistible swarms of midges attack them, so that the whole population has to take refuge in the swamps. These insects destroy the lions, not so much by their bites—though these are bad enough—as by their shrill unending buzz which the animals cannot endure. Let this be put on record as something both new and out of the common. For what could be more remarkable than that lions should be overcome by midges, while men escape with their lives from the same danger?

51   The Hulophagoi [Wood-eaters] are found near the people we have just described, and do not differ much from them, for they also live on green food. They eat, even in the hot weather, the fruits that fall from the trees; or else they pick a plant which grows in shady valleys, of a hard consistency and with a stalk like a turnip: this they call bounias;[11] the soft and tender part of it is what they eat. At night they sleep in places which are safe from wild beasts and at the same time suitable for sleeping in.

In the morning, as soon as the sun rises, they all come down from the trees with their wives and children and strenuously exert themselves to obtain the tenderest shoots, which they eat with relish. And this is their whole mode of life. Their arboreal movements might be thought incredible, and the skill of their hands, fingers, feet, and other limbs also is amazing. They leap without difficulty from branch to branch, and even in the most dangerous places one will snatch up a broken branch for another. This tribe, in fact, exhibits such powers that an observer, himself struck dumb with amazement, would not dare to describe them to those who have not seen them. No branch has any sap in it but they crush it with their teeth and digest it in their stomachs. On account of their thinness they suffer little injury to their bodies when they fall from a height. They all go naked; and the offspring of their women is shared by all, both as regards paternity and rearing. Sometimes they engage in inter-tribal warfare. Most of them, as a result of the effects of hunger, exchange life for death when their sight is clouded with cataract, which happens about their fiftieth year.

52 Beyond them are the people whom their neighbours call the Kunēgetai [hunters]. These people have their lodging in the trees because of the great numbers of wild beasts in the country. They capture game in snares and eat it. They are also skilled in archery. When it happens that they are short of food and unable to kill or trap any game, they remedy the deficiency from the skins of previous kills, which are soaked in water and covered lightly with hot embers, and thus roasted are divided among the people to be eaten.

53 Beyond these, but separated by a wide stretch of country, and more towards the west, are the people who gain their food by hunting elephants. Certain of them sit up in the trees and watch the movements of the animals. As an animal passes by, they descend swiftly, and pushing its left thigh with their feet

they cut the tendons of the right knee with an axe made specially for this purpose; and thus with one hand they inflict such wounds and with the other they grasp the tail so firmly, that it is as if a life and death struggle is in progress, for they must either kill or be killed. As soon as the beast has fallen, from the force of the blow and from loss of blood, the hunter's companions appear on the scene, and while the animal is still alive they cut the flesh from its quarters and feast thereon with joy. The beast subdued in this way suffers a long and painful death.

54 The Elephantophagoi [Elephant-eaters] therefore live among great dangers. Others of them have a different method of capturing the animals. Three men equipped with one bow and plenty of arrows dipped in snake-poison station themselves in a glade where the elephants come out. When an elephant approaches, one of the men holds the bow and the other two draw the bowstring with all their force, releasing the arrow which is aimed at the middle of the animal's flank, so that on striking it will penetrate the inner parts, cutting and wounding as it goes in. Hence even so great a beast grows feeble and falls, convulsed with pain.

55 There is a third group of Elephant-hunters who hunt in this manner: When the elephants go to rest after eating their fill, they do not sleep lying on the ground, but lean against the largest and thickest trees so that the weight of the body is supported by the tree; so that you might call this a spurious rather than a true way of resting because the deepest sleep is troubled by the possibility of destruction through falling, for once these animals have fallen they cannot raise themselves. Therefore when the Elephant-hunters wandering in the forest see one of these resting-places they cut through one side of the tree with a saw in such a way that it will neither fall on its own nor support a weight, but will take only a very slight strain.

The beast returning from pasture to its accustomed sleeping-place leans against the tree, which immediately gives way, and so a meal is provided for the hunters. The flesh from the quarters is cut away and the animal dies from loss of blood; the rest of the meat is then distributed among the hunters.

56 Ptolemy king of Egypt ordered these hunters by an edict to refrain from killing elephants, so that he himself might be able to have them alive; and he promised them great rewards for obedience. But not only could he not persuade them to obey, but they answered that they would not change their mode of subsistence for the whole kingdom of Egypt.

57 The Simoi [Flat-nosed] hunters are called 'the unclean ones' by the Nomads. Part of them lives towards the west; and another part towards the south, smaller in numbers and known as Strouthophagoi [ostrich-eaters] for they subdue ostriches both by trickery* and with clubs. These birds provide them with the means of life, for they yield materials for food, clothing, and beds. The Flat-noses are enemies of the Ostrich-eaters and raid them. They use for spear-heads the horns of the oryx antelope which are long and sharp enough to pierce. Their country is full of these animals.

58 Separated from them by a small tract of country are the Akridophagoi [Locust-eaters], a tribe shorter in stature than the others; they are thin and emaciated and their skins are very black. At the approach of the spring equinox, when the south-west and west winds blow, countless swarms of large locusts fly with the wind from countries hitherto unexplored. These creatures differ little from birds in their powers of flight, but much in appearance. The people feed on them at all times,

* This suggests that they used the Bushman method of putting the skin of an ostrich on their heads, and, thus disguised, approaching the birds without scaring them.

and eat them salted and prepared in other ways. They are caught by means of smoke, which stupefies them and brings them to the ground.[12] The people are said to be agile and swifter of foot than their neighbours. They do not live beyond forty years because of the dryness of their food, and they die more hardly than they live. For when old age approaches, swarms of flying lice appear on their bodies, insects not unlike ticks, but a little smaller. They begin on the breast and belly- and devour the whole body and face. The first onset of this trouble is like an attack of the itch, and as time goes on people scratch themselves in torment. At last when the disease has run its course, the unhappy people are unable to bear the misery caused by the eruption of the insects and the efflux of diseased blood. And such is the end of the Locust-eaters, whether it be due to the dryness of the body, to the kind of food they eat, or to the air.

59 Next to the Locust-eaters there is a country full of a wonderful variety of pasturage, but utterly uninhabited, not because it has always been so, but because of the large numbers of scorpions and venomous spiders, which some call 'four-jaws' and ascribe to the heavy rainfall. When the inhabitants could no longer resist these plagues they fled, preferring the safety of exile to their own country, so that it has been uninhabited ever since. In the same way it has happened elsewhere that the people have had to leave their own country, as when there was a plague of field-mice in Italy; of sparrows eating all the corn in Media; and of lions in North Africa. Many unlooked for calamities have left the countries they attacked empty of inhabitants.

60 Lastly, towards the south, live the people called Kuna-molgoi [Dog-milkers] by the Greeks, who have long hair and beards, and breed large dogs like the Hyrcanians, with the help of which they hunt cattle which wander from India into their

country.[13] Large numbers of these cattle are to be seen from the winter solstice to midwinter. The people also milk the bitches and live on their milk, though they feed also on the flesh of wild beasts. Of what is to be found south of these, we have no information.

61   The social organization of the Trōglodytes is as follows. Some of the tribes are under despotic chiefs. Wives, and children as well, they have in common, except that they may not have affairs with the wives of chiefs; the penalty for this offence is a fine of one sheep. Their manner of life is this: in winter, that is about the time of the Etesian winds when their land is blest with abundant rains, they live on blood and milk, which, stirred together in one filthy mixture, they warm on the fire in jars. If the hot weather harasses them, they stay in damp places fighting among themselves for pasturage; then they eat their old and diseased cattle, which are slaughtered by the butchers, whom they call 'unclean'. No living creature is dignified with the title of parent save only the bull and the cow, the one being called father and the other, mother. The same dignity is accorded to the ram and the ewe. On that account their custom is to take their daily food not from their parents but from their live-stock. The mass of the common people drink an infusion of the plant paliurus; the chiefs drink a preparation from a certain flower which yields a wine of poor quality. Their buttocks are girt with skins, the rest of the body being left uncovered. Some have the custom of mutilating their genital members, as do all the Egyptians. And those whom the Greeks call *koloboi*, that is, mutilated, remove from infants with a razor all that part which others merely circumcise out of obedience to religious law; whence they have received the designation.

63   Their burial customs are as follows. They bind the necks of the dead to the legs with cords made of paliurus fibre; then,

placing them on a hillock or mound, they cover them with stones of a size that can be carried by hand, not without facetious and derisive talk, until they are completely covered up. An antelope horn is then stuck on the top as a grave post, and the crowd departs laughing, without any display of emotion. Thus they wisely transpose the usual funeral custom, as if it was advisable not to afflict oneself with grief on account of happenings which are themselves devoid of grief. When sudden quarrels arise about pasturage and they come to blows, this indeed being all that they fight over among themselves, the old women rush between the fighters and separate them, soothing their angry minds with soft words. They do not sleep as other men do, but are always moving round with their herds. The male animals carry bells fastened to their horns so that the noise they make may keep off wild beasts. At nightfall they drive them into enclosures roofed with mats of palm-fibre, to which the women betake themselves with the children. The men sit round fires lit outside and keep themselves awake by singing. Thus in many of them habit overcomes nature through the necessity of performing their duties. Those who from old age—which overtakes all—are unable to follow the herds are strangled by being hung with an ox-tail round their necks. If a man's life should be unduly prolonged, any person who wishes may speed his end, and while chiding the man for his refusal to die may kill him in the prescribed manner. Nor is it only those who through old age are debarred from herding who are thus put to death, but those also who are afflicted with lingering diseases or any bodily infirmity.

71   The rhinoceros

In size the rhinoceros is no smaller than the elephant, but he is lower in stature. He is of the colour of boxwood, and his skin is thinner to the touch. He carries on his nose a horn which curves backwards, nearly as strong and as rigid as iron. When fighting with the elephants, with whom he wages unending war over grazing-grounds, he rips open their bellies with this horn, thus causing their death. But if he cannot manage to reach the elephant's belly, he loses his strength and falls, lacerated by the tusks and trunk of the elephant, from which he differs much in strength and power.

72   The giraffe

In the Trōglodyte country there is an animal called Kamēlo-pardalis by the Greeks, a name derived from the composite nature of the beast. For from the leopard it derives its spotted skin, and from the camel its long neck. It is very thickset and has a very long neck, so long in fact that it can eat the tops of the trees.

73 The monkeys called Sphinx, Kunokephalos, and Kēpos.[14] These monkeys are exported to Alexandria from the Trōglodyte country and from the rest of Aithiopia. The sphinx is like those painted by artists, except that it is covered all over with hair. It has a good disposition, but is full of cunning, and so can learn to do various things with very little teaching.

74 The Kunokephalos is represented in art with a human body of ugly appearance; it has a dog's face and a voice not unlike the squeak of a mouse. But it is an exceedingly fierce animal and cannot be tamed by any method. Its face has a harsh appearance owing to its eyebrows and eyes. Such is the male. The female is peculiar in that its womb is external.

75 The Kēpos has the face of a lion, the body of a panther, and the size of a gazelle. And since it is dappled it has been given the name of Kēpos, that is, garden.

76   The carnivorous bull[15]

Of all the animals that I have mentioned the wild bull is the fiercest and least tameable, because it eats flesh; it is also thicker, heavier, and swifter than the domestic kind, and is of a remarkable red colour. Its mouth extends up to its ears and its eyes are redder than those of the lion. It can move its horns just as it moves its ears, but in a fight it can make them rigid and immovable. The arrangement of its hair is the opposite to that of other living creatures. It approaches even the strongest of beasts, and hunts all others; in particular it does great damage to the domestic herds of the people. It alone is invulnerable by lance or bow, and for this reason nobody has been able to subdue it, though many have tried. But if it falls into a pit or other trap it is soon stifled because of its savage temper. Therefore it is rightly considered by the Trōglodytes that one who is endowed with the courage of the lion, the speed of the horse, and the strength of the wild bull knows not how to yield to the sword.

77   The wild Krokottas

The Krokottas is so called by the Aithiopians, from whose language the name is derived, because it is a mixture of dog and wolf, but much fiercer than either, and exceeding all animals in voracity and power of teeth. For it can break any bones with ease, and having torn its prey in pieces eats it at once. It is not easy to tell how it digests the food in its stomach. But we do not believe those who say that it can imitate the human voice.[16] They say that it calls men by name at night, and that those who go out, as in answer to a man's voice, are attacked by the krokottas and devoured.

78   Of gigantic snakes[17]

It is said that in Aithiopia there are snakes of stupendous size and of many kinds, which all live by what they can kill. The biggest which we ourselves have seen was forty-five feet long. Every snake, even the largest, can be tamed if it is oppressed and weakened by hunger. For Agatharkhidēs bears witness to the fact that he saw snakes which had been placed in baskets for his inspection lose their ferocity while their desire to eat increased and at length, no matter how fierce normally, become so quiet and tame that no animal could be milder or less terrible.

80   Of hot springs

Since there are many things to marvel at, far removed from reality, I will proceed to describe some places which have features worthy of commemoration. First, then, a man who sails down the coast from Arsinoē will see the Hot Springs on his right hand, where the water falls into the sea from a high rock flowing as it were through narrow-mouthed pipes; this water is not sweet, but bitter and brackish. After this, the traveller comes to the Nile[18] which flows from a lake through a channel in soft and spongy ground into a lowlying hollow.

81   Beside the lake, and rising out of a wide plain, is a hill in which there is a mine of red ochre, which, even if there were nothing else remarkable about it, is spread over the top of the hill and blinds those who gaze at it for any length of time. In this part lies the great harbour, first called Muos Hormos and later the Port of Aphroditē. Here also are three islands, two of them covered thickly with olive trees; the third, which is less wooded, is a haunt of the birds called meleagrides.[19]

82   Beyond is a bay called Foul Bay; and when you have sailed past it there appears in the open sea an island called Snake Island, because at one time it was full of all kinds of snakes, though to-day there are none left. The precious stone well-known by the name of topaz is found here. It is transparent, like glass, and is a pleasing sight when set in gold. The inhabitants, who by royal edict are the guardians and collectors of the stones, obtain it in the following way. They wander about at night with mattocks of various sizes, because by daytime the sunlight obscures the stones and they cannot be seen; but at night they can be seen to shine, and when they have

been observed, the miner places over them vessels of such a size as to cover them. When it is day he comes back and digs out the rocks in which the stones lie, handing them over afterwards to the stone-cutters.

83   After this the sea becomes very shallow, being not more than two fathoms in depth. It is also green in colour, not from the nature of the water, but from sea-weed which transmits its colour to the water. Hence there are multitudes of sea-dogs[20] here; and warships and other vessels propelled by oars find this route easy and suitable, for there are no storms here, nor is the surface swept by waves rolling in from the outer sea; moreover it furnishes an incredible supply of fish. In other parts disasters to the elephant ships [of the Ptolemies] bring much misery to the people concerned, for the ships are either dashed on to the rocks by the waves or else they run aground on sandbanks, leaving the sailors no means of escape.

84   The country has been explored as far as the Headland of the Bulls and Ptolemaïs;[21] the further parts do not offer a passage to everyone. The land beyond lies more to the east than to the south. Springs rise in the Psebean Hills[22] which they call mountain torrents. The tract of country which faces the interior is full of elephant, rhinoceros, wild bull, and pig. Round the bay there are many islands, but they produce nothing, though thronged with birds of species as yet unknown. After that the sea becomes deep and navigable. In it are whales so enormous as to strike the beholder with terror; they do not, however, harm sailors unless they happen to get in their way.

NOTES

1   Ptolemy II Philadelphos.
2   He wrote a history of Argolis, though his date is uncertain.

3 Son of Bēlos, and a mythical king of Aithiopia; he was the husband of Kassiopeia.

4 An ancient capital of Persia, north of Persepolis.

5 The Greek name for Africa.

6 Greek κάσας, 'a skin to sit on', 'a saddle'.

7 Pliny mentions three groups of Autei: the first lived in Arabia, somewhere near the Homēritai; the second in Egypt, apparently between Pelusium and Arsinoē; the third, those referred to by Agatharkhidēs, on the Red Sea coast south of Muos Hormos. It would seem that Agatharkhidēs has confused the Arabian Autei with those on the Troglodytic coast in Africa, and thus brought in an erroneous reference to Persian rule. Pliny calls both the second and third groups *Arabes* (*Nat. Hist.* VI, 32 and 33).

8 The Atbara.

9 The 'island' of Meroē is formed by the White or true Nile on the west, the Blue Nile on the south, and the Atbara on the east.

10 Sirius, the Dog Star, rises towards the end of July.

11 Greek βουνιάς, 'turnip'.

12 Locusts can fly only with the wind, not against. While Agatharkhidēs says that smoke stupefies them, Strabō says that the darkness which it produces makes them drop to the ground (XVI. iv. 2). In actual fact, smoke, if thick enough, may drive them away unless they are hungry, though sudden darkness, as when a cloud obscures the sun on a bright day, does make them drop to the ground. A diet of locusts and nothing else would certainly produce emaciation, and it is doubtful if people could exist entirely on them.

13 In the 2nd century B.C. India was still thought by some to be contiguous to Africa. The Hyrcanians lived on the south side of the Caspian Sea.

14 It is uncertain what type of monkey the Sphinx was; the

OED gives 'sphinx-baboon', used in 1607. The Kunokephalos, 'dog-headed', was probably a baboon; and Kēpos, 'garden', is a fancy name instead of the proper word κῆβος, kēbos, a kind of monkey.

15 By wild bull is perhaps meant the buffalo, one of the most savage of African animals, though it is not carnivorous.

16 See note 1 to chapter 50 of the *PME*.

17 Perhaps pythons.

18 The occurrence of 'Nile' for rivers other than the river of Egypt in the geographers suggests that they may have sometimes used it as a general term for any big river, though in some cases they may have believed that branches of the real Nile occurred in several places, or even that some of the rivers so called were the Nile.

19 Guinea-fowl.

20 Sea-dogs: dog-fish or small sharks.

21 Ptolemaïs Thērōn.

22 Even if these were the highlands of Ethiopia (the Lake Psebō of Strabō is supposed to be Lake Tana) they are a long way from Ptolemaïs.

What Agatharkhidēs has to say about the Ikhthuophagoi may be supplemented by a more detailed account of a similar people who lived on the coast of Gedrōsia as described by Nearkhos and included in Arrian's *Indika*, chapter 29:

The people, as their name imports, live upon fish. Few of them, however, are fishermen, and what fish they obtain they owe mostly to the tide at whose reflux they catch them with nets made for this purpose. These nets are generally about 2 stadia long, and are composed of the bark (or fibres) of the palm, which they twine into cord in the same way as the fibres of flax are twined. When the sea recedes, hardly any fish are found among the dry sands, but they abound in the depressions of the surface where the water still remains. The fish are for the most part small, though some are caught of a considerable size, these being taken in the nets. The more delicate kinds they eat raw as soon as they are taken out of the water. The large and coarser kinds they dry in the sun, and when properly dried grind into a sort of meal from which they make bread. This meal is sometimes also used to bake cakes with. The cattle as well as their masters fare on dried fish, for the country has no pastures, and hardly even a blade of grass. In most parts crabs, oysters and mussels add to the means of subsistence.... Certain of their communities inhabit deserts where not a tree grows, and where there are not even wild fruits. Fish is their sole means of subsistence. In some few places, however, they sow with grain some patches of land and eat the produce as a viand of luxury along with the fish which forms the staple of their diet. The better class of the population in building their houses use, instead of wood, the bones of whales stranded on the coast, the broadest bones being employed in the framework of the doors. Poor people, and these are the great majority, construct their dwellings with the backbones of fish. (McCrindle's translation, which forms the second part, pp. 153–224, of his *Commerce and Navigation of the Erythraean Sea.*)

McCrindle adds in a footnote: 'This description of the natives, with that of their mode of living and the country they inhabit, is strictly correct even to the present day.'

Bibliography

ANCIENT

1. *Editions and translations of the* PME *in order of date*

GELENIUS, Sigismundus. *Arriani Periplus Euxini Ponti. Eiusdem Erythraei.* Basel, 1533. [Title in Greek.]

STUCKIUS, Iohannes. *Arriani historici et philosophi Ponti Euxini et Maris Erythraei Periplus.* Geneva, 1577.

BLANCARDUS, Nicolaus. *Arriani . . . Periplus Ponti Euxini, Periplus Maris Erythraei,* etc. Amsterdam, 1683. [Title in Greek.]

HUDSONUS, Johannes. *Geographiae Veteris Scriptores Graeci Minores.* Vol. 1. Oxford, 1698.

FABRICIUS, B. *Arriani Periplus Maris Erythraei.* Dresden, 1849.

MÜLLER, Carolus. *Geographi Graeci Minores.* Paris, 1855. Vol. 1, pp. 257–305.

FABRICIUS, B. *Der Periplus des Erythräischen Meeres.* Leipzig, 1883.

FRISK, Hjalmar. *Le Périple de la Mer Erythrée.* Göteborg, 1927.

Translations

VINCENT, William. *The commerce and navigation of the ancients in the Indian Ocean.* Vol. II. *The Periplus of the Erythraean Sea.* London, 1807.

McCRINDLE, J. W. *The commerce and navigation of the Erythraean Sea.* Bombay, 1879. (Reprinted 1973.)

SCHOFF, W. H. *The Periplus of the Erythraean Sea.* New York, 1912.

2. *Agatharkhidēs*

On the Erythraean Sea. Text in Hudson, *above*, vol. I.

On the Erythraean Sea. Text in Müller, *above*, vol. I.

On the Erythraean Sea. Text in Phōtios, *below*.

3. *Other classical authorities*

AGATHĒMEROS—PSEUDO-AGATHĒMEROS. Text in Müller, *above,* vol. II.

ANTONINE ITINERARY. G. Parthey et M. Pinder, *Itinerarium Antonini Augusti*. Berlin, 1858. The page references to Wesseling mean the edition by P. Wesseling (*Vetera Romanorum Itineraria*, Amsterdam, 1735), whose pagination Parthey and Pinder used, without otherwise citing his book.

DITTENBERGER, W. *Orientis Graeci inscriptiones selectae: Supplementum sylloges inscriptionum Graecarum.* Vol. I, Leipzig, 1903.

HĒRODOTOS. Text: ed. K. Hude, Oxford, 1927. Trans.: Rawlinson, ed. 4, London, 1880.

KOSMAS INDIKOPLEUSTĒS. Text: ed. E. O. Winstedt, Cambridge, 1909. Trans.: J. W. McCrindle, *The Christian Topography of Cosmas*, Hakluyt Soc., 1897.

PHILOSTORGIOS. Text in Reading's edition of Theodoret and Euagrios, Cambridge, 1720.

PHŌTIOS. *Bibliotheca.* Berlin, 1824, 5.

PLINY. *Naturalis Historia.* Valpy, London, 1826. (Delphin edition.)

PTOLEMY. C. Müller, *Claudii Ptolemaei Geographia.* Paris, 1883–1901.

STRABŌ. Text by Siebenkees and Tzschucke, Leipzig, 1811; text and trans. by H. L. Jones, Loeb Classical Library, 1917–32.

MODERN

BECKINGHAM, C. F. and G. W. B. HUNTINGFORD, *The Prester John of the Indies . . . by Father Francisco Alvares* (Hakluyt Society, Cambridge, 1961).

BECKINGHAM, C. F. and G. W. B. HUNTINGFORD, *Some Records of Ethiopia, 1593–1646* (Hakluyt Society, London, 1954).

BENT, J. T., *The Sacred City of the Ethiopians* (London, 1893).

BIVAR, A. D. H., 'The sequence of Menander's drachmae', *J.R.A.S.* (1970).

BLOCH, J., 'Sur quelques transcriptions de noms indiens dans le Périple de la Mer Erythrée', in *Mélanges d'Indianisme offerts ... à M. Sylvain Lévi* (Paris, 1911).

BURTON, R. F., *First Footsteps in East Africa* (London, 1856).

CALDWELL, R., *A Comparative Grammar of the Dravidian or South Indian family of languages*, 2nd ed. (London, 1875).

CHITTICK, N., 'An archaeological reconnaissance of the south Somali coast', *Azania*, IV (1969).

CHRISTIE, A., 'An obscure passage from the *Periplus*', *B.S.O.A.S.*, XIX (1957).

COOLEY, W. D., *Claudius Ptolemy and the Nile* (London, 1854).

COTTRELL, L., *Concise encyclopaedia of archaeology* (London, 1970).

CRAWFORD, O. G. S., *Ethiopian Itineraries, circa 1400–1524* (Hakluyt Society, Cambridge, 1958).

CRAWFORD, O. G. S., 'Some medieval theories about the Nile', *Geographical Journal* CXIV (1949).

DAINELLI, G. and O. MARINELLI, 'Le prime notizie sulle rovine di Cohaito', *Boll. Soc. Afric.*, XXVII (1908).

DAMES, M. Longworth, *The Book of Duarte Barbosa* (Hakluyt Society, London, 1918).

DAVIES, O., Article 21 in *Man* (February, 1929).

DRAKE-BROCKMAN, R. E., *British Somaliland* (London, 1912).

EUTING, J., *Nabatäische Inschriften aus Arabien* (Berlin, 1885).

FREEMAN-GRENVILLE, G. S. P., *The medieval history of the coast of Tanganyika* (London, 1962).

GIBB, H. A. R., *The Travels of Ibn Battuta*, vol. 2 (Hakluyt Society, Cambridge, 1962).

GLASER, E., *Skizze der Geschichte und Geographie Arabiens* (Berlin, 1890).

GROTTANELLI, V. L., *Pescatori dell' Oceano Indiano* (Roma, 1955).

Guida dell' Africa Orientale Italiana (Milano, 1938).

GUILLAIN, C., *Documents sur l'histoire, la géographie et le commerce de l'Afrique orientale* (Paris, 1856).

HANSMAN, J., 'Charax and the Karkheh', *Iranica antiqua* VII (1967).

HAYWOOD, C. W., 'The Bajun Islands and Birakau', *Geographical Journal* LXXXV (1935).

Hobson-Jobson. See YULE, H., and A. C. BURNELL.

HOLLIS, A. C., *The Nandi* (Oxford, 1909).

HORNELL, J., 'The origins and ethnological significance of Indian boat designs', *Memoirs of the Asiatic Society of Bengal*, VIII (1920).

HUNTINGFORD, G. W. B., *The Nandi of Kenya* (London, 1953).

HUNTINGFORD, G. W. B., *The Southern Nilo-Hamites* (London, 1953).

HUNTINGFORD, G. W. B., 'Three notes on early Ethiopian geography', *Folia Orientalia*, XV (1974).

JOHNSTON, H. H., *The opening up of Africa* (London, 1911).

KAMMERER, A., *Essai sur l'histoire antique d' Abyssinie* (Paris, 1926).

KING, C. W., *The Natural History of Precious Stones* (London, 1867).

LE STRANGE, G., *Lands of the Eastern Caliphate* (Cambridge, 1930).

LIDDELL, H. G. and R. SCOTT, *Greek-English Lexicon* (Oxford, 1935).

MACDOWALL, D. W., 'The early western satraps and the date of the Periplus', *Num. Chron.*, 7 ser. IV (1964).

MACDOWALL, D. W. and N. G. WILSON, 'The references to the Kuṣāṇas in the Periplus and further numismatic evidence for its date', *Num. Chron.*, 7 ser. X (1970).

MADAN, A. C., *Swahili-English Dictionary* (Oxford, 1903).

MASPERO, G., *The Dawn of Civilization* (London, 1910).

MEREDITH, D., 'Annius Plocamus: two inscriptions from the Berenice road', *J. Roman Stud.*, XLIII (1953).

MILLER, J. Innes, *The Spice Trade of the Roman Empire* (Oxford, 1969).

MONFREID, H. de, *Les Secrets de la Mer Rouge* (Paris [1931]).

OLIVER, R., and MATHEW, G., (edd.) *History of East Africa*, vol. I (Oxford, 1963).

Paulys Real-Encyclopädie der classischen Altertumswissenschaft . . . Neue Bearbeitung (Stuttgart, 1893–).

PIRENNE, J., 'Le Royaume sud-arabe de Qatabân et sa datation', *Bibliothèque du Muséon*, XLVIII (1961).

RÉVOIL, G., *La Vallée du Darror* (Paris, 1882).

SALT, H., *A Voyage to Abyssinia and travels into the interior of that country* (London, 1814).

SCHWANBECK, E. A., 'Ueber den Periplus des Erythräischen Meeres', *Rheinisches Museum*, Neue Folge VII (1850).

SLEEN, W. G., van der, 'Ancient glass beads', *Journal of the Royal Anthropological Institute*, 88 (1958).

SMITH, V. A., *The early history of India*, 4th edition (Oxford, 1924).

SMITH, W., (ed.) *Dictionary of Greek and Roman Biography*, 3 vols (London, 1844–9).

SMITH, W., (ed.) *Dictionary of Greek and Roman Geography*, 2 vols (London, 1873–8).

STARCKY, J., 'Un contrat nabatéen sur papyrus', *Revue Biblique*, 1951.

STEERE, E., *Handbook of the Swahili language* (London, 1884).

TAYLOR, W. E., *African Aphorisms; or Saws from Swahili-land* (London, 1891).

THOMSON, J. O., *A History of Ancient Geography* (Cambridge, 1948).

VILLIERS, A., *Sons of Sinbad* (London, 1940).

WAINWRIGHT, G. A., 'Obsidian', *Ancient Egypt* (Sept. 1927).

WARMINGTON, E. H., *The Commerce between the Roman Empire and India* (London, 1928).

BIBLIOGRAPHY

Wellsted, J. R., *Travels in Arabia* (London, 1838).

Wheeler, R. E. Mortimer, *Rome beyond the Imperial Frontiers* (London, 1954).

Yule, H., and A. C. Burnell, *Hobson-Jobson*, new ed. (London, 1903).

MAPS

1/500,000 (7.89 miles to 1 inch)

AFRICA

GSGS. sheets ND 372, ND 373, ND 384, NC 381, NC 382, NC 383, NC 391, NC 392, NC 395, NB 391, NB 394, NA 383, NA 385, SA 381, SA 376, SB 372, SB 375.

1/1,000,000 (15.78 miles to 1 inch)
International World Map

AFRICA

NE 37	Port Sudan	NA 38	Mogadiscio
NC 38	Harar	SA 37–38	Mombasa
NC 39	Alula	SB	Dar es salaam
NB 39	Obbia		

ARABIA

ND 38	Aden	NE 40	Salala
ND 39	Socotra	NF 40	Muscat-Masira

PERSIA

NG 40   Bandar Abbas

INDIA

NG 41	Makrān	NC 43	Coimbatore
NG 42	Sind	NC 44	Madura
NF 42	Kāthiāwār	ND 44	Madras
NF 43	Ahmadabad	NE 44	Hyderabad
NE 43	Bombay	NE 45	Puri
DN 43	Bangalore	NF 45	Calcutta

Indian Government Tourist Maps [IGTM]
1959. 1/2,534,400 (40 miles to 1 inch)

SW region: [Rann of Kutch to Goa.]
S region: [Goa, Comorin, Madras.]
SE region: [Madras–Masulipatam.]
E region: [Ganges.]

Index of Places, Tribes, and Persons Named in the Text

References to chapter numbers in the *Periplus* are given first it italics, followed by page numbers in roman. Names are transliterated from the Greek spelling used in the text.

Abēria (Gujarat), *41*, 43, 85, **109**, 153
Adouli, *3*, *4*, *17*, *24*, 20, 30, 34, 60, 64, 81, 83, **87-9**, 90, 123, 124, 148-50, 163, 170
Agriophagoi, *2*, 19, 59, 143
Aigialos mikros kai megas (Greater and Lesser Strand), *15*, *51*, 29, 49, 94
Aigidiōn island, *53*, 50, 70, 76, **115**
Akabarou, *52*, 49, 76, 81, 85, **113**, 155
Akannai, *11*, 26, 83, 93, 124, 170
Alalaiou islands, *4*, 21, 76, **90**
Alexandreia (Alexandria in Egypt), *26*, 7, 35, 127, 191
Alexandros (Alexander the Great), *41*, *47*, 44, 46, 47, 68, 69, 106, 112
Apokopa mikra kai megala (Lesser and Greater Bluffs), *15*, 29, 94
Apollodotos, *47*, 47, 154
Apologou (Al-Ubulla), *35*, 40, 76, 81, **105**, 152
Arakhousioi (usually Arakhōsioi), *47*, 46, 85, 154
Aratrioi, *47*, 46, 85
Argalou (Uraiyur), *59*, 53, 76, 85, **118**, 156
Ariakē, *6*, *14*, *41*, *54*, 8, 22, 28, 43, 50, 68, 85, **109**, 112, 122, 153
Arōmatōn emporion kai akrōtērion (Mart and Cape of Spices; Olok,

Gardafui), *12*, *30*, *57*, 4, 11, 25 26, 37, 53, 58, 66, 81, 83, 93, 124, 173-4
Asabōn (Musandam), *35*, 39, **105**, 152
Asikhōnos, *33*, 38, **104**
Astakapra (Hathab), *41*, *43*, 44, **110**
Aualitēs (Zeyla), *7*, *8*, *25*, 22, 23, 34, 58, 61, 83, **90**, 124, 144, 146
Ausineitic coast, *15*, 29, 97, 148
Azania, *15*, *16*, *18*, *31*, *61*, 4, 29-31, 37, 54, 62, 83, 95, 99, 119

Baiōnēs (Peram), *42*, 44, **110**
Bakarē (Vaikkarai), *55*, *58*, 51, 53, 85, **116-18**, 156
Baktrianoi (Bactrians), *47*, *64*, 46, 56, 69
Balita, *58*, 53, **118**
Barakē, *40*, *41*, *55*, 43, 51, 85, **109**
Barbaria, *5*, *25*, 21, 34, 83, 99
Barbarikē, Barbarikon, *38*, *39*, 41, 44, 59, 84, **108**, 125, 164
Barbaroi, *2*, *4*, *7*, *17*, 19, 20, 23, 30, 59, 129-30, 143, 146, 147
Bargusoi, *62*, 55, 156
Barugaza (Broach), *14*, *21*, *27*, *31*, *36*, *40-52*, *56*, *57*, *64*, 11, 28, 32, 35, 38, 40, 43-51, 53, 56, 85-7, **110-12**, 122, 123, 125, 138, 142, 154, 155, 164

Bernikē, *1*, *2*, *18*, *19*, *21*, 5, 19, 31, 32, *58*, 64, 65, 80, 81, 83, **86–7**, 168

Boukephalos Alexandreia, *47*, 46, 68, **112–13**

Buzantion (Vijayadurg), *53*, 50, 85, **114**, 155

Dakhinabadēs (Deccan), *50*, *51*, 49, 85, **113**, 155

Dēsarēnē, *62*, 55, **120**, 123, 156

Didōrou nēsos 4, 20, 76, **89**

Diodōrou nēsos (Perim), *25*, 34, 76, 84, **102**

Diōrukhos (the Channel, i.e. the Siyu Channel), *15*, 29

Dioskouridou nēsos (Socotra), *30*, *31*, 37, 76, 84, **103**, 123, 124, 151

Diospolis (Diopolis), *6*, *7*, 22, 23, 61, 136, 138

Eirinon (Rann of Kutch), *40*, 42, 43, 85, **108–9**

Eleazos (Ili-azz), *27*, 9, 35, 103, 151, 152

Elephas, Cape (Ras Filuk), *11*, 26, 27, 93, 169

Erannoboas, *53*, 50, 83, 85, **114–15**

Eruthra thalassa (Erythraean Sea). See General Index

Eudaimōn Arabia (Aden), *26*, *27*, *57*, 8–10, 34, 35, 52, 58, 84, **102**, 151

Euphratēs, river, *35*, 40

Gandaraoi (Gandharans), *47*, 46, 85, 154

Gangēs, city, *63*, 55, 86, **120**, 125, 156

Gangēs, river, *47*, *50*, *60*, *63*, *64*, 46, 49, 54–6, 69, 86, **120**, 124, 156

Gedrōsians, Bay of the, *37*, 40, **106**, 153

Hērōnē, *43*, 44, **112**

Hippalos, *57*, 52, 70–1

Hippioprosōpoi, *62*, 55, 156

Homēritai (Himyarites), *23*, 1, 33, 59, 100, 148, 151

Hōraia, *37*, 41, 84, **108**, 125, 153

Ikhthuophagoi, *2*, *4*, *20*, *27*, *33*, 19, 21, 31, 35, 39, 59, 143, 150, 169, **180–4**, **196–7**

Kaineitōn nēsos, *53*, 50, 76, **115**

Kaisar (Caesar), *26*, 8, 10, 35

Kalaiou islands, *34*, *35*, 39, **104**

Kalliena (Kalyana), *52*, *53*, 8, 10, 49, 50, 81, **114**, 155

Kalon, mount, *35*, 39, **104–5**

Kamara (Kaviripaddinam), *60*, 54, 74, **118**, 156

Kammōni, *43*, 44, **112**

Kanē (Hisn Ghurab), *27*, *29*, *32*, *33*, *36*, *57*, 35, 36, 38–40, 52, 53, 66, 84, **102–3**, 124, 142

Kanraïtai, *20*, 32, 150

Kaspia thalassa (Caspian Sea), *64*, 56, 75

Katakekaumenē nēsos (Burnt island), *20*, 32, **100**

Kēprobotos, *54*, 50, 155

Kharibaēl, *23*, *26*, *31*, 33, 34, 37, 100, 151

Khersonēsos, *53*, 50

Kholaibos, *22*, 32, 100, 102, 148, 150

Khrusē, *56*, *60*, *63*, 52, 54, 55, 86, **120**, 123, 156

Kirradai, *62*, 55, 74, 156

Kolkhoi (Korkai), *59*, 53, 85, **118**, 156

Koloē (Qohayto), *4*, 20, **89–90**, 149

Komar, Komarei (Cape Comorin, Kanya Kumari), *58*, *59*, 53, 58, 73, 85, **118**

Kottanarikē, *56*, 156

Kuēneion (Sennar), *4*, 20, 83, **90**, 149

Lamnaios, river (Narbada), *42*, 44, 85, **110**, 112

Leukē Kōmē (Yanbu' al-bahr), *19*, 8, 31, 58, 83, 84, **100**, 150

Leukē nēsos (White island), *53*, 50, **115**

Libanōtophoros (Hadramaut), *27*, *29*, *31*, 36, 37, 151, 152

Limurikē (Tamil country), *31*, *32*, *47*, *51*, *53*, *56*, *60*, *64*, 38, 46, 49, 50, 52–4, 56, 85, 110, 113, **116**, 122–5, 155, 164

Maiōtis, lake, *64*, 56, 75

Maïs, river, (Mahi), *42*, 44, **110**

Malaō (Berbera), *8*, *9*, 23–5, 58, 59, 83, **90**, **92**, 124, 134, 146, 162, 163

Malikhas, king, *19*, 8–10, 31, 150

Manbanos (Nahapāna), king, *41*, 8, 10, 43, 69, 85, 112, 153–5

Mandagora (Bankot), *53*, 50, 83, 85, **114**, 155

Mapharitis, Mopharitis (Ma'afir), *16*, *22*, *31*, 30, 32, 37, 148, 150

Masalia (Masulipatam), *62*, 54, 86, **119**, 131, 156, 162

Melizeigara (Jaigarh), *53*, 50, 83, 85, **114**, 155

Menander, king, *47*, 47, 154

Menouthias, island, *15*, 11, 29, 84, **97–9**, 141 n.1, 158, 159, 174

Meroē, *2*, 19, 59, 87, 93, 149, 184

Mētropolis Axōmitē (Aksum), *4*, 20, 60, 89, **90**, 148–50

Minnagar, Minnagara (Mandasor), *38*, *41*, 41, 44, 84, 108, **110**, 149

Mopharitis. *See* Mapharitis above

Moskha (Salala), *32*, *33*, 38, 58, 81, 84, **104**, 124, 152

Moskhophagoi, *2*, *3*, *5*, 19, 21, 59, 143

Mosullon, *10*, *11*, 11, 24, 26, 83, **92**, 93, 124, 134

Moundou, *9*, *10*, 24, 26, 76, 83, **92**, 124, 134, 146

Mouza (Maushij), *7*, *16*, *21*, *24*, *28*, *31*, 23, 30, 32–4, 36, 38, 58, 65, 72, 81, 84, **100**, 122, 124, 148, 163

Mouziris (Cranganore), *53*, *54*, 50, 72, 75, 85, **116**

Muos Hormos, *1*, *19*, 5, 19, 31, 58, 77, 80, 81, 83, **86**, 168, 193

Nabataioi (Nabataeans), *19*, 8–10, 31, 100, 129, 150

Naoura (Cannanore), *53*, 50, 85, **115**

Neiloptolemaiou, *11*, 26, **92–3**, 170

Neilos (Nile), *4*, *63*, 5, 20, 55, 78–80, 93, 169, 173–6, 193, 196

Nelkunda (Kottayam), *53*, *54*, *55*, 50, 51, 71, 85, **116**

Nikōnos dromos (Nikōn's course), *15*, 3, 29, **95**

Okēlis (Sheikh Sa'id), *7*, *25*, *26*, 23, 34, 58, 61, 65, 72, 75, 84, **102**, 116, 124, 128, 134

Omana (Oman) (in Arabia), *32*, 38, 104, **106**, 122, 142, 152

Omana, Ommana (in Persis), *27*, *36*, 35, 40, 84, **106**, 152

Opōnē, *12*, *13*, *15*, 26, 28, 29, 62, 83, **94**, 124, 134, 142, 152

Oreinē, *4*, 20, **89**

Orneōn nēsos (Birds' island), *27*, 35, 102

Ozēnē, (Ujjain), *48*, 47, 70, 85, **113**, 154

Paithana (Paithan), *51*, 49, 70, 85, **113**, 155

Palaipatmai (Dabhol), *53*, 50, 83, 85, **114**, 155

Palaisimoundou (Ceylon, Sri Lanka), *61*, 54, 64, 74, 86, **119**, 123, 156

Pandion (Pāndya), *54*, *58*, *59*, 11, 50, 53, 71, 85, 116, 118, 156

Papikē, *41*, *43*, 44, **110**

Paralia, *58*, 53

Parsidōn khōra (country of the Persians), *37*, 40, 84, 106

Parthoi (Parthians), *38*, 41, 153

Pasinou Kharax, *35*, 40, **105–6**

Persikos kolpos (Persian Gulf), *35*, 39, 40

Persis (Persia), *27, 33, 36, 38,* 35, 39, 40, 152

Petra, *19,* 8–10, 31, 100, 150

Podoukē (Arikamedu), *60,* 54, 58, 74, 85, **119**

Poklaïs. *See* Proklaïs below

Pontos, *64,* 56, 75

Proklaïs (Charsadda), *47, 48,* 7, 46, 47, 68, 69, 75, 85, **112**, 154

Ptolemaïs tōn thērōn (Ptolemaïs of the Huntings), *3, 4,* 20, 83, **87**, 163, 168, 172, 194

Puralaōn islands, *15,* 29, 76, 95, **97**

Purron oros (Red Mountain), *58,* 53, **118**

Rhambakia, *37,* 41, **108**, 153

Rhapta, *16,* 11, 30, 63, 64, 84, **99–100**, 123, 124, 146–9, 158, 163, 173, 174

Sabaïtai (Sabaeans), *23,* 33, 100, 127, 151

Sakhalitēs, *29, 32,* 36, 38, 84, **103**, 152

Sandanēs, *52,* 8, 10, 50, 155

Saphar, *23,* 33, 84, 100, 149, 151

Saraganēs (Gautamīputra Śrī Śatakarṇī), *52,* 8, 10, 50, 154, 155

Sarapidos nēsos (Island of Sarapis, Masira), *33,* 39, **104**

Sarapiōnos dromos (Sarapiōn's course), *15,* 3, 29, **95**, 174

Saubatha (Shabwa), *27,* 35, 84, **102–3**, 149, 151

Sauē, *22,* 32, 84, **100**, 148, 150

Semirameōs hupsēlon (Height of Semiramis), *35,* 40, **105**

Sēmulla (Chaul), *53,* 50, 83, 85, **114**, 155

Sēsatai, *65,* 56, 75, 156

Sēsekreienai islands, *53,* 50, **115**

Sinthos, river, (Indus), *38, 40,* 41, 42, 67, 84, **108**, 153

Skuthia (Scythia), *27, 38, 41, 48, 57,* 35, 41, 43, 47, 53, 67, 84, **108**, 136, 153, 164

Sōpatma, *60,* 54, 58, 74, 86, **119**

Souppara (Sopara), *52,* 49, 83, **113**, 155

Suagros (Ras Fartak), *30, 32,* 37, 38, 58, 72, 84, **103**

Surastrēnē (Kathiawar), *41, 44,* 43, 45, 85, **109**, 110, 153

Tabai *12, 13,* 11, 28, 83, **94**

Tagara (Ter), *51,* 49, 70, 85, **113**, 155

Tapatēgē, *11,* 26, 93

Taprobanē. *See* Palaisimoundou above

This, Thina (China), *64, 65,* 56, 86, **120**, 124, 125, 156

Toparon, *53,* 50, 83, 85, **114–15**

Troullas, *27,* 35, 102

Tundis (Tanor), *53, 54,* 50, 71, 75, 85, **116**

Zēnobios islands (Kuria Muria), *33,* 39, **104**

Zōskalēs, *5,* 21, 147–9

Index of Greek Words

ἀγκυροβόλιον, 58
ἄγναφα, 129
ἀκριβὴς, 60
ἁπλοῦς, 130

βασιλεύειν, 60
βουνιάς, 184, 195
βριάριον, 73

γράαι, γραῖαι, 67
γυργάθοις, 62

ἑκατοντάρχης, 64
ἐλαφρὰς, 67–8
ἐμπόρια, 81–2
ἐξαρτισμοῖς, 65

θήρα 172

κάσας, 195
κοινή, 7
κροκόττας, 70

κυνήγιον 172

λιμὴν, 58

μέλαν ἰνδικὸν, 67

ναύπλιος, 64
νόθος, 60
νῶτα, 66

ὅρμος, 58

παραλήπτης, 64

στάδιον, 58–9
σκοτουλᾶτος, 130
σχεδία, 61

τισηβαρικὴ, 59

φαλάγγων, 66
φρούριον, 73

Index of Trade-Goods Mentioned in the Text

This index is arranged under the Greek words used in the text for the commodities named; cross-references under the English equivalents follow. References to chapter numbers in the *Periplus* are given first, followed by page numbers in roman.

ἀβόλλαι, cloaks, *6*, *24*, 21, 33, 60

ἀδάμας, diamond, *56*, 52

ἀλόη, aloes, *28*, 36, 122, 124

ἀνδριάντες, statues, *28*, 36

ἀργυροῦς, silver, *8*, 24, 122. See also χρῆμα below.

silver money, *49*, 48

ἀργυρώματα, silver ware, *6*, *24*, *28*, *39*, *49*, 22, 33, 36, 42, 48

σκεύη ἀργυρᾶ, objects of silver, *10*, 24

ἀρσενικόν, yellow orpiment, *56*, 51

ἄρωμα, spices in general, *7*, *10*, *12*, *13*, *23*, *25*, 28, 61, 122, 124, 136, 141, 150

ἀσύφη, cinnamon, *12*, 28, 124. See also γιζειρ, δουακα, κασία, μαγλα and μοτὼ below.

βδέλλα, fragrant gum, *37*, *39*, *48*, *49*, 41, 42, 47, 48, 125, **132**. See also εὐωδία and μοκροτου below.

βούτυρον, ghi, *14*, *41*, 28, 43, 122, 133, 136

γαυνάκαι, unlined garments, *6*, 22, **130–1**

γιζειρ, fine cinnamon, *12*, 28, 124, 133. See also ἀσύφη above, and κασία, μαγλα and μοτω below.

δέρματα σιρικὰ, Chinese skins, *39*, *42*, 122

δηνάριον, money, *6*, *8*, *49*, 22, 24, 48. See also 122 and χρῆμα below.

δικρόσσια, fringed mantles, *6*, 21

δοκοί, beams, *36*, 40

δουακα, cinnamon, *8*, 24, 124, 133. See also ἀσύφη and γιζειρ above, κασία, μαγλα and μοτὼ below.

δουλικά, slaves, *13*, 28. See also 61, 142 and σώματα below.

ἔλαιον, oil, *32*, 38, 136

ἔλαιον σησάμινον, sesame oil, *14*, *41*, 28, 43, 122, **135–6**

ἔλεφας, ivory, *3*, *4*, *6*, *10*, *16*, *17*, *49*, *56*, *62*, 20–23, 25, 30, 48, 52, 55, 122, 123, 141

ἔριον, raw silk, *64*, 56

εὐωδία, fragrant gums in general, *10*, 25, 122, 124, 133, 141

ζῶναι, sashes, *49*, 48

ζῶναι σκιωταὶ, striped sashes, *24*, 33

ἡμίονοι, mules, *24*, 33

ἱμάτια βαρβαρικὰ ἄγναφα, unfulled Barbaric cloth, *6*, 21

210

ἱμάτια βαρβαρικὰ σύμμικτα, miscellaneous Barbaric cloth, 7, 23
ἱματίων ἀβόλλαι, cloth cloaks, 6, 22
ἱματισμός, clothing, 24, 28, 36, 39, 49, 56, 33, 34, 36, 40, 42, 48, 51, 122, 130
ἵπποι, horses, 24, 28, 33, 36

κάγκαμον, cancamum, medicinal product, 8, 24, 124, 129, 133–4
καλλεανὸς λίθος, turquoise, 39, 42, 140
κάρπασος, flax cloth, 41, 43, 68
κασία, casia (cinnamon), 8, 10, 12, 13, 24, 28, 122, 124, 127–8, 134. See also 141, 169 and ἀσυφη and δουακα above, and μαγλα and μοτώ below.
κασσίτερος, tin, 7, 28, 49, 56, 23, 36, 47, 51, 122
κέρατα, sail-yards, 36, 40, 139
κιννάβαρι ἰνδικόν, cinnabar, 30, 37, 122, 124, 132
κοράλλιον, coral, 28, 39, 49, 56, 36, 42, 47, 51
κόστος, a spice, 39, 48, 49, 42, 47, 48, 125
κρόκος, saffron, 24, 33, 137
κύπερος, aromatic plant, 24, 33, 136

λάκκος, coloured lac, 6, 22, 136
λέντια, linen, 6, 21, 131
λίβανος, frankincense, incense, 12, 27, 28, 29, 30, 32, 36, 39, 28, 35, 36, 37, 40, 42, 122, 126–7, 133, 141, 142, 151, 169
λίβανος περατικός, incense from beyond the Straits of Bab al-Mandab, 8, 10, 11, 24, 26
λίβανος σαχαλιτικός, incense from South Arabia, 32, 38, 124
λιθιά διαφανής, precious stones, 56, 61, 52, 54, 122
λιθίας ὑαλῆς, glassware, 6, 7, 17, 21, 23, 30
λόγχη, spears, 17, 30
λύγδος, marble, 24, 34, 141

λύκιον, medicinal product, 39, 49, 42, 48, 125, 134
λώδικες, blankets, 24, 33
μαγλα, cinnamon, 12, 28, 124. See also ἀσυφη, δουακα, and κασιά above and μοτώ below.
μαδαράτε. See Boats, sewn, in General Index.
μάκειρ, macir, medicinal product, 8, 24, 124, 126, 134
μαλάβαθρον, malabathrum, aromatic leaf, 56, 63, 65, 51, 52, 55, 56–7, 122, 125, 134–5, 157
μαργαρίτης, pearls, 56, 52. See also πινικόν below.
μαχαίρια, μάχαιραι, swords, 6, 17, 22, 30
μέλαν ἰνδικόν, Indian ink (indigo?), 39, 42, 122
μελιέφθα χαλκά, soft copper, 6, 8, 21, 24, 138
μελίλωτον, clover, 49, 48, 140
μοκροτου, fragrant gum, 9, 10, 24, 25, 133. See also βδέλλα and ευωδία above.
μολόχινα, mallow cloth, 6, 48, 49, 51, 22, 47–9, 130
μόλυβος, μόλιβος, lead, 49, 56, 47, 51
μοναχή, Indian broadcloth, 6, 14, 22, 29
μορρίνη, μουρρίνη, murrhine ware, 48, 47, 122, 138–9
μοτώ, cinnamon, 12, 13, 28, 124, 135. See also ἀσυφη, δουακα, κασία, and μαγλα above.
μουσικά, musicians, 47, 48, 141
μύρον, perfume, 24, 49, 33, 48

ναργίλιος, coconut, 17, 31, 132
νάρδος, spikenard, 39, 48, 49, 56, 63, 42, 47, 48, 52, 55, 122, 125, 136
νῆμα σιρικὸν, Chinese silk yarn, 39, 49, 64, 42, 48, 56

ξύλον σαντάλινον, sandalwood, 36, 40, 139

ὀθόνιον, Indian cotton cloth, 24, 32, 39, 33, 38, 42, 122, 129

ὀθόνιον ἰνδικὸν — μοναχὴ καὶ σαγματογῆναι, 6, 14, 31, 22, 29, 38

ὀθόνιον μοναχή, 6, 14, 22, 29

ὀθόνιον παντοῖον, assorted Indian cloth, 49, 48

ὀθόνιον σηρικὸν, silk, 49, 56, 64, 48, 52, 56, 122

ὀθόνιον χυδαῖον, common cloth, 41, 48, 51, 43, 47, 49

οἶνος, wine, 6, 7, 17, 24, 28, 37, 39, 49, 56, 22, 23, 30, 33, 36, 41, 42, 47, 48, 51, 60, 122, 123, 189

ὀνυχίνη λιθία, onyx, 48, 49, 51, 47–9

ὀπήτια, awls, 17, 30

ὄρυζα, rice, 14, 31, 37, 41, 28, 38, 41, 43, 122

παρθένοι, girls, 49, 48

πελύκια, axes, 6, 17, 22, 30

πέπερι, πίπερι, pepper, 49, 56, 48, 51, 52, 71, 125, 135, 156

περιζώματα, belts, 6, 14, 22, 29

πινικόν, pearls, 35, 36, 59, 61, 63, 39, 40, 53, 54, 140, 142. See also μαργαρίτης above.

πλοιάρια ῥαπτὰ. See Boats, sewn, in General Index.

πολύμιτα, brocades, 39, 49, 56, 42, 48, 51

πορφύρα, purple cloth, purple dye, 24, 36, 33, 40, 122

ποτήρια, cups, 6, 8, 22, 24

πυρός, corn, 28, 36, 136. See also σῖτος below.

ῥινόκερως, rhinoceros horn, 6, 17, 22, 31, 122, 124, 137

σαγματογῆναι. See under ὀθόνιον above.

σάγοι, cloaks (Arsinoitic), 8, 23, 129

σάκχαρι, sugar cane, 14, 29, 122, 126, 137

σανδαράκη, red orpiment, 49, 56, 48, 51

σάπφειρος, lapis lazuli, 39, 42

σίδηρος, iron, 6, 8, 21, 22, 24, 122

σινδόνες, σινδόναι, muslins, 6, 61, 62, 22, 54–5, 131

σινδόνες ἀργαρίτιδες, from Argalou, 59, 53

σινδόνες γαγγιτικαὶ, from the Gangetic region, 63, 55

σινδόνες ἰνδικαὶ, Indian, 48, 47

σινδόνων παντοῖα, assorted, 51, 49

σῖτος, corn, wheat, 7, 14, 17, 24, 31, 32, 36, 37, 41, 56, 23, 28, 30, 33, 38, 41, 43, 52, 122, 132, 136. See also πυρός above.

σκέπαρνα, adzes, 6, 22

σμύρνα, myrrh, 7, 8, 10, 24, 49, 23–5, 34, 48, 124, 125, 127, 135, 169

στακτή, oil of myrrh, 24, 34, 124, 136

στίμι, antimony, 49, 56, 48, 51, 140

στολαὶ ἀρσινοϊτικαὶ, Arsinoitic robes, 6, 21

στόμωμα, steel, 6, 22

στύραξ, storax, 28, 39, 49, 36, 42, 48, 125, 137

σώματα, slaves, 8, 31, 36, 24, 38, 40. See also δουλικά above.

ὑάκινθος, sapphire, 56, 52

ὑαλᾶ σκεύη, glassware, 39, 42, 122. See also λιθίας ὑαλῆς above.

ὑέλος ἀργὴ, crude glass, 49, 56, 48, 51

φάλαγγες ἐβενίνοι, ebony sticks, 36, 40

φάλαγγες σησάμινοι, shisham beams, 36, 40, 137

φοῖνιξ, dates, 36, 37, 40, 41, 133

χαλκός, copper, 28, 36, 49, 56, 36, 40, 47, 51

χαλκουργήματα, copper ware, 24, 34
χελώνη, χελωνάρια, tortoiseshell, 3, 4,
  6, 7, 10, 13, 15, 16, 17, 30, 31, 33,
  56, 61, 63, 20, 22, 23, 25, 28–31,
  37–9, 52, 54, 55, 122, 123, **125–6**,
  141
χιτῶνες, tunics, 8, 23
χρῆμα, money, 24, 28, 39, 56, 33, 36,
  42, 51. See also δηνάριον above.

χρυσόλιθον, topaz?, 39, 49, 56, 42, 47,
  51, 139
χρυσός, gold, 8, 36, 63, 24, 40, 55, 122
  gold money, 49, 48
χρυσώματα, gold articles, 6, 24, 22, 33
χυλὸς ὄμφακος, unripe olives, 7, 23,
  122, 137

ὠρόχαλκος, a copper alloy, 6, 21, **139**

Adzes, σκέπαρνα
Agate, μορρίνη, μουρρίνη
Aloes, ἀλόη
Antimony, στῖμι
Awls, ὀπήτια
Axes, πελύκια

Beams, δοκοί
Belts, περιζώματα
Blankets, λώδικες
Boats, sewn, μαδαράτε, πλοιάρια
  ῥαπτὰ
Brocades, πολύμιτα

Casia, κασία
Cinnabar, κιννάβαρι ἰνδικὸν
Cinnamon, ἀσυφη, δουακα, γιζειρ,
  μαγλα, μοτω
Cloaks, ἀβόλλαι
Cloth, ὀθόνιον
Clothing, ἱματισμός
Clover, μελίλωτον
Coconut, ναργίλιος
Copper, χαλκός
Copper, soft, μελιέφθα χαλκὰ
Copper alloy, ὠρόχαλκος
Coral, κοράλλιον
Corn, πυρός, σῖτος
Cups, ποτήρια

Dates, φοῖνιξ
Diamonds, ἀδάμας
Dye, purple, πορφύρα

Ebony sticks, φάλαγγες ἐβένινοι

Flax cloth, κάρπασος
Frankincense, λίβανος

Garments, γαυνάκαι
Ghi, βούτυρον
Girls, παρθένοι
Glass, crude, ὕελος ἀργὴ
Glassware, λιθίας ὑαλῆς, ὑαλᾶ σκεύη
Gums, fragrant, βδέλλα, μοκροτου
Gums, fragrant, in general, εὐωδία

Horses, ἵπποι

Incense, λίβανος
Indigo?, μέλαν ἰνδικὸν
Ink, Indian?, μέλαν ἰνδικὸν
Iron, σίδηρος
Ivory, ἐλέφας

Lac, λάκκος
Lapis lazuli, σάπφειρος
Lead, μόλιβος, μόλυβος
Linen, λέντια

Malabathrum, μαλάβαθρον
Mantles, fringed, δικρόσσια
Marble, λύγδος
Medicinal products, κάγκαμον, λύκιον
Money, δηνάριον, χρῆμα
Mules, ἡμίονοι
Murrhine ware, μορρίνη, μουρρίνη

INDEX OF TRADE-GOODS MENTIONED IN THE TEXT

Musicians, μουσικά
Muslins, σινδόνες, σινδόναι
Myrrh, σμύρνα

Oil, ἔλαιον
Oil of myrrh, στακτή
Olives, unripe, χυλὸς ὄμφακος
Onyx, ὀνυχίνη λιθία
Orpiment, red, σανδαράκη
Orpiment, yellow, ἀρσενικὸν

Pearls, μαργαρίτης, πινικόν
Pepper, πέπερι, πίπερι
Perfume, μύρον
Precious stones, λιθία διαφανὴς

Rhinoceros horn, ῥινόκερως
Rice, ὄρυζα
Robes, στολαὶ

Saffron, κρόκος
Sail-yards, κέρατα
Sandalwood, ξύλον σαντάλινον
Sapphire, ὑάκινθος

Sesame oil, ἔλαιον σησάμινον
Shisham beams, φάλαγγες σησάμινοι
Silk, raw, ἔριον
Silk yarn, Chinese, νῆμα σιρικὸν
Silver, ἀργυροῦς
Silver ware, ἀργυρώματα
Skins, Chinese, δέρματα σιρικὰ
Slaves, δουλικὰ, σώματα
Spears, λόγχη
Spices in general, ἄρωμα
Spikenard, νάρδος
Statues, ἀνδριάντες
Steel, στόμωμα
Storax, στύραξ
Sugar cane, σάκχαρι
Swords, μάχαιραι, μαχαίρια,

Tin, κασσίτερος
Topaz, χρυσόλιθον
Tortoiseshell, χελώνη
Tunics, χιτῶνες
Turquoise, καλλεανός λίθος

Wheat, πυρός, σῖτος
Wine, οἶνος

General Index

Abalitic Gulf, 144
Abhīra, 109
Abu sharm al-qibli, 86
Abu Zaid Hassan, 103
Adanē, 102
Addi Qayeh, 89
Aden. *See* Eudaimōn Arabia in Index of Places etc.
Adulitanum, Monumentum. *See* Monumentum Adulitanum
Aelius Gallus, 3, 10
'Afar (Danakil), 143
Afilas, king of Aksum, 89
Afrodito, watering-place, 80
Agatharkhidēs, 1, 3, 14, 86, 143, 147, 166; extracts from, 167–8, 177–97
Agathēmeros, 3, 4
Aguēzāt, 149
Akestimos the Cretan, 172
Akridophagoi, 143, 187
Aksum. *See* Mētropolis Axōmitē in Index of Places etc.
Alawa, African tribe, 147
Alexander the Great. *See* Alexandros in Index of Places etc.
Alexander, son of Sundaios, of Oroanda, 171
Alexandreia (Alexandria), in Susiana, 106
Alexandria, in Egypt. *See* Alexandreia in Index of Places etc.
Almeida, Manoel de, cited, 68
Alvares, Francisco, cited, 103, 115
Amazons, 74
Andhra, 154, 155

Anjanwel, river, 114
Anjediva, island, 115
Antiphilos, port, 90, 168, 170
Antonius (*sic*) Pius, Roman emperor, 95
Aphroditē's Harbour, later name of Muos Hormos, 86, 168, 193
Apoasis, son of Miorbollos of Etenna, 171
Apollodōros, 74
Apollonos hydreuma, 80
Apollo's river-land, 169
Aqiq, 87
Arabia emporion, name of Aden, 102
Arakan, 120
Arakhōsia. *See* Arakhousioi (*sic*) in Index of Places etc.
Argeste, Cape, 128
Arikamedu. *See* Podoukē in Index of Places etc.
'Arish, El-. *See* Rhinokoloura
Aristonis hydreuma, 80
Aristotle, 77
Arkhippos, 3, 61
arrack, 115
Arrian, 6, 7, 13, 106, 108, 112, 115; extract from, 196–7
Arsinoē, in Egypt, 5, 60, 79, 80, 122, 129
Arsinoē, in Trōglodutikē, 168, 169, 193
Artemidōros, son of Apollōnios of Pergē, 172
Asbas, ruler of Adouli, 150
Ascitae, 61, 147

Assab, 170
Assabinus, Arabian god, 128
Assal, Lake, 170
Astabara (Atbara), river, 184
Aswan, 80
Atbara, river. *See* Astabara
Athana, name of Aden, 102
Atramitai, 103, 151
Auē, 60
Augustus, Roman emperor, temple of, at Cranganore, 116
Ausan, 148, 151
Autaioi, 180
Autei, 195
awesia, type of ship, 162
Azania. *See* Index of Places etc.
Azov, Sea of. *See* Maiōtis, lake, in Index of Places etc.

Bab al-mandab, straits of, 65, 102, 170
Babbs, the, name for Bab al-mandab, 102
Baboons. *See* Kunokephalos
Babylon, in Egypt, 79
Bacare. *See* Bakarē in Index of Places etc.
Bactriana, 132
bagala, type of ship, 162
Bāḥrnagāsh, 148, 149
Bahrein, 162
Baluchistan, 106
Bandar Abbas, 153
Bandar Alula, 83, 93
Bandar Harshau, 92
Bandar Kasim, 83, 92
Bandar Tank, 106
Bandar Ziada, 83
Bankot. *See* Mandagora in Index of Places etc.
Bantu, 147
BaNyamwezi, 175
Baragaza, 11
Barawa, 95
Barbosa, Duarte, 114

Bari, Sudanese tribe, 145
Barraqa Island, 102
Bassein, 113
batela, type of ship, 162
Bautahara, 104
Beads, 142
bedeni, type of ship, 160
Beeston, A. F. L., 9
Beni Asab, 105
Beni Jenabi, 104
Berber, on the Nile, 87
Berbers, 59, 146
Berenikē. *See* Bernikē in Index of Places etc.
beryl, 71
Bēsatai, 75
Bharraky, 109
Bharukacha, original name of Broach, 110
Billah, 104
Birds' Island. *See* Orneōn nēsos in Index of Places etc.
Bitter Lakes, 5, 77, 79
Bivar, A. D. H., 153 n., 154–5
Black Sea, 75
Blood and milk, drinking, 145, 189
Bluffs of Azania. *See* Apokopa mikra kai megala in Index of Places etc.
Boats, sewn, 29, 40, 122, 140, 142, 158–60
Bongo, Sudanese tribe, 145
Bosaso, Somali name for Bandar Kasim, 92
Boukephalos, 112
Boxos, 178
Brahmagiri, 142
Brava (Barawa), 95
Broach. *See* Barugaza in Index of Places etc.
Bubastis, 77
buffalo, 196
buggalow. *See* bagala
bull, carnivorous, 191–2
bull, wild, 194, 196
Bulls, headland of the, 194

Burikao (Bur Kavo, Bur Gao, Port Durnford), 95, 174
Burma, 75, 120
Burnt Island. See Katakekaumenē nēsos in Index of Places etc.
Burnt Islands, 115
Burungi, African tribe, 147

Cabalsi, watering-place in Egypt, 80
Cael, 118
Caesar. See Kaisar in Index of Places etc.
Cambay, Gulf of, 85, 110
camels, 32, 35, 151
Cambyses, 167
camelopardalis, 191
Canary Islands, 132
Cannanore. See Naoura in Index of Places etc.
cannibals, 55, 157
canoes, dug-out, 159
Cape of Spices, Ptolemy's name for Cape Gardafui, 93
Caspian Sea. See Kaspia thalassa in Index of Places etc.
Catois, Guy, 130
caulking, 158, 162
Celobothras, 155
Cenon hydreuma, 80
Ceylon. See Palaisimoundou in Index of Places etc.
Channel, the Siyu. See Diōrukhos in Index of Places etc.
Charsadda. See Proklaïs in Index of Places etc.
Chastana, dynasty, 154
Chaul. See Sēmulla in Index of Places etc.
Chera kingdom (Kerala), 116, 155
China. See Thina in Index of Places etc.
Chola kingdom, 86, 118, 156
Cholamandalam (Coromandel), 118, 156, 162
Chryse, 120

circumcision, 144, 145, 189
Clysmo. See Klusma
Comorin, Cape. See Komar, Komarei in Index of Places etc.
Compasi, watering-place in Egypt, 80
Constans, Roman emperor, 97
Constantine I, Roman emperor, 97
Constantine II, Roman emperor, 97
Constantine XI, Byzantine emperor, 95
Constantine XII (*sic*), Byzantine emperor, 95
Correa, Diogo, 115
Cosmas Indicopleustes. See Kosmas
Cooley, W. D., 173
Cottonara, 171
Courses of Azania. See Azania in Index of Places etc.
crabs, 67, 197
Cranganore. See Mouziris in Index of Places etc.
Crawford, O. G. S., 175–6
crocodiles, 29, 37, 99, 169

Dabhol, Dabul. See Palaipatmai in Index of Places etc.
Dahlak Islands. See Alalaiou islands in Index of Places etc.
Daimaniyat Island, 104
Damirikē, Damurikē, 85, 110, 116
Danakil. See 'Afar
Daphnē, port of, 169
Daraba, Darada, 168
Darius the Great, Hystaspes, king of Persia, 77, 152
Dar es salaam, 99
dau (dhow), 162
dead, disposal of the, 183, 189-90
Deccan. See Dakhinabadēs in Index of Places etc.
Dehej, 110
Deinias, 178
Deirē, 169, 170, 172
Delemme Island, 89
Delgado, Cape, 2, 174

demani, name of a season in E Africa, 165
Dēmētrios, Watch-towers of, 168
Devagadh, Devagarh, 114
Didime, watering-place in Egypt, 80
Didinga, Sudanese tribe, 145
Diogenēs, navigator, 3, 11, 99 n.1, 173
Dioskoridēs, 133, 134
Dissei Island, 89
dog-fish, 194
Dog milkers. *See* Kunamolgoi
Dōsarēnē, 120
Dōsarōn, river, 120
Durgā, 73
Durnford, Port. *See* Burikao
Dvīpa Sukhadara, Sanskrit name of Socotra, 103
Dvaraka, Dwarka, 109

Eil, 94
El-'Arish. *See* Rhinokoloura
El-Dere, 95
elephants, 20, 49, 60, 190–1, 194
Elephant eaters. *See* Elephantophagoi
Elephant hunting, 166–9, 177, 185–7
Elephantophagoi, 168–9, 185–7
Elisar, conjectural S Arabian ruler, 10
Ēpiodōros, conjectural name of an island, 73
Eratosthenēs, 3, 59
Erranoboam, river, 115
Eruthras, 1, 178–9
Erythraean Sea, derivation of name, 1, 177–9
Erythras. *See* Eruthras
Essina, 11
Eumēdēs, founder of Ptolemaïs, 168
Eumenēs, Wood of, 168, 169
Eyasi, Lake, 147

Fabricius, B., 7
Fahal Island, 104
Falacro, watering-place in Egypt, 80
field mice, 188

Filuk, Ras. *See* Elephas, Cape, in Index of Places etc.
Fish eaters. *See* Ikhthuophagoi in Index of Places etc.
fishing, methods of, 29–30, 62, 180–1, 196–7
fish, preparation of, for food, 180–1, 196–7
Flat-noses, 187
Foul Bay, 87, 168, 193
'four jaws', spiders, 188
Frisk, Hjalmar, 12, 13

Gabaz, sub-kingdom of Aksum, 149
galawa, type of canoe, 159
Galen, 134
Galla, 145, 176
Gandhara, 85, 154. *See* also Gandaraoi in Index of Places etc.
Ganga, Ganges, river. *See* Gangēs in Index of Places etc.
gangi, type of ship, 162
Gardafui, Cape. *See* Arōmatōn emporion kai akrōtērion in Index of Places etc.
Gautamīputra Śrī Śātakarṇī, Indian king. *See* Saraganēs in Index of Places etc.
Gaza, in Africa, 93
Gazē, sub-kingdom of Aksum, 149
Gebanitae, 128, 151
Gedrōsia, 106, 196
Gelenius, Sigismund, 13
George, St, Island of, 115
giraffe, 191
Godavari, river, 85, 113, 155
Gorowa, African tribe, 147
Guadel, Cape, 106
guinea fowl, 193
Gujarat. *See* Abēria in Index of Places etc.

Habb, river, 108, 153
Haddas, river, 87
Hadramaut, 103, 151–2. *See* also

Libanōtophoros in Index of Places etc.

Hadrian, Roman emperor, 95

Hadza Bushmen, 147

Halania Island, 102

Halki, 139

Hanfila Bay, 90, 170

Hanno, 6

Haqlē, king of Aksum, 149

Hasik, 104

Hastavakapra, Hathab. See Astakapra in Index of Places etc.

Hatshepsut, Queen, 62, 81

Hawakil Bay, 90

Haywood, Capt. C.W., 95–6

Heis, 92

Heliopolis, Heliu, 79

Hēraios, Kushan king, 69

Hero, Hērōöpolis, 77, 79

Hērodotos, 1, 2, 36

Himyarites. See Homēritai in Index of Places etc.

Hippados, name of the sea beyond Cape Gardafui, 72

Hippalos, Hippalus, 3, 4, 72

Hippalus wind, 52, 72, 116

hippopotamus, 61, 169

Hippuros, port in Ceylon, 64

Hisn Ghurab. See Kanē in Index of Places etc.

Hog Island, 115

Honavar, 115

Horace, 136

Hulophagoi, 184–5

hyaena, 49, 70, 192

Hyrcanians, 195

ibis, 169

Ibn Battuta, 104, 115

Idrisi, 112, 113

Ili-azz. See Eleazos in Index of Places etc.

Indus, river. See Sinthos in Index of Places etc.

Iovis hydreuma, 80

Iraqw, African tribe, 145, 147

Isis, river-land of, 169

Jaigarh. See Melizeigara in Index of Places etc.

Jask, Cape, 106

Jamsanda, 114

Jaygad, river, 114

Jaz Jun Island, 104

Jebel Khamir, 176

Jebel Khiyabar, 106

Jebel Lahrim, 105

Jebel Sha'am, 105

Jerome, St, 167

Jhelum, Jihlam, 112–13

Josephus, 89

Juba, king of Mauritania, 145–6

Justinian, Byzantine emperor, 59

Kabolitai, 70

Kabul, 70

Kach, Rann of. See Eirinon in Index of Places etc.

Kailobothras (Keralaputra), 155

Kaïsos, the Homērite, 59

kaltis, gold coin, 55, 74

Kalyana. See Kalliena in Index of Places etc.

kamēlopardalis, 191

Kandahar, 85, 155

Kannanur. See Naoura in Index of Places etc.

Karamojong, Ugandan tribe, 145

Karur. See Vanji

Karwar, 115

kasikazi (NE monsoon), 164–5

Katabanoi, 151

Kathiawar. See Surastrēnē in Index of Places etc.

Kaviripaddinam. See Kamara in Index of Places etc.

Kayal (Cael), 118

Kēbos monkey, 196

kenge, giant water-lizards, 99

Kenya, Mt, 175

Kēphēnia, name for Ethiopia, 178
Kēpos monkey, 191, 196
Kerala, Keralaputra, 85, 116, 155, 156
Kērobotros, 155
Khabirun, place named by Idrisi, 113
Kharakēnē, 106
Kharax Spasinou, 105–6
Kharimortos, 170–2
Khatramotitai, 9, 151
Kiamboni, 95
Kilimanjaro, Mt, 174–6
Kim, 112
kipupwe, season in E Africa, 165
Kirāta, forest people of Nepal and
    Sikkim, 74
Kirwan, Sir Laurence, 106
Kisiju, 99
Kismayu, 95
Klusma, 5, 79, 80
Kobē, 11
kolandiophōnta, 54, 163
Kolkai. See Kolkhoi in Index of
    Places etc.
Kollam. See Quilon
Koloboi, 189
Komaria, 118
Konōn, Altars of, 168
Koptos, 64, 80, 86, 87
Koraos, fort and hunt of, 168
Korkai. See Kolkhoi in Index of
    Places etc.
Korravai, S Indian demon, 73
Kosmas Indikopleustēs, 4, 62, 89,
    148, 150, 166–7
kotia, type of ship, 162–3
Kottanara. See Kottonara
Kottayam. See Nelkunda in Index of
    Places etc.
Kottiara, 71
Kottiaris, river, 4
Kottonara, 71, 156
kotumba, type of ship, 162
Kreophagoi, 169
krokottas, 70, 192
Kṣaharāta, Indian dynasty, 154

Kunamolgoi, 188–9
Kunēgetai, 185
K'un lun people, 163
Kunokephalos (baboon), 191, 196
Kuria Muria Islands. See Zēnobios
    Islands in Index of Places etc.
Kuṣāna, Kushan, Indian dynasty, 69
kusi, season in E Africa, 164–5
Kutch, Rann of. See Eirinon in Index
    of Places etc.
Kuṭṭam, 71, 156
Kwaihu, 95

Ladhikiya, 61
Lamu, 97
Laodikeia, 61
Larak Island, 105
Lāstā, 175–6
laughter at funerals, 145, 190
Leōn, 169, 170
Leonnatos, Macedonian general, 163
leopards, 49
lice, flying, 187
Licinius, Roman emperor, 97
Likhas, 169–71
lions, 17, 81, 84, 188
lizards, giant, 37, 99
Locust eaters. See Akridophagoi
locusts, 19, 59, 143, 187, 195
Lysas, freedman of Annius Plocamus,
    64

Ma'afir. See Mapharitis in Index of
    Places etc.
Madras, 119
Madura, 156
Mafya Island, 97
Mahi, river. See Maïs in Index of
    Places etc.
Maisolia, Ptolemy's name for Masu-
    lipatam, 119
Mait, 92
Makasi, 95
Malikhas, Maliku, king of the

Nabataeans. *See* Malikhas in Index of Places etc.
maleleji, season in E Africa
Malvan, 115
Mamelukes, of Egypt, 95
Manda Island, 97
Mandangad, 114
Mandasor. *See* Minnagar in Index of Places etc.
Manpalli, 118
Marawa, Galla tribe, 176
Mariaba (Marib), 10
Marinos, of Tyre, 3, 4, 11, 12, 99n.1, 173-4
Markianos, of Hērakleia, 3, 4
Marora, 176
Marsuabai, 10
Mary Ann, brig, 61
Masai, 145
mashua, type of boat, 162
Masira Island. *See* Sarapidos nēsos in Index of Places etc.
masula, type of boat, 162
Masulipatam. *See* Masalia in Index of Places etc.
Mauas, Maues, Indian king, 153
Mauro, Fra, 176
Maushij. *See* Mouza in Index of Places etc.
Mauza', 100
Maximin, Roman emperor, 95
Maximin II, Roman emperor, 97
McCrindle, J.W., 10, 13
mchoo, Lesser Rains in E Africa, 165
meleagrides (guinea fowl), 193
Mēlinos, 168
Memphis, 78, 79
Menippos, of Pergamon, 6
Meregh, 94, 95
Mersa Fatma, 90
midges, 184
Minagara, Ptolemy's spelling of Minnagara, 110
Minaioi, 136
Mkulumuzi, river, 99

Mnaseas, of Patara, 6
Modoura, 156
Modusa, 156
Mogadishu, 94, 95
monsoons, 72, 163-5
Monumentum Adulitanum, 89, 166-167
Monze, Cape, 106
Moro, Sudanese tribe, 145
Mosul, 131
Mosyllon. *See* Mosullon in Index of Places etc.
Mounds, of stones, 145
Mountain of the Moon, 173-6
Mousa, Ptolemy's spelling of Mouza, 100
Msasani, 99
mtepe, type of ship, 159-60
mtumbwi, type of canoe, 159
Mukalla, 102, 103
mulberry, 169
Mulhule, 65
Müller, C., 7, 13
Murle, Sudanese tribe, 145
Musandam, Ras. *See* Asabōn in Index of Places etc.
musimu (monsoon), 164
Mussel Harbour. *See* Muos Hormos in Index of Places etc.
mussels, 197
Muziris. *See* Mouziris in Index of Places etc.
mwaka, Greater Rains in E Africa, 164-5

Nahapāna, Indian king. *See* Manbanos in Index of Places etc.
Namados, river, 110
Nandi, 70, 145
Narbada, river. *See* Lamnaios in Index of Places etc.
Nāsik, 154
Nearkhos, 2, 196-7
Necos. *See* Nekhō II
Nekhō II, Pharaoh, 2, 77

Nero, Roman emperor, 95
night-blindness, 66
Niki, 174
Nile, river. *See* Neilos in Index of
   Places etc.
Nogal, river, 94
Nonnosos, 59
Notou Keras, 11, 169, 170
nyctalopia, 66

Obbia, 94
obsidian, 60
Ocelis. *See* Okēlis in Index of Places
   etc.
ochre, mine of red, 193
Olok. *See* Arōmatōn emporion in
   Index of Places etc.
Oman. *See* Omana (in Arabia) in
   Index of Places etc.
opsian stone, 21, 60
Ōreitai, 108, 153
Orissa, 120
Ormara, 106
oryx, 187
Ostrich eaters, 187
Oyster Rock, 115
oysters, 197

Paithan. *See* Paithana in Index of
   Places etc.
Palaesimondo, 119
Palaesimundum, river, 119
paliurus, 144, 189
Palma, A. Cornelius, 9
Pāndya kingdom, *See* Pandion in
   Index of Places etc.
Pangani, 99, 132
Panjab, 85
Panōn Kōmē, 11
Parali, old name for Travancore, 73
Parthians. *See* Parthoi in Index of
   Places etc.
Pasargadai, 178
Pasinēs, son of Sogdonaios, 106
Pasirees, 106

Patale, 72
Pate Island, 97
Pemba Island, 84, 97, 99
Peninsula, The. *See* Khersonēsos in
   Index of Places etc.
Peram, Piram. *See* Baiōnēs in Index
   of Places etc.
Perim Island. *See* Diodōrou nēsos in
   Index of Places etc.
Periplus of the Erythraean Sea, author-
   ship, 6, 7; date of, 8–12; editions
   of, 12–14, 198; manuscripts of, 12,
   13
Periplus, other works so called, 5, 6,
   57 n.
Periyar, river, 71, 116, 155
persea tree, 169
Perseus, 178
Petra, 8, 9, 100, 150
Peucolais, 75, 112
Peukelaōtis, 112
Peutinger Table, 116
Philip's Island, 169
Philostorgios, 102, 173
Philōtera, 77, 168
phleōs, 169
Phōtios, 14, 60; extract from, 177–97
pig, 194
Pigeon Island, 115
piracy, 30, 50, 61, 63, 64, 146–7
Piram Island. *See* Baiōnēs in Index of
   Places etc.
Pliny, 1, 3, 6, 11, 60, 61, 64, 67, 71, 72,
   75, 77, 93, 102, 112, 115, 116, 118,
   119, 120, 132, 134–8, 145–6, 155,
   156, 195; extracts from, 125–9, 151
Plocamus, Annius, 64
plough, 63, 64
Poeniconon, watering-place in Egypt,
   80
Polubios, 167, 172
Pondicherry, 119
poplar grove, 169
Pōros, Indian king, 177
Port Durnford. *See* Burikao

Portus Mosyllicus, 11, 12
Prason, Cape, 2, 174
Prokopios, 158
Psebean Hills, 194
Psebō, Lake, 196
Psugmos, 169
Ptolemy, the geographer, 2–4, 11,
    62, 70–2, 75, 93, 99, 100, 102, 103,
    105, 109–10, 112–14, 116, 118–20,
    144, 149, 156, 170, 173–4
Ptolemy II, Philadelphus, of Egypt,
    3, 6, 77, 79, 86, 166, 168, 177, 187
Ptolemy III, Euergetēs I, of Egypt, 89,
    95, 166–7
Ptolemy IV, of Egypt, 95, 170–1
Ptolemy V, of Egypt, 95
Ptolemy VII, Phuskōn, of Egypt, 14
Puhar. See Kamara in Index of
    Places etc.
Punt, 62, 81, 94, 158
Purali, river, 108, 153
Puṣkalāvati, 112
Puthangelos, 169, 170, 172
Puthalaos, 169, 170

Qamar Bay, 104
Qataban, 9, 151
Qohayto. See Koloē in Index of
    Places etc.
Qosseir, Qusair, 77, 86
Quilon, 77, 86
Qurna, 106

Raheita, 170
Rameses II, Pharaoh, 77
Rann of Kutch. See Eirinon in Index
    of Places etc.
Ras al-Hadd, 104
Ras al-Asidah, 102
Ras al-'Usēde, 102
Ras Asir, 93
Ras Delgado, 174
Ras Dumeira, 170
Ras Fartak. See Suagros in Index of
    Places etc.

Ras Filuk. See Elephas, Cape, in Index
    of Places etc.
Ras Hafun, 94
Ras Hasik, 104
Ras Jardafun, 94
Ras Kimbiji, 174
Ras Shenagef, 94
Red Cliffs, 118
Red Mountain. See Purron oros in
    Index of Places etc.
Redesieh, 171, 172
Rhapton, Cape, 99, 173–4
Rhapton, river, 99, 174
rhinoceros, 20, 190–1, 194
Rhinokoloura (El-'Arish), 150
Rome, 123
Rosalgat, Cape, 104
Rufiji, river, 99–100
Ruvu, river, 99
Ruwenzori, 174

Saba, port of, 168
Sabaeans. See Sabaïtai in Index of
    Places etc.
Sabai, town of, 168
Sabat, place named by Ptolemy, 100
Sabbatha, Ptolemy's spelling of
    Saubatha, 102
Sabin, Arabian god, 151
Sabota, capital of the Atramitae,
    151
Saēsadas, variant of Sēsatai, 75
Saho, 143
Saidapat, 119
Śaka, Śakastan, 108, 153, 155
Salala. See Moskha in Index of
    Places etc.
Salama, 95
Salgu, on Fra Mauro's map, 176
Sandawe, African tribe, 147
sangara, type of boat or raft, 54, 163
Sapa, Pliny's name for the incense
    country, 151
Sapedanes, Parthian prince in India,
    153

Sapphara, 100
Saranē, 149
Sariba, variant of Sapa, 151
Sasan, Parthian prince in India, 153
Satavastra, Parthian prince in India, 153
Saturos, 77, 168
Saurashtra. *See* Surastrēnē in Index of Places etc.
Savitri, river, 114
Schoff, W. H., 12, 13
Scenae Veteranorum, 79
scorpions, 188
Scythians. *See* Skuthia in Index of Places etc.
Seleukos II, Kallinikos, 167
Ṣellari, river, 176
Sennar. *See* Kuēneion in Index of Places etc.
Serapium, 79
Serjeant, R. B., 100
Serikē, 75
Sesōstris, Pharaoh, 77
Shabwa. *See* Saubatha in Index of Places etc.
sharks, 196
Sheikh Saʻid. *See* Okēlis in Index of Places etc.
Shihr, 103
ships, 80–1, 158–63
Sigi, river, 99
Sikha Island, 102
Simoi, 187
Simoundou, 119
Simulla, 114
Sinai (i.e. Chinese), 4, 75, 120
Sirius, 195
Siyu Channel. *See* Diōrukhos in Index of Places etc.
Skopas, 172
Skulax, of Karuanda, 5
snakes, 37
snakes at sea, 41, 43, 51, 67
snakes, gigantic, 49, 192–3
Snake Island, 193

Socotra, *See* Dioskouridou nēsos in Index of Places etc.
Sopara. *See* Souppara in Index of Places etc.
Sorath, 109
Sosaeadae, 75
souspha birds, 62
South Wind, Headland of the. *See* Notou Keras
sparrows, 188
Sphinx monkey, 191, 195–6
Spices, Mart of. *See* Arōmatōn emporion in Index of Places etc.
spiders, venomous, 188
springs, hot, 193
Sri Lanka. *See* Palaisimoundou in Index of Places etc.
stade, definition of, 58–9
St George's Island, 115
Strabō, 3, 5, 10, 14, 77, 87, 90, 112, 119, 141, 143, 146, 147, 151, 172, 195, 196; extracts from, 144–5, 168–70
Strands of Azania. *See* Aigialos mikros kai megas in Index of Places etc.
Strongulos, 105
Strouthophagoi, 187
Suadi Island, 104
Suakin, 87
Subaha, 104
Suez. *See* Klusma
Sumatra, 120
Surastra, 109
Surath, 109
Syagros. *See* Suagros in Index of Places etc.
Syēnē, 80

Tajura, Bay of, 90, 170
Takkazi, river, 176
Tamil coast, Tamilakam. *See* Limurikē in Index of Places etc.
Tamna, 151
Tamraparṇī, river, 118

Tana, Lake, 196
Tando Muhammad Khan, 153
Tanga, 99
tanga mbili, season in E Africa, 165
Tanor. *See* Tundis in Index of Places etc.
Targi, pl. Tuareg, 146
tarum, 129
Taxila, 85, 154
Taylor, W. E., extract from, 164–5
Ter. *See* Tagara in Index of Places etc.
Terabdōn, 106
Thair. *See* Tagara in Index of Places etc.
Theophilos, navigator, 3, 11, 99 n.1 173
Thomas, St, 103
This (name of China?), 120
Thomna, 151
Thou, place in Egypt, 79
tigers, 49
Timosthenēs, of Rhodes, 3, 6
Timoula, 114
Tohen, 94
Togaron, 114
Toniki, 11, 174
topaz, 193–4
towing boats, 45, 68
Trajan, Roman emperor, 10, 79, 95
Trajan's canal, 3, 4, 5, 79
trappaga, type of ship, 162
traps, fish, 29, 30, 62
Travancore, 73, 85
Trichinopoly, Old, 118
Trivandrum, 118
Trōglodutikē, Trōglodytes, Trōgo-
    dytes, 14, 77, 83, 126, 127, 129,
    134, 143–6, 166, 168, 172, 173,
    189–92
Tseimwal, 114
Tuareg, 146
Tutikorin, 118

Ubulla, al-. *See* Apologou in Index of Places etc.
Udain, 100
Ujjain. *See* Ozēnē in Index of Places etc.
Umm el-ketef, 87
Uraiyur. *See* Argalou in Index of Places etc.

Vaikkarai. *See* Bakarē in Index of Places etc.
Vanji (Karur), 116, 155
Vasai, 113
Vashishti, river, 114
Vembanad, Lake, 71, 116
Vengurla Rocks, 115
Vicus (Vico) Iudaeorum, 79
Vijayadurg (Visadrog). *See* Buzantion in Index of Places etc.
Vincent, W., 13
Vishishti, river, 114
vuli, Latter Rains in E Africa, 165

water lizards, 99
whales, 183, 194, 197
wren, 145
Wood eaters. *See* Hulophagoi

Xavier, St Francis, 103
Xenophōn, 6

Yanbu' al-bahr. *See* Leukē Kōmē in Index of Places etc.
Yerim, 100

ZaHaqlē, king of Aksum, 145
Zande, of the Sudan, 145
Zanzibar, 84, 97, 99, 162
Zebayir, 100
Zeyla. *See* Aualitēs in Index of Places etc.
Zingis, 11
Zula, Gulf of, 87, 89